Not
Your Mother's®
Make-Ahead and
Freeze Cookbook

Not Your Mother's® Make-Ahead and Freeze Cookbook

Jessica Fisher

The Harvard Common Press
Boston, Massachusetts

THE HARVARD COMMON PRESS
535 Albany Street
Boston, Massachusetts 02118
www.harvardcommonpress.com

Printed in the United States of America
Printed on acid-free paper

Library of Congress Cataloging-in-Publication Data
Fisher, Jessica (Jessica Getskow)
   Not your mother's make-ahead and freeze cookbook / Jessica Fisher. — 1st ed.
      p.   cm.
   Includes index.
   ISBN 978-1-55832-756-6 (alk. paper)
   1. Make-ahead cooking.   2. Frozen foods.   3. Quantity cooking.   I. Title.
   TX652.F4985   2012
   641.5'55—dc23   2012004607

Special bulk-order discounts are available on this and other Harvard Common Press books.
Companies and organizations may purchase books for premiums or resale, or may arrange a
custom edition, by contacting the Marketing Director at the address above.

Cover recipe: Spinach and Feta Manicotti with Lemon and Oregano, page 200
Spine recipe: Pulled Pork Sandwiches with Asian Slaw and Tangy Barbecue Sauce, page 160
Back cover recipe: Pork Chile Verde with Hominy and Carrots, page 154

Book design by Ralph Fowler / rlf design
Cover photography and prop styling by Sabra Krock; food styling by Carrie Purcell

10 9 8 7 6 5 4

Not Your Mother's is a registered trademark of The Harvard Common Press.

To my husband, Bryan,

who has truly been my partner in all things.

From kids to cookbooks (and everything in between),

life has been such a joy to share with you.

Contents

Acknowledgments

When I was just a little girl, I dreamt of writing a book—a cookbook, no less. It's amazing to me that so many years later that dream has come true. I could not have done it without the help of some wise and witty folk. Many thanks are due.

Thank you to the team at The Harvard Common Press, who embraced this project and patiently walked this rookie author through the paces: Bruce Shaw, for his enthusiasm for quality books; Adam Salomone, for the energy he brought to the project; Dan Rosenberg, for his encouragement and humor throughout the process; Valerie Cimino and Jane Dornbusch, who partnered with me to craft the best book possible; Pat Jalbert-Levine, for her amazing attention to detail and infectious enthusiasm; and the entire production crew for making it so spiffy and fun to look at.

Thanks to my agent, Alison Picard, for believing in the project and connecting me with such a great group of people.

Thank you to my wonderful readers at my blogs Life as MOM and Good Cheap Eats. You make writing and cooking fun! Thanks to those friends who tested recipes or offered counsel, including but not limited to: Aimee, Allie, Amy G., Amy McG., Amy N., Caroline, Cathy, Cristina, Crystal, Dawn, Erin, Jamie, Janel, JessieLeigh, Jessika, Joy, Lauren, Lynn, Mandi, Marilyn, Michelle, Patti, Phoebe, Prerna, Shaina, Sheila, and Tsh. Thank you to Mom and Dad, Jace and John, and endless friends for your willingness to be my guinea pigs—er, taste testers.

Special thanks to my six sweet children, who willingly made my project theirs. The Cookbook was a group endeavor, and I'm so thankful for your excitement about it—and your willingness to eat batch after batch of ice cream sandwiches until the recipe was "just right." You make taste testing a joy.

Deep gratitude goes to my precious husband, who washed lots of dishes, flew solo on kid duty, cleaned up endless messes, orchestrated bedtimes, and cheered me on throughout it all. You are my rock. Thank you for encouraging me in all my wild dreams.

And ultimate thanks to Jesus, who gave me all good things.

Introduction

This is *Not* Your Mother's Make-Ahead and Freeze Cookbook

Dinnertime. The word can evoke memories of lively voices, cozy suppers, and candle-light; images of forks chasing the last morsels of this or that on the plate; flavors blending in a happy symphony; satisfied hearts and tummies. Contentment.

But the notion of dinnertime can also bring to mind that frantic feeling when you come home tired, the dog is barking, the phone is ringing, and the entire house-hold is clamoring, "What's for dinner?" Stress.

You grope for an answer. Fast food? TV dinners? Canned soup? These are all quick fixes, but at what cost? All have excess sodium and additives, dubiously sourced ingredients, and questionable taste. What can you do to make meal-times more enjoyable without resorting to less-than-best menu options? How can you make contentment, not stress, the norm at dinnertime?

Turn to your freezer—what Alton Brown calls "the most potent food-preservation device ever devised." That precious appliance can save your bacon when it comes to putting healthy, whole-some meals on the table in record time. I've been preparing make-ahead and freeze meals for 15 years now, since I was a young high-school teacher with no one to feed but my husband and myself. Today I cook for a small army of eight: me, my husband, and our six children, aged tot to teen. And while I have my fair share of "Calgon, take me away" moments, mealtimes are usually pleasurable at our house.

Good eating has always been part of our family culture, from enjoying upscale Santa Barbara restaurants during our dating years to laughing as our first-born, at 10 months, devoured peach salsa from a spoon to grilling pizzas today on the backyard barbecue for a pack of famished children. For us, mealtimes are an event.

And while I love to cook, as a work-at-home mom, I also like to enjoy time with my family. Making many meals ahead of time allows me to have the best of both worlds. I regularly spend focused time in the kitchen, cooking up a storm and stashing the results away in the freezer for later use. The outcome? Perfect homemade convenience foods that serve us well, without undue stress.

In as little as an hour a week, you, too, can stock your freezer with make-ahead meals and meal components that are tasty, filling, healthy, and budget-friendly.

But don't worry: These are not your mother's—or your grandmother's—frozen casseroles. Drawing on modern technology and a global food market full of diverse ingredients, the recipes that follow feature a wide variety of flavor profiles and cooking methods. They appeal to modern taste buds, and they can all be prepared in bulk to help you save time in the kitchen. These meals will put the lively voices and cozy suppers back into your dinner times.

The Case for Make-Ahead and Freeze Meals

Home cooks lead busy lives. Students, single parents, stay-at-home moms, work-at-home parents, working professionals, retired grandparents—all are looking for delicious meals that are easy and affordable. They crave tasty meals, but due to lack of planning, lack of knowledge, or lack of cooking mojo, they settle for less than the best. Deep down, lots of folks feel there must be a better and easier way to eat well. Many of our mothers practiced "cook and freeze" methods. Whether they engaged in a once-a-month marathon kitchen session or spent a harvest season preserving the surplus vegetables and fruits on hand, the cooks who came before us were known to stash

meals and meal components away in the deep freeze.

Unfortunately, many of those dishes were forgotten in deep storage and developed a serious case of frostbite. Or, worse, they weren't all that tasty to begin with. If you remember the heavy, starch-laden casseroles of yesteryear, you might say "No, thanks" to homemade frozen entrées.

But times, technology, and tastes have all changed. And a freezer packed with ready-to-go breakfasts, lunches, and dinners can be a boon to any home cook. Taking a different approach to food preparation and storage could change your kitchen, your mealtimes, and your life.

Many of today's home cooks either are intimidated by the prospect of cooking many meals at once or simply don't know where to start in freezing foods for later enjoyment. Some have never even heard of "freezer cooking." Others may enjoy cooking but lack the time and energy to spend hours in the kitchen, especially after a full day of work.

But freezer cooking can provide a handy solution to dinner dilemmas. Imagine enjoying inexpensive, healthy, tasty meals any night of the week. Imagine having a freezer stocked with several weeks' worth of easy, versatile dinners that please any palate, young or old. Imagine preparing a multitude of meals in just a few hours.

I started my "cook and freeze" adventure the traditional way, spending 8 to 24 hours shopping, chopping, and hopping about my kitchen, trying to get 30 meals ready to freeze at once. Fifteen years ago,

I was seven months pregnant with my first child and preparing to quit my job as a high-school teacher. My friend Jessika and I had read *Once a Month Cooking,* the grandmother of all freezer cookbooks, and we decided to give it a go. My pregnant, swollen feet got a workout, but it all seemed worth it when I ended up with 40 meals stashed in the freezer for the coming month and beyond.

Jessika and I now have 8 kids and 180 miles between us, but we both still practice freezer cooking, often swapping recipes and freezer-meal ideas via phone, email, or text, even though it's been quite some time since we've had the opportunity to cook in the same kitchen.

Over the years, as my family grew from one little baby to six active children, I needed the convenience of premade meals all the more. But I often found myself utterly exhausted by the effort it took to get it all done in a day or two. I needed to find ways to fill my freezer without spending an inordinate amount of time doing it. Typical shortcuts like canned soups and sauces didn't fit my desire to feed my family less-processed, healthier foods. I wanted it all.

I sought simpler ways to fill the freezer, like doing double-batch cooking to make two lasagnas instead of one and mini cooking sessions wherein I'd create a range of meals built around one main ingredient. I wanted to find the most efficient methods for cooking ahead of time.

One day, another friend, Crystal, shared her idea of tackling her freezer cooking in two hours. Two hours? What a great way to streamline my efforts even more!

After years of freezer cooking the traditional way, I've realized that it can be more streamlined, that I can have home-cooked meals ready and waiting, and that I don't have to spend days in the effort to pull it off—unless I want to. Instead, I have found ways to condense my cooking tasks and develop bulk cooking plans that I can pull off in less than five hours.

We live in an age of instant gratification. While hard work is still important, ours is a fast-paced society. But good home cooking still has a place in it. Through careful planning and making use of modern technologies, I'm now able to prepare 20 to 30 breakfasts, lunches, or dinners in a matter of hours.

Donna Reed, it's time to meet Jane Jetson. While we may not have machines producing food to order the way the Jetsons did, we can have tasty, healthy meals at the ready without an inordinate amount of work.

Efficient freezer cooking is the wave of the future—and it's definitely not your mother's frozen dinner.

Quick-Start Guide
Instructions for Big-Batch Cooking

Every four to six weeks, I take time out of my schedule to prepare several meals for the freezer. It's a little gift to myself, to make dinnertime easier in the weeks ahead. I might spend an hour or two cooking on a lazy afternoon, or I might wake up with the sun on a weekend day and cook all morning. It really depends on what our household needs at any given moment and what I feel like doing that day.

The one constant is the time that it saves me throughout the month as I go to the freezer for a pan of enchiladas or pop some homemade scones into the oven in a matter of seconds. My family avoids the drive-through, and we eat exceptionally well with minimal last-minute work.

On a recent Saturday afternoon, I was sorely tempted to "run for the border"—or at least the closest taco stand. After thinking through my options, I headed for my kitchen instead. I pulled a container of taco meat and a pan of enchiladas from the freezer. While those reheated in the microwave, I chopped lettuce, shredded cheese, and laid out tubs of sour cream and salsa. Within five minutes, I had assembled a complete taco bar and fed my family a feast that certainly beat anything the local taco joint had to offer. And it was thanks to make-ahead meals in my freezer.

Some folks might thumb their noses at "cook and freeze" meals. Perhaps they've had bad experiences; maybe they're haunted by a memory or two of Mom's Mystery Meat Casserole. However, those are relics of the past! I am a self-proclaimed food snob, yet after finding and developing recipes that really work for my family, I've found bulk cooking to be a happy compromise between a busy life, a tight budget, and a desire for good, home-cooked food.

Perhaps you've heard or read about this freezer-cooking thing. But it's a bit overwhelming, and you just don't have the time to figure it all out. It sounds complicated; it involves lots of charts; it takes too much time. Or maybe you're just so eager to get started that you don't want to spend time reading.

It's easier than you think. Big-batch cooking is as simple as preparing a double batch of tonight's dinner and freezing half for another night. It only takes a few minutes longer to make that second helping, but the rewards are huge, as there's no cleanup or prep work when you serve that meal in a few weeks' time.

If you want to put away 8 to 12 meals at one time, here's a quick-start guide to cooking, freezing, and enjoying homemade meals in the weeks ahead.

1. Copy or print out a Freezer Cooking Master Plan (page 61).

2. Choose one protein, such as chicken, to cook for this round. Write that in the first square under "main ingredient/protein." (Next time, you can make different kinds of dishes, but we're doing baby steps here.)

3. List your four favorite chicken recipes in the next column. Check out the chicken chapter, which starts on page 103, for inspiration.

4. Create a grocery list in column three, based on the recipes you chose. You're going to prepare double or triple batches of each of these items, so adjust your grocery list accordingly. Check your pantry to see what you have and what you will need to buy.

5. Go shopping. Make sure there's enough room in the fridge to store all the perishables.

6. Prior to your freezer-cooking session, prep all your vegetables and any other ingredients that might need chopping, slicing, and dicing.

7. Let the freezer cooking begin! Prepare each recipe in assembly-line fashion. Don't forget that you're doubling or tripling recipes. For each of the four recipes, lay out two or three baking dishes to fill and put them together quickly and efficiently. Then continue with the next recipe.

8. Wrap, label, and freeze as you go. Make sure that food cools to room temperature before freezing. To enable quicker freezing and a better result, completely chill the food in the refrigerator before placing it in the freezer.

9. By the time you're done, you should have 8 to 12 dinners ready to go for the coming weeks. If you choose four simple recipes, you'll be done in a few hours. And you'll be amazed at how much time you just bought yourself.

The Basics of Freezer Cooking

When convenience-food items and home refrigeration units started to come on the scene in the first part of the twentieth century, they offered a welcome respite from all the hard work it took to put food on the table. Home cooks have always welcomed convenience, from store-bought sliced bread (1920s) to a complete frozen entrée (1940s). We are no different from our predecessors in wanting shortcuts to get

us to dinnertime faster and more economically. However, modern-day "convenience" items are no longer "the best thing since sliced bread." They can take a huge bite out of one's budget, and they usually aren't the healthiest food choices around. There is a better way.

Make your favorite foods ahead of time to store in the freezer for the perfect, customized convenience meals. Not only will you save time and money by cooking in bulk, you'll also be able to feed your fam-

ily exactly what you want to feed them instead of settling for second best.

Chill Out:
What Can You Freeze?

The short answer: a lot. The variety of foods that can be partially or completely prepped ahead of time is vast. Many of your favorite meals or meal components can be made weeks in advance and stored in the freezer, enabling you to have the home-cooked meals you crave any night of the week. You will be surprised at the choices available to you.

Complete Main Dishes

○ Meatloaf. I like to mix and form the loaf, and then wrap and freeze it prior to baking. It tastes fresher than a loaf that's been cooked and then frozen.

○ Meatballs. Use the same meat mix you use for meatloaves. Form the balls, bake them in the oven, and then freeze family-size portions in freezer bags. Later you can turn them into simple spaghetti and meatballs with Easy Slow Cooker Red Sauce (page 205) or try the variations such as Swedish Meatballs with Dill (page 100), Barbecue Sauce for Meatballs (page 98), and *Boules de Picolat* (page 101).

○ Hamburger patties. Quick-freeze the uncooked patties on a baking sheet lined with plastic wrap. Once the patties are frozen, place them in a freezer bag. When you're ready to serve them, the burgers can be placed on the grill without thawing, making for quick cookouts.

○ Marinated meat and poultry. Place the uncooked meats along with the marinade in a freezer bag or freezer-safe container. Freeze the marinade and meat. The meat will marinate as it thaws later in the refrigerator. Cook as you normally would.

○ Casseroles, lasagnas, and enchiladas. Assemble several pans at once to freeze for later baking.

○ Burritos. Prepare the burritos and seal them in freezer bags. Thaw and heat them in the microwave or crisp them on a stovetop griddle. Burritos can also be heated directly from the freezer.

○ Tamales. Leave the steamed tamales in their cornhusk wrappings. Seal them in a freezer bag. Re-steam them right before serving (no need to thaw).

○ Taquitos. Quick-freeze assembled taquitos on baking sheets, and then seal them in a freezer bag. When ready to serve, bake them without thawing.

○ Stews, soups, and chili. Freeze these dishes in freezer-safe containers. Consider freezing individual portions in small containers for quick lunches and snacks.

Meal Components and Basic Ingredients

Meal components are simply parts of meals that are precooked or premixed in order to help you get a head start on dinner. Precooking and freezing a few meal components can save you valuable minutes in the kitchen. Seasoned ground beef, tomato sauce, marinades, meats and poultry cut for stir-fries or to add to salads and sandwiches, compound butters, baking mixes, and spice blends are all homemade convenience items that you can prepare in bulk and store in the freezer for later use.

- Seasoned ground beef. Cool the cooked meat and store in a freezer bag or freezer-safe container. Incorporate this later into tacos, chili, casseroles, nachos, burritos, and more.

- Meat and chicken pre-cut for stir-fries. Trim and slice the meat and seal it in a freezer bag or freezer-safe container. Thaw in the refrigerator before using in your favorite recipes.

- Cooked chicken. Cook chicken in the slow cooker or oven or poach it on the stovetop (pages 107 and 109). Chop or shred the cooked chicken and seal it in a freezer bag to use later in chicken salads, soft tacos, burritos, Asian dishes, soups, sandwich fillings, and more.

- Carnitas and shredded beef or pork. Place cooked meat in freezer bags or freezer-safe containers. Use it in tacos, burritos, nachos, soups, and barbecue sandwiches.

- Pasta sauce. Cook up a big batch of sauce, with or without meat, and store it in whatever size freezer-safe containers you like.

- Cooked beans. Prepare a big batch of dried beans and store them in 2-cup portions in freezer bags or freezer-safe containers.

- Pizza dough, sauce, and toppings. As soon as you've allowed the dough to rise for a short time, seal the dough ball(s) in freezer bags and freeze. The pizza sauce and toppings can be packaged in freezer bags or freezer-safe containers. Put together a kit so you can pull just one package out of the freezer when you're planning pizza for dinner.

- Club warehouse purchases. Bulk packs of cheeses, meats, and breads can be repackaged for storage in the freezer, helping you make the most of the bulk savings. Shredded cheeses like mozzarella, cheddar, Monterey Jack, and Parmesan freeze well, as do some softer cheeses, such as goat cheese. Crumbled cheeses, including Gorgonzola, blue, and feta, also hold up well when frozen.

- Surplus produce. If you belong to a produce co-op or CSA, you may find yourself inundated with fresh produce at times. While enjoying it fresh from the farm is divine, letting it go to waste because you can't eat it fast enough is not. Diced or sliced bell peppers and onions, berries, and chopped or whole bananas can all be frozen without much extra preparation; just seal them in freezer bags. Other vegetables, like green beans and snap peas, can easily be blanched, cooled, and frozen for later use.

- Dinner kits. Grocery stores sell meal kits, packages of ingredients to put together before serving. Why not make your own? Consider preparing "dinner kits" for easy-to-assemble meals such as tacos, sloppy Joes, burritos, or pizza. Cook and season meat or beans. Steam a pot of rice. Portion out the cheese. Package each of these components in meal-size portions and place all the bags for a certain meal in one larger bag. Label the bag and freeze it for later use. Transfer the bag to the refrigerator the day before serving, and the work is practically done for you come dinnertime.

○ Baking mixes and other baked goods. If you love to bake but find yourself pressed for time, assemble your own baking mixes. When you have your dry ingredients already measured and mixed, pancakes, muffins, waffles, biscuits, brownies, and quick breads can be ready in a flash. Pre-formed frozen scones and biscuits bake quickly, making for a delicious morning treat. Whole-Grain Cinnamon Rolls (page 311) and Chocolate Butterhorn Rolls (page 316) can be pulled from the freezer to thaw in the refrigerator over-

Taking Freezer Meals on the Road

My family and I love to eat! Good eating is definitely part of our family culture. And we're not afraid to spend money on dining out, as long as we get what we pay for. Unfortunately, we've had a few too many overpriced, tasteless restaurant meals. It makes vacation eating a little challenging: Eating out in unfamiliar places can be difficult to navigate if you don't know which restaurants are worthy of your patronage.

Whether we are going for a week at the lake or a weekend at Grandma's house, we generally want to rest, relax, and eat well in our leisure time. Freezer meals help make that happen—and save us from those overpriced restaurant disappointments.

If you are heading out on vacation, packing several meals in the cooler will serve you well.

- You will know what you're eating. This is particularly helpful if you have folks with special diets or food aversions in your group.

- You can save money. By packing meals for a recent three-day trip to the mountains, our family easily saved $200. We ate like kings with food we knew we liked, and we kept a lot of change in our wallet.

- With the money you save, you can splurge on other things. On that three-day trip, we were able to upgrade to more deluxe accommodations, which included a complete gourmet kitchen for cooking our meals. You could also apply your savings toward a couple of higher-end restaurant meals.

- If you're visiting family or friends, bringing a meal or two to share takes the burden off your host and helps you all enjoy the visit a little more.

night, providing you with freshly baked breads for breakfast or brunch the next day.

What Can't You Freeze?

There are a few things that are better left unfrozen. Here's my short list:

○ White potatoes. Don't think you can chop up a bunch of uncooked potatoes and freeze them for later use. They generally discolor and lose texture. The best way to freeze white potatoes successfully is to cook them first, as for Potatoes Stuffed with Caramelized Onions and Dubliner Cheese (page 193) or Cream Cheese Mashed Potatoes (page 82).

○ Recipes containing mayonnaise. This category includes dips, chicken salads, casseroles with mayo, and so

- You can eat on your schedule. Packing snacks and meals on vacation allows you to eat when you're hungry. If your kids wake long before the hotel breakfast—or Grandma—is ready, you can easily serve them some Milk and Honey Granola (page 253) or Breakfast Sliders (page 280) without disrupting the flow of those around you.

Some things to remember when taking meals on the road:

- Don't bring more than you can store or eat at your destination. You don't want to pack stuff only to waste it due to insufficient refrigeration, cooking facilities, or mouths to feed. Make sure that you will have a refrigerator/freezer and at least a microwave in your condo, cabin, or hotel or that Grandma has enough room to store what you're bringing.

- Avoid bringing heavily spiced foods. If you have picky eaters or ones with sensitive stomachs, leave the spicy foods at home. No one wants to deal with fussy kids or indigestion on vacation.

- Bring meals that are easy to prepare. Casseroles and soups are great for traveling since they reheat easily. The fact that they are virtually one-dish dinners also helps.

- Frozen meals can go camping, too! Chicken burritos, stuffed potatoes, and waffles and pancakes can be reheated over a hot fire. Pasta and red sauce are easy to cook on the camp stove. And of course, marinated or spice-rubbed meats and fish will cook well on the grill. You can pack a feast for camping and have very little work to do once you reach your destination.

on. The mayonnaise tends to separate, and the texture and flavor of the dish suffer.

O Lettuce, greens, and other vegetables to use raw. Lettuce and other salad greens should not be frozen. Most other vegetables can be frozen if they are to be cooked later, but otherwise, it's Sog City, baby.

O Block cheeses and sliced cheeses. These do not generally freeze well—they crumble upon defrosting—but shredded cheese can be frozen successfully. Very soft cheeses like Brie and Camembert should not be frozen.

Frozen Assets: Approaches to Freezer Cooking

In the 1990s, once-a-month-cooking hit the scene. It is a method of cooking 30 meals in a day or two and freezing them for later use. And it works! I started using this technique years ago and have found it to be a great way to save time, money, and brain power. I save time when I use the assembly-line method; I save money by buying and cooking in bulk; and I save brain power by not having to think too much about what's for dinner. I can go to the freezer and grab a pan of enchiladas or a bag of taquitos for a quick dinner, thereby avoiding the fast-food trap.

There are lots of ways to approach make-and-freeze cooking:

Double Duty

This is perhaps the easiest and most painless way to fill your freezer. Simply double tonight's dinner and freeze the extra. Do this for several nights, and your freezer will be stocked with a variety of meals. All the recipes in this book can be easily doubled or tripled, making it simple to create a freezer stash quickly.

Short but Sweet

Mini sessions are short cooking sessions focused on preparing several meals around a certain protein or key ingredient. You might do this once a week or do several mini sessions over the course of several days. Either way, over time you will have built a massive stockpile of meals in your freezer. Grab an hour or two and do some assembly-line cooking!

Cook for a Month

In the early days of freezer cooking, cooks spent several days shopping, chopping, and cooking up a month's worth of meals, many of them casseroles. Today's lifestyles don't always afford such lengthy cooking sessions. With careful planning, however, three to five hours of efficient cooking time can result in a month's worth of meals and meal components without a lot of fuss. There are several cooking plans in this book that will help you prepare 20-plus meals in less than a day.

Make a Day of It

But there's no rule that says you can't spend a day in the kitchen if you'd like to! The method you choose depends on your inclination and the time you have available. There's no "right" way to do it, except the way that works for you this month.

The cooking plans in the next chapter will walk you through every step. They are varied in length and intensity, so you can choose one that best suits your schedule. Or you can build your own plan following the suggestions in a later chapter (page 57). And if you're someone who just wants to get cooking, consult the Quick-Start Guide (page 1) and get to work.

Keep Your Cool: Proper Freezing Techniques

Freezing preserves food because it inhibits the action of microorganisms that would otherwise lead to spoilage. Food stored in the freezer shouldn't go "bad," as the enzyme action is effectively halted while the food is frozen. As long as you start with fresh food in the first place and the food stays frozen for the entire storage time, you shouldn't have to worry about spoilage. In fact, the USDA says that "frozen foods remain safe indefinitely," provided they are stored at 0°F. But taste and texture can be adversely affected depending on how a food is frozen and how long it is kept in cold storage.

Additionally, it can be difficult to keep a home freezer at a steady 0°F because typically the door is opened fairly frequently. So it's a good idea to serve foods within a reasonable amount of time to ensure the best taste and texture. A general rule of thumb is not to store items longer than two to three months in the freezer compartment of a refrigerator or six months in a dedicated deep freezer.

Often, folks worry that their frozen foods will have a funny taste or develop unsightly ice crystals. These problems are easily prevented if food is cooled, packaged, and stored correctly. An understanding of the freezing process can help you maximize and preserve your food's quality.

The colder the food is before it hits the freezer, the faster it will freeze. Quick freezing keeps ice crystals small, leading to better quality control, less cell damage, and less loss of moisture upon thawing. Large ice crystals, formed during slow freezing, can hurt the texture of the food, causing it to lose moisture and resulting in dry, tasteless food. Therefore, chilling a dish in the refrigerator before freezing it is always a good idea.

Your goal is to have food taste as good or better on the other side of freezing. (And yes, some flavors do improve upon freezing.) Warm food releases moisture or steam into the air. If you cover the food before it has had a chance to cool, the steam will condense on the inside of the lid. Warm food placed in the freezer will take longer to freeze, and upon freezing, it will have lots of large unsightly ice crystals.

One approach, which I recommend, is to allow hot foods to cool slightly, uncovered, at room temperature, before refrigerating them. While hot foods can be refrigerated safely, your refrigerator will have to work harder to cool them. Once a food has cooled slightly at room temperature, you can chill it thoroughly in the refrigerator before freezing it. Keep in mind that perishable food should never stand at room temperature longer than two hours.

Frozen food should stay at 0°F or colder. A freezer thermometer is essential to keeping your food fresh. A freezer alarm is even better. An inexpensive gadget, a freezer alarm will alert you when the freezer's temperature rises to an unsafe temperature. There is almost nothing more discouraging to a cook than finding a freezer full of food thawing and spoiling due to a power outage, blown fuse, or a freezer door inadvertently left slightly open.

That's a Wrap: A Variety of Packaging Methods

There are several ways that you can package food for freezing. What you use depends on the storage space available and the foods you are preparing to freeze.

Zip-top freezer bags are great for storing meats, baked goods, and other items that hold their own shape. You can save space by putting soups, stews, or beans in

these as well—but there is a possibility of leakage. Always thaw a zip-top freezer bag full of food on a tray in the refrigerator to catch any drips.

One of the benefits of zip-top bags is that they can be laid flat, frozen, and then lined up like books on a shelf or stacked like pancakes. They provide a great way to store a lot of food in a small amount of space. You can reuse bags that you've used for baked goods and baking mixes; simply store the empty bags in the freezer until next time. But never reuse bags that have held raw meat, poultry, or seafood.

When using zip-top freezer bags, be sure to remove as much air as possible from the bag before sealing it. You can easily use a straw to suck out the air from bags holding fruits, vegetables, or baked goods. Seal the bag almost completely, squeezing out as much air as you can with your hands. Then insert a plastic drinking straw into a small gap in the seal. Suck out any remaining air, pinching the bag's seal and the straw closed as the plastic encloses itself around the food. Remove the straw and seal the bag quickly to prevent air from reentering the bag. While this may seem like an odd method, it is quite effective in removing excess air from the bags. Do not use this technique with uncooked meats or seafood, to avoid contact with bacteria.

There are also commercial freezer bags with valves available, but they are rather expensive compared to the handy duo of freezer bag and drinking straw.

Quick freezing or open freezing is the practice of individually freezing items like scones, berries, or burgers on trays and then transferring them to a freezer bag or container for longer-term freezing. When foods are frozen this way, it isn't necessary to thaw the entire package to use two or three items. You can simply remove the number of items you plan to serve while leaving the rest in the freezer. Freezer bags are ideal for storing quick-frozen items.

Reusable/disposable plastic containers with lids are wonderful for storing foods like sauces, soups, and stews. These are leak-proof, making them ideal at thawing time and quick for reheating. Since slightly frozen foods will pop out easily from the container into the stockpot for stovetop reheating, you won't need to wait for them to thaw completely.

Disposable aluminum baking pans are very convenient, especially if you know you'll be giving meals as gifts or taking them to potluck dinners. Some brands come with sturdy aluminum lids that make wrapping especially quick and easy and add extra stability for stacking in the freezer. While disposables are not everyone's favorite because they are sometimes hard to reuse, they are convenient.

Glass or metal baking dishes are the longest lasting of the freezer-friendly packaging choices. If you have a large supply, these are your best bet. But you might not want to have all your pans sitting in the freezer when you decide to bake an impromptu cake. I have a lot of pans, so this is one of my favorite ways to store mashed potatoes, lasagna, and other meals that I want to pop straight into the oven. Some

glass bakeware comes with plastic lids for storage, reducing the need for foil or other wrappings. These are wonderful options, as they are completely reusable and stack beautifully in the freezer.

Vacuum-sealing machines that encase your food in airtight plastic are also available. These are said to protect extremely well against freezer burn. However, they are costly to purchase, as are the special plastic bags they require. These machines generally work best for food items that hold their shape, such as steaks or loaves of bread. They cannot be easily used for liquids.

However you package your foods, be sure to label them with the date, the name of the contents, and the cooking or reheating instructions, if applicable. It's easy to forget once something's been in cold storage for a while. And some foods change color when frozen. The last thing you want to do is confuse mushroom gravy with chocolate fudge sauce.

A Tight Squeeze: What About Freezer Space?

Although I do currently own a large deep freezer, that hasn't always been the case. I know from years of personal experience that you don't need a dedicated freezer to make freezer cooking work. In fact, when I started practicing this mode of cooking, I owned the smallest refrigerator known to man. It was only one step up from a dorm fridge, but it regularly held the makings of a dozen or more meals.

Here are some suggestions for making it work with whatever freezer you have:

○ Start with a mostly empty freezer. You won't be able to store several weeks' worth of meals in it if it already holds multiple containers of ice cream, loaves of bread, and packages of hamburger. Consider "eating from your freezer" prior to a big cooking session so that you can reduce what is already there. Hold off on buying a lot of other frozen foods until you know how much space you will need for homemade dinners. Remember, since you're going to be making your own convenience foods, you won't need the store-bought versions anyway.

○ If you already have a stockpile of frozen meats and poultry, use them as the building blocks of your make-ahead and freeze meals. Uncooked meat can be thawed, cooked, and re-frozen without loss of taste or texture. Good recipes to try would be Best-Ever Chicken Pot Pie (page 121) or Oven-Baked Beef Taquitos (page 69). You won't need much extra space for these meals; you're simply going to take the frozen hamburger or chicken out, thaw it, cook it up, give it a makeover, and put it back where it was, transformed from a frozen raw ingredient into a frozen convenience food.

○ Use freezer bags. Zip-top freezer bags, designed for cold temperatures and durability, can hold many kinds of frozen foods. These are especially useful for meats in marinades, taco fillings, pizza dough, and some thicker stews and chilis. As you cool, label, and freeze the food in these bags, seal them and lay them flat in your freezer. Once they are frozen, you will be able to stand them on end and line them up like books on a shelf, making the best use of your storage space. Make sure that you remove as much excess air as possible before sealing the bag in order to avoid freezer burn.

○ Use similarly shaped plastic containers. For liquids, like pasta sauce, use containers that are all the same shape and size. These will stack well and make the best use of your space. Square containers fill space more efficiently than round ones, but use what you have or add to your collection over time.

○ Organize like with like. If you have three 9 × 13-inch pans, stack those on top of each other. Stash all your sauce containers in one spot. Line up all your freezer bags like books on a shelf. Not only will those meals be easier to find, you'll also make the most of your space.

○ Consider freezing meal components. Casseroles are big and bulky. Your average refrigerator-freezer can only hold so much, but if you use meal components as a preferred dinnertime shortcut, you can make the most of it, stashing a vast quantity of meats, vegetables, grains, and other building blocks in a small amount of space.

Good Labeling

Accurate labeling is key to enjoying your frozen meals to the fullest. Be sure to include the following:

1. Date, so that you can eat the food within 2 to 3 months, ideally.

2. Recipe name: no mystery meat!

3. Baking/serving instructions, so that you don't have to hunt down the recipe in order to figure out how to serve the meal.

Breaking the Ice: Proper Thawing

What about thawing? Some foods, like unbaked pies, don't need to be thawed prior to baking and serving. Soups and chilis can be thawed and reheated in a pot on the stove. Frozen burritos can be baked or microwaved directly from the freezer.

But other foods, like lasagna, meats, and casseroles, do best when completely defrosted prior to cooking. This should be done in the refrigerator, not on the counter, so that the thawing food does not get too warm. Place zip-top freezer bags and foil-wrapped packages on a tray to catch drips before stowing them in the refrigerator. A slow thaw also allows the food to reabsorb some of the moisture it lost when it was frozen.

You'll have a better-tasting meal if it's had adequate time to thaw, so plan ahead and pull out two or three meals at a time to defrost in the refrigerator. Some will thaw more quickly than others. If you have a variety of items thawing in the refrigerator, you'll have some options come dinnertime.

Cash for Your Cache: Freezer Cooking Can Save You Money

One of the most tangible benefits of freezer cooking is that it can save you money. Here's how:

○ You can buy in bulk. Ever shake your head in wonder at folks who shop at warehouse clubs and come home with ginormous packages of food? Large families like mine go quickly through a bulk pack of chicken breasts or a 5-pound bag of shredded cheese, items that can often be a terrific bargain. But smaller households may have a harder time using up those huge packages. With freezer cooking, you can easily reap the cost savings from that bulk package. Divide a 5-pound bag of cheese into smaller meal-size bags for tacos, burritos, or pizzas. Divvy up the bulk pack of chicken breasts into zip-top freezer bags, add a marinade to each bag for good measure, and you're halfway to dinnertime.

○ You can avoid processed foods. Processed foods have one major thing going for them—convenience. They help us save time and get us from hungry to fed in short order. But there's a cost involved. Although, thanks to coupons and sales, processed foods can sometimes be inexpensive to buy, their regular prices are actually quite high. And they aren't always the best tasting or healthiest choices. By putting a few hours of work into cooking and freezing foods prepared from scratch, you can avoid processed foods.

○ You can limit your takeout. Although I love to have someone else do the cooking, I know that eating too many restaurant meals isn't good for our health or our pocketbooks. Having a stash of freezer meals on hand helps us avoid takeout and keeps some extra cash in our pockets.

○ You can go grocery shopping less often. Since I do big shopping trips to do big cooking, I go grocery shopping less frequently. Frequent shopping can lead to impulse buys, so staying out of the store saves me money by helping me avoid those unnecessary purchases.

How to Swing the Deal

Although your overall monthly grocery bill will probably be lower when you switch to freezer cooking, it can initially be difficult to fund a bulk cooking session. Many months I've been able to feed my family of eight on less than $600, a figure well below the national average, because I was practicing big-batch cooking and making good use of my deep freeze. However, that one grocery bill for a month's worth of meals can seem daunting. There are several ways that you can swing economical batch cooking, even on a fixed budget.

○ Use what you have on hand, and don't make recipes that call for ingredients that might not fit your budget during this pay period. Instead, scan your fridge, freezer, and pantry for what's already on the shelves and build your menu plan from there.

○ Practice stockpiling. Buy ingredients you use frequently in larger quantities when they are on sale, rather than paying full price later when you need the item. If you make this a regular practice, you'll find that you can keep a fuller pantry. This is not hoarding we're talking about. Provided you don't buy more than you will use in a reasonable length of time, this is simply wise investing. If my local store has a great price on chuck roast one week, I will probably buy several packages and store them in the freezer until my next bulk cooking session, when I will turn them into Beef Stew with Eggplant and Carrots (page 226), Mexican Beef Tortas (page 71), and Beef and Barley Soup with Dill (page 217). If you know that you use a jar of salsa each week, buy six the next time it goes on a great sale. Good sale prices tend to repeat every six weeks. This kind of stockpiling works for all ingredients except some fresh produce items or other foods that have a short shelf life.

- Straddle the sales. Find out the beginning and ending dates of your local grocery stores' sales. Build your menus around the sale items from two consecutive weeks. Usually, you can get an ad for the new sale the night before it starts, sometimes sooner. Just check your junk mail or ask at your store. If you don't mind going shopping on back-to-back days, you can take advantage of two weeks' worth of sales in one week. Some stores even offer "double-ad days" where they overlap the two weeks' sales for one day. Shop the week you plan to cook to maximize the ingredients' freshness.

- Cook enough meals or meal components to last longer than one month. If you find a great deal on a main ingredient, buy enough for two months of meals. For instance, at the beginning of one month, I can make enough Easy Slow Cooker Red Sauce (page 205) to last us six to eight weeks. With proper packaging and storage, I know it will be fresh tasting for even longer. Not only does this provide us with a little more

variety in our menus for both months, it also helps me offset my costs because I cooked a sale-priced item in greater quantity.

- Make in-season recipes. It just makes sense to cook what is in season and on sale. Roasted Vegetable Quiche (page 196) and Easy Stovetop Ratatouille (page 188) are ideal for the summer harvest season. Sales on boneless chicken breasts are also abundant during the summer months. November and December are ideal months to prepare turkey recipes. A few birds will make several batches of enchiladas, tamales, and a turkey version of Chicken Divan with Cheddar Crust (page 124). In winter, chuck roast is often a butcher's special; use it to make stews, chilis, and ragus.

- Build your freezer meals to feature items that you can reliably get for a good price. Meat can be expensive, but eggs, beans, rice, and pasta are almost always good deals. You can easily make many meals based on these ingredients. Spinach and Feta Manicotti with Lemon and Oregano (page 200), Green Chile Rice Casserole (page 186), and Red Lentil Dal (page 190) are not only meatless, they're also built on economical ingredients.

Meal Planning: Dinnertime and Beyond

Most home managers know that having a meal plan is key to a smoothly running

How Freezer Cooking Helps Me

My dad was born and raised on a farm in Minnesota, and his parents grew most—if not all—of what they ate. I remember stories of my grandmother and my aunts working long days in their hot farmhouse kitchen, putting up jars and jars of preserves and pickles, freezing the summer's produce, and preparing big batches of food to get them through the winter months. Not only was it part of the agrarian society they lived in, it was also necessary in order to put food on the table.

Times have changed. While we may have a wider variety of foods and healthier eating options today, many of the old ways are worth holding on to. My grandma had it right when she cooked ahead. Bulk cooking is a great way to eat well and save money. And there are lots of ways to tweak bulk cooking to fit your lifestyle. Here's what readers of my blog, LifeasMOM.com, had to say about it, in response to these questions: How does freezer cooking help you? How does it help your family eat better? How do you make it work for your life?

Freezer cooking helps me in the mornings. We are always rushed to get going out the door, so I keep the freezer stocked with our favorites so I don't have to tell the kids, "I don't have time." Pancakes, waffles, and muffins are popular freezer items around here. I make time for freezer cooking by making larger batches. For instance, instead of making "just enough" waffles for breakfast on a Saturday morning, I will triple the recipe and save the extras in the freezer. **—Katie Goodman, GoodLifeEats.com**

Freezer cooking helps me make sure my family is eating well, even though I'm juggling working full time, mothering two kids under three, and spending time with my husband. On nights when I get home just in time for dinner, knowing that the freezer is well stocked helps me avoid the temptation of grabbing fast food or expensive takeout on the way home. And if I have to miss dinner for a meeting, I can leave instructions for my husband so that he and the kids still eat real food. (Left to their own devices, it'd be frozen pizza for sure!) **—Kate Snyder, GreenAroundtheEdges.net**

I cook with whole and fresh foods in large quantities. For example, I prefer making my own bread dough in five minutes and using it for a multitude of breakfast, snack, lunch, and dinner items. I can use natural and organic ingredients without breaking the bank. My family is eating food without preservatives or additives and with whole-food ingredients we can pronounce. **—Jackie Brown, MomOnaMission.me** household. If you know what the dinner plan is, you can avoid the fast-food drive-through on the way home from soccer practice. The kids won't be crying for something to eat while you stare dazedly into the cupboards. And you can put the lively voices and candlelight back into dinnertime.

Having a freezer stocked with home-made meals facilitates meal planning. You can scan the freezer contents at the beginning of the week and decide what to serve, working around the week's activities.

But freezer meals can go beyond just dinnertime. Ginger-Coconut Scones (page 302) make a delicious breakfast. Freezer Smoothies (page 269) are quick on-the-go snacks. Foods like Chipotle Chicken and Onion Wraps (page 132) and Cheesy Butternut Squash Soup with Herbs (page 211) are great packed into a lunch box and reheated at work or school. You can work freezer cooking into good eating all day long.

These make-ahead meals can go on vacation with you, help a friend who's just had a baby, or comfort the neighbors who've just lost a loved one. Stocking your freezer does more than just provide dinner: It can improve the quality of your life, your budget, and your friendships.

Keys to Efficiency

Efficiency in bulk cooking combines the best of all worlds. You can get home-cooked food the way you want it. You have convenience on the nights you need it. You conserve valuable resources (like money, utilities, and packaging) by buying and cooking in bulk. And you don't have to spend an inordinate amount of time stocking the freezer if you use some timesaving techniques.

Here are the keys to efficient freezer cooking:

- Cooking in bulk

- Planning your meals around common ingredients and core proteins

- Making good use of the tools and technology (that is, small appliances) at your fingertips

- Using the assembly-line method to prepare several batches of a recipe at one time

Cooking in Bulk

If you cooked 30 different meals in one day, you'd have a month's worth of dinners in the freezer, but you would not have saved any time and you would be utterly exhausted. Efficient freezer cooking relies on cooking in bulk and making several "copies" of the same thing. It won't save you time unless you prepare double or triple batches of the recipes you've chosen.

You may be concerned that you will get bored with your meal choices over the month's time. But if you surveyed your eating habits over the past month, you'd probably find that you had several meals more than once. People do that.

And if you include meal components in your cooking plan, you'll find that a few variations can really change up your suppers. A triple batch of seasoned taco meat can go into tacos one night, fill Mexican-style omelets another night, and top off Six-Layer Nachos (page 185) on a third night. That triple batch doesn't seem so boring after all, does it? You can mix and match meal components to create a huge variety of meals.

Common Ingredients

One of the best ways to save time during a bulk cooking session is to combine common ingredients in different ways. The humble chicken breast can be transformed into Tandoori Chicken (page 115), Not Your Mother's Chicken Noodle Soup (page 210), Creamy Chicken Enchiladas (page 123), and Best-Ever Chicken Pot Pie (page 121). All four meals vary in flavor, but they come from the same starting point.

Using common ingredients can also help you take advantage of grocery-store sales. If you find ground beef or steaks on special, then stock up, prepare them in different ways, and stash them in the freezer for later. You'll eat well for a few bucks instead of having to pay full price when you have a hankering for a certain food—and it's not on sale.

Tools to Help You

Efficiency is the goal in freezer cooking, not only on serving day but during your cooking session as well. There are a number of tools that can make quick work of your cooking tasks or even take them off your hands completely, so that you can work on other recipes in your meal plan.

You probably already have basic cookery tools at your disposal, but the following are especially suited to making your bulk cooking sessions more efficient. If there's something on this list you don't own, consider borrowing from a friend for your cooking session or investing in the item if you have the space to store it.

Slow Cookers
The slow cooker is a home cook's best friend. Who else simmers a stew for you while you turn your attention to other tasks? Using one or two large slow cookers during your cooking session will not only result in several prepared meals, it will also free up valuable stovetop real estate for other dishes.

Large Stockpots
While the slow cooker works on a stew, the stockpot on your stove can be busy with soup or red sauce. It is also helpful for browning large batches of ground beef. Having one or even two large stockpots is helpful when cooking up a storm.

Bread Machine
The bread machine is an efficient kitchen servant that can work wonders. In less than 2 hours, it can prepare dough for 4 pizzas or 32 rolls. Since yeast dough freezes best without long rising times, you can instead run your bread machine through more than one mixing cycle in a short amount of time.

Keep a Freezer Inventory

After you spend good time and money planning, shopping, and cooking, you want to make sure that you enjoy those frozen assets in a timely manner. Frozen food, properly stored at 0°F, will keep indefinitely. But eventually, texture and taste can break down under cold storage.

A good rule of thumb is to consume your frozen meals within two to three months. Good labeling is key, so that you know when you made a certain dish and what that dish is. No mystery meat allowed!

Depending on what kind of freezer storage you are using, you may want to keep track of your freezer meals by posting a list of some kind in a prominent spot. If you cross off the items as you use them and add to the list as you add to your freezer inventory, you should always have a good idea of what meals are available to you.

Stand Mixer

A stand mixer is ideal for mashing large batches of potatoes or mixing up mega batches of cookie dough. It can also knead bread dough and whip up a cheesecake in a matter of minutes. A stand mixer can reduce your prep time tremendously.

Food Processor

A food processor is a whiz at shredding cheeses and chopping vegetables quickly, helping you get your food from the grocery bag to the freezer in the shortest time possible. It's also great for blending sauces and soups.

Immersion Blender

An immersion, or stick, blender can quickly puree a smoothie or soup—no need to transfer the mixture to a blender or food processor. It also reduces the number of items to wash, getting you out of the kitchen even faster.

A Home-Kitchen Assembly Line

Henry Ford probably never dreamed that his assembly-line practices of sequential organization and minimal worker motion would help out a home cook a century later. Ford realized that creating many of the same items in succession saves time and money because the worker is simply repeating a motion many times over instead of starting from scratch each time. The same holds true for bulk cooking.

Assembling a lasagna from start to finish might take 30 minutes. But assembling four lasagnas does not take two hours. Mass production takes less time than making several single items one after another.

By creating a sequence in food prep and having all your ingredients within arm's reach, you can prepare bulk batches of any number of recipes and decrease the effort and time that it takes.

Batch cooking can free you up to have your cake and eat it, too. You can enjoy home-cooked meals any night of the week without a lot of fuss. You don't need to spend a lot of time in the kitchen in order to fill your freezer and make things easier for yourself in the days and weeks ahead. A little efficiency goes a long way.

Work It—for *You*

Freezer cooking can work for any household, budget, or size of freezer. Explore the different modes of packaging, purchasing, and preparation until you find the ones you like the best. With proper planning and equipment, you can easily prepare delicious meals at home, on a budget, and in accord with your own dietary preferences. Make-ahead and freeze cooking can enable you to have home-cooked meals whenever you want them, without the marathon cooking sessions of our mothers' kitchen days.

Cooking Plans
to Fit Your Needs

It's certainly true that you can run through the grocery store, pile your cart high, rush home, cook up a storm, and stash your results in the freezer, without following any particular plan. I've done this kind of spontaneous cooking myself.

However, it may take longer than you think. You may find yourself missing key ingredients. And you may discover that a 15-pound turkey cannot be cooked on a sheet pan instead of in your misplaced roasting pan. Ask me how I know.

Truth be told, it's always better to have a plan. Whether you are traveling across the country, looking toward retirement, or simply filling your freezer with homemade convenience foods, a plan will serve you well. It will ensure that you have everything you need, and it will also help you use your time in the most efficient man-

ner. Freezer cooking is all about saving time so that you can enjoy the rest of your life—as well as your mealtimes.

The following plans produce 10 to 30 meals each. In determining the number of meals each plan makes, I've used the recipe yields as my guideline; exactly how many meals each plan produces will depend on the portion sizes you prefer and the extent to which you supplement your meals with side dishes. The plans will walk you through the shopping, cooking, and freezing phases of bulk cooking. Consult the chapter entitled Creating Your

Own Cooking Plan, page 57, for tips on how to develop your own plan and adapt your recipes for freezing.

These plans range in duration from one hour to all day. If you have only an hour or two to cook, make the most of it and get a head start on 10 meals and meal components to help you get through the next couple of weeks without a lot of fuss. If you've got a free day to spend in the kitchen, then stock that freezer up with homemade convenience to feed you and your family throughout the month!

The time frames suggested assume that you have already purchased the groceries listed, own or can borrow all the appliances needed, and have completed your prep list. The grocery lists include the specific amounts needed for each plan in parentheses after the item in question. Where there are additional shortcuts to take, those are noted as well. In some cases, certain ingredients in a given recipe are not in the meal plan, because those ingredients aren't added until the day the dish is served. (For example, in the Everything Plan III, I haven't listed the salmon that goes into the fish chowder, because you freeze the chowder base without the fish.) Read the recipes carefully to make sure you've got whatever ingredients are needed to finish the dish when you serve it, and read each cooking plan and each recipe involved prior to shopping. That way, you'll have a view of where you're headed in terms of finished meals and know what tasks are in store.

Breakfast Plan I (2 hours or less)

Breakfast Plan II (3 to 4 hours)

Meatless Plan I (2 hours or less)

Meatless Plan II (3 to 4 hours)

Beef Plan (2 hours or less)

Poultry and Seafood Plan
 (2 hours or less)

Meat and Poultry Plan (3 to 4 hours)

Everything Plan I (1 day)

Everything Plan II (1 day)

Everything Plan III (1 day)

10-plus meals serving at least 4 people

Individual Greek Egg Casseroles, page 197, 8 servings
Better Instant Oatmeal Packets, page 257, 24 packets
Bulk-Batch Pancake mix, page 258, 2 batches
Cinnamon Banana Bread, page 290, 3 dozen mini breads
Mix-and-Match Muffin mix, page 294, 2 batches

Grocery List

FRESH PRODUCE:

☐ Bananas (6)

DAIRY:

☐ Eggs (19)

☐ Crumbled feta cheese (2⅔ cups)

☐ Milk (1 quart)

☐ Half-and-half (1½ cups)

FROZEN:

☐ Frozen chopped spinach (two 9-ounce packages)

CANNED/BOTTLED/DRY GOODS:

☐ Unbleached all-purpose flour (12 cups)

☐ Whole-wheat pastry flour (7 cups)

☐ Quick-cooking rolled oats (6 cups)

☐ Granulated sugar (2½ cups)

☐ Light or dark brown sugar (2¾ cups)

☐ Raisins, dried cranberries, or dried blueberries (optional; 1½ cups)

☐ Vegetable oil (¾ cup)

☐ Instant dry milk powder (optional; ½ cup)

☐ Baking powder (5 tablespoons plus 2 teaspoons)

☐ Baking soda (4½ teaspoons)

SEASONINGS:

☐ Ground cinnamon (1½ teaspoons)

☐ Salt and freshly ground black pepper

BAKERY:

☐ Italian bread (1 large loaf, for 8 cups bread cubes)

TO SAVE MORE TIME, PURCHASE:

☐ Cubed bread in the bakery department

Packaging

☐ 24 snack-size zip-top bags, labeled Instant Oatmeal (if you prefer not to label each bag, simply collect them all in a large, labeled canister to store in the pantry or freezer)

☐ 4 quart-size zip-top freezer bags, labeled Pancake Mix (2) and Mix-and-Match Muffin Mix (2)

☐ 3 gallon-size zip-top freezer bags, labeled Cinnamon Banana Breads

☐ Eight 2-cup ramekins with lids, labeled Greek Egg Casseroles

Gadgets and Small Appliances

Three 12-cup muffin pans and papers for lining

Prep List

1. Assemble the storage containers and ingredients.

2. Thaw the spinach.

3. Cube the bread.

Cooking Plan

1. Preheat the oven to 350°F. Prepare a batch of cinnamon banana bread, pour the batter into the lined muffin tins, and put them in the oven.

2. Assemble the Greek egg casseroles. Cover and place in freezer. [EGG CASSEROLES DONE]

3. Prepare the instant oatmeal packets. [OATMEAL PACKETS DONE]

4. When the timer for the banana breads rings, remove the breads from the oven and allow them to cool on a rack.

5. Assemble all the baking-mix ingredients and prepare two batches each of pancake and muffin mixes. [PANCAKE MIXES AND MUFFIN MIXES DONE]

6. Clean up while you wait for the banana breads to finish cooling.

7. Package the cooled breads in zip-top freezer bags and store the bags in the freezer. [BANANA BREADS DONE]

8. Finish up by wiping down the counters. Put away any remaining ingredients.

Breakfast Plan II: 3 to 4 Hours

18-plus meals serving at least 4 people

Cranberry-Orange Granola, page 255, 1 batch
Better Instant Oatmeal Packets, page 257, 24 packets
Lemon-and-Honey Flax Waffles, page 264, 2 batches
Buttered French Toast Casserole with Almonds and Ginger, page 266, 2 batches
Savory Ham and Swiss Clafouti, page 277, 2 batches
Lemon-Blueberry Scones, page 300, 2 batches
Whole-Grain Cinnamon Rolls, page 311, 1 batch

Grocery List

FRESH PRODUCE:
- [ ] Lemons (2)
- [ ] Orange (1)
- [ ] Parsley (2 tablespoons chopped)

DAIRY:
- [ ] Butter (about 1½ pounds)
- [ ] Milk (2 cups)
- [ ] Buttermilk (1 quart)
- [ ] Eggs (12)
- [ ] Half-and-half (5 cups)
- [ ] Swiss cheese (8 ounces; 2 cups shredded)

FROZEN:
- [ ] Frozen blueberries (3 cups)

MEAT:
- [ ] Ham (1 pound)

CANNED/BOTTLED/DRY GOODS:
- [ ] Unbleached all-purpose flour (14 cups)
- [ ] Whole-wheat pastry flour (12 cups)
- [ ] Quick-cooking rolled oats (6½ cups)
- [ ] Old-fashioned rolled oats (5 cups)
- [ ] Whole-wheat flour (1 cup)
- [ ] Granulated sugar (2¾ cups)
- [ ] Light or dark brown sugar (2½ cups)
- [ ] Dried fruit, such as raisins, dried cranberries, or dried blueberries (optional; 1½ cups)
- [ ] Instant dried milk powder (optional; 1 cup)
- [ ] Nuts of your choice (1 cup chopped)
- [ ] Baking powder (½ cup plus 2 tablespoons)
- [ ] Baking soda (2 teaspoons)
- [ ] Vegetable oil (½ cup)
- [ ] Raisins—dark, golden, or a combination (½ cup)
- [ ] Sliced almonds (¼ cup)
- [ ] Dried cranberries (¼ cup)
- [ ] Crystallized ginger (¼ cup chopped)
- [ ] Active dry yeast (3¾ teaspoons)
- [ ] Vanilla extract (2½ teaspoons)
- [ ] Dijon mustard (2 teaspoons)

(continued)

Grocery List *(continued)*

SEASONINGS:

- [ ] Salt and freshly ground black pepper
- [ ] Ground cinnamon (2 tablespoon)
- [ ] Dried parsley flakes (2 teaspoons), if not using fresh herb

BAKERY:

- [ ] Italian or brioche bread (2 large loaves)

TO SAVE MORE TIME, PURCHASE:

- [ ] Diced ham
- [ ] Shredded cheese
- [ ] Chopped nuts

Packaging

- [ ] 24 snack-size zip-top bags, labeled Instant Oatmeal (if you prefer not to label each bag, simply collect them all in a large, labeled canister to store in the pantry)
- [ ] 7 gallon-size zip-top freezer bags, labeled Lemon-Blueberry Scones (2), Cranberry-Orange Granola (1), Whole-Grain Cinnamon Rolls (2), Lemon-and-Honey Flax Waffles (2)

- [ ] Two 9 × 13-inch pans with lids or heavy-duty aluminum foil to cover, labeled French Toast Casserole
- [ ] Two 8-inch pie or cake pans with lids or heavy-duty aluminum foil to cover, labeled Ham and Swiss Clafouti

Gadgets and Small Appliances

Bread machine

Food processor

Several baking sheets that will fit in your freezer

Prep List

1. Assemble the storage containers and ingredients.
2. Slice the bread into 1½-inch slices.
3. Dice the ham.
4. Shred the cheese.
5. Zest the lemons and orange.
6. Chop the parsley, if using fresh.

Cooking Plan

1. Preheat the oven to 300°F. Begin the cinnamon roll dough in the bread machine. Allow the kneading cycle to run, scraping down the sides so that all the ingredients are incorporated.

2. Mix up the granola and start it baking in the oven.

3. Check the cinnamon roll dough and make sure that all the ingredients are incorporated and that the dough ball is formed. Allow the machine to finish the dough cycle.

4. Mix up one batch of scones, form them, and freeze them on trays.

5. Stir the granola.

6. Make the second batch of scones, form them, and freeze them on trays. (20 min.)

7. Check the granola.

8. In assembly-line fashion, prepare the instant oatmeal packets. [OATMEAL PACKETS DONE]

9. Mix up the ham and Swiss clafoutis. Wrap and freeze. [CLAFOUTIS DONE]

10. The granola should be done. If so, remove it from the oven and allow it to cool.

11. The scones should be firm. Remove the scones from the freezer and transfer them to zip-top freezer bags. Return them to the freezer immediately. [SCONES DONE]

12. Form the cinnamon rolls. Freeze on trays.

13. Assemble the French toast casseroles. Wrap and freeze. [FRENCH TOAST CASSEROLES DONE]

14. Assemble the waffle mix in two zip-top freezer bags. Store in the freezer. [WAFFLE MIXES DONE]

15. Place the cooled granola into the labeled gallon-size zip-top freezer bags. [GRANOLA DONE]

16. Remove the cinnamon rolls from the freezer and transfer them to the labeled zip-top freezer bags. Return the bags to the freezer immediately. [CINNAMON ROLLS DONE]

17. Clean up the workspace. Wipe down the counters.

Meatless Plan I: 2 Hours or Less

10-plus meals serving at least 4 people

Jamie's Spice Mix, page 90, 1 batch
Pepper Jack and Chile Burritos, page 187, 1 batch
Easy Stovetop Ratatouille, page 188, 1 batch
Sun-Dried Tomato Pesto, page 206, 1 batch
Basic Pizza Dough, page 234, 1 batch
Tomato and Herb Pizza Sauce, page 236, 1 batch
Easy-Peasy Cheesy Pizza kit, page 237, 4 kits
Parmesan Herb Blend, page 240, 2 batches

Grocery List

FRESH PRODUCE:

- [ ] Onion (1 medium, for 1 cup chopped)
- [ ] Garlic (1 head, for 2 tablespoons plus 2 teaspoons chopped)
- [ ] Red bell pepper (1)
- [ ] Green bell pepper (1)
- [ ] Zucchini (1 medium)
- [ ] Yellow squash (1 medium)
- [ ] Eggplant (1 medium)
- [ ] Mushrooms (4 ounces)
- [ ] Lemon (1)
- [ ] Basil (about ½ cup plus 2 tablespoons chopped)
- [ ] Parsley (about 2 tablespoons chopped)

DAIRY:

- [ ] Parmesan cheese (12 ounces; 3 cups finely shredded)
- [ ] Mozzarella cheese (12 ounces; 3 cups shredded)
- [ ] Monterey Jack cheese (12 ounces; 3 cups shredded)
- [ ] Pepper Jack cheese (8 ounces; 2 cups shredded)

CANNED/BOTTLED/DRY GOODS:

- [ ] Petite diced tomatoes (one 28-ounce can plus two 14.5-ounce cans)
- [ ] Unbleached all-purpose flour (4½ cups)
- [ ] Refried beans (two 15-ounce cans)
- [ ] Sun-dried tomatoes (16 ounces; 2 cups)
- [ ] Olive oil (1½ cups)
- [ ] Pine nuts or walnuts (¾ cup)
- [ ] Tomato paste (one 6-ounce can)
- [ ] Chopped green chiles (one 4-ounce can)
- [ ] Honey (2 tablespoons)
- [ ] Active dry yeast (1 tablespoon)

SEASONINGS:

- [ ] Dried basil (3 tablespoons), if not using fresh herb
- [ ] Kosher salt, fine sea salt, and freshly ground black pepper
- [ ] Garlic powder (2 tablespoons plus 2 teaspoons)
- [ ] Onion powder (2 tablespoons)
- [ ] Paprika (1½ tablespoons)

Grocery List *(continued)*

- ☐ Dried oregano (1 tablespoon plus 1 teaspoon)
- ☐ Dried parsley flakes (2 teaspoons), if not using fresh herb
- ☐ *Herbes de Provence* (1½ teaspoons)
- ☐ Celery seeds (1 teaspoon)
- ☐ Crushed red pepper flakes (½ teaspoon)
- ☐ Dried thyme (½ teaspoon)
- ☐ Cayenne pepper (½ teaspoon)

BAKERY:

- ☐ Burrito-size flour tortillas (12)

TO SAVE MORE TIME, PURCHASE:

- ☐ Chopped onions
- ☐ Chopped garlic
- ☐ Sliced mushrooms
- ☐ Shredded cheese

Packaging

- ☐ 4 snack-size zip-top freezer bags, labeled Parmesan Herb Blend for Pizzas
- ☐ 6 sandwich-size zip-top bags, labeled Pizza Dough (4), Jamie's Spice Mix (1), Parmesan Herb Blend (1)
- ☐ 14 pint-size zip-top freezer bags, labeled Pizza Sauce (9), Sun-Dried-Tomato Pesto (5)
- ☐ 4 quart-size zip-top freezer bags, labeled Pizza Cheese
- ☐ 6 gallon-size zip-top freezer bags, labeled Pizza Kit (4), Bean and Cheese Burritos (2)
- ☐ Two 5-cup plastic containers with lids, labeled Ratatouille

Gadgets and Small Appliances

Bread machine

Food processor

Immersion blender

Prep List

1. Assemble the storage containers and ingredients.
2. Chop the onions and garlic.
3. Chop the herbs.
4. Shred the cheeses if they are not already shredded.
5. Chop the vegetables for the Easy Stovetop Ratatouille.
6. Zest the lemon.

Cooking Plan

1. Start the pizza dough in the bread machine.

2. Prepare the pizza sauce on the stove.

3. Check the pizza dough to make sure that all the ingredients have been incorporated into the dough ball. Scrape the sides of the dough pan, if necessary. Once the kneading cycle is over, set the timer for 30 minutes.

4. Prepare two batches of the parmesan herb blend. Place 1 cup in the sandwich bag labeled Parmesan Herb Blend. Divide the remainder between the 4 snack-size bags labeled Parmesan Herb Blend for pizza. Put one of the 4 bags in each of the gallon-size pizza kit bags. [PARMESAN HERB BLEND DONE]

5. Start the ratatouille on the stove.

6. Finish up the pizza sauce. Portion and cool the pizza sauce. Each of 9 bags should have ½ cup sauce. Chill the sauce in the refrigerator before freezing.

7. Portion the pizza cheese: ¾ cup Monterey Jack cheese and ¾ cup mozzarella cheese in each pizza cheese bag. Place one bag of cheese in each large pizza kit bag.

8. The pizza dough hits the 30-minute mark. Divide the dough into four portions and place in sandwich-size bags. Add one dough ball to each large pizza kit and place the kits in the freezer immediately. [PIZZA KITS DONE]

9. Make the sun-dried tomato pesto. Portion the pesto into the 5 marked bags. Freeze. [SUNDRIED TOMATO PESTO DONE]

10. Prepare a batch of Jamie's spice mix. Bag and freeze. [JAMIE'S SPICE MIX DONE]

11. The ratatouille is done. Portion and cool the ratatouille. Chill the containers in the refrigerator before freezing. [RATATOUILLE DONE]

12. Prepare the burrito filling. Assemble the burritos. Bag and freeze the burritos. [BURRITOS DONE]

13. Wipe down the counters. Put away the herbs, spices, and other ingredients. Once the pizza sauce is chilled, add one container to each pizza kit bag already in the freezer. The remaining bags of pizza sauce can be frozen and used for other pizzas or on pasta, as well as for dipping sauce for garlic bread. Transfer the containers of ratatouille to the freezer once they are chilled.

15-plus meals serving at least 4 people

Quick and Easy Cheese Enchiladas, page 183, 1 batch
Green Chile Rice Casserole, page 186, 2 batches
Tahini Vegetable Patties, page 192, 2 batches
Broccoli Gratin with Tarragon and Buttered Bread Crumbs, page 195, 2 batches
Tomato Sauce with Oregano and Kalamata Olives, page 201, 1 batch
Black Bean Soup with Jalapeño, page 219, 1 batch
Homemade Cream of Celery Soup for Cooking, page 223, 4 batches
Oatmeal–Chocolate Chip Pancake mix, page 259, 2 batches
Spiced Whole-Grain Waffle mix, page 262, 2 batches

Grocery List

FRESH PRODUCE:

- [ ] Broccoli florets (3 pounds)
- [ ] Onions (3 medium, for 2½ cups chopped)
- [ ] Celery (3 ribs, for 1½ cups chopped)
- [ ] Carrots (3, for 1 cup shredded)
- [ ] Red bell pepper (1, for 1 cup chopped)
- [ ] Zucchini (1, for 1 cup shredded)
- [ ] Russet potato (1 medium, for 1 cup shredded)
- [ ] Jalapeno peppers (2, for about ⅓ cup chopped)
- [ ] Garlic (4 to 6 cloves)
- [ ] Scallions (1 bunch, for ¼ cup sliced)
- [ ] Orange (1)
- [ ] Lemon (1)

DAIRY:

- [ ] Milk (1 quart)
- [ ] Sour cream or plain Greek yogurt (4 cups)
- [ ] Cheddar cheese (2½ pounds; 10 cups shredded)
- [ ] Parmesan cheese (1 ounce; ¼ cup finely shredded)
- [ ] Eggs (4)
- [ ] Butter (1¼ cups)

CANNED/BOTTLED/DRY GOODS:

- [ ] Unbleached all-purpose flour (10 cups)
- [ ] Whole-wheat pastry flour (6 cups)
- [ ] Oat flour (2 cups)
- [ ] Brown rice (2 cups, to yield 6 cups cooked)
- [ ] Quick-cooking rolled oats (1½ cups)
- [ ] Chopped green chiles (two 4-ounce cans)
- [ ] Light or dark brown sugar (1 cup)
- [ ] Mini chocolate chips (1 cup)
- [ ] Baking powder (½ cup plus 2 tablespoons)
- [ ] Cornmeal (½ cup)
- [ ] White wine (¼ cup)
- [ ] Baking soda (2 teaspoons)
- [ ] Petite diced tomatoes (two 14.5-ounce cans or one 28-ounce can) *(continued)*

Grocery List *(continued)*

- [ ] Black beans (four 15-ounce cans)
- [ ] Reduced-sodium vegetable broth (6 cups; 48 ounces)
- [ ] Garbanzo beans (two 15-ounce cans)
- [ ] Tomato sauce (one 15-ounce cans)
- [ ] Enchilada sauce (one 28-ounce can)
- [ ] Sliced black olives (one 2.25-ounce can)
- [ ] Kalamata olives (⅓ cup chopped)
- [ ] Tahini (¼ cup)
- [ ] Vegetable oil
- [ ] Olive oil (5 tablespoons)

SEASONINGS:

- [ ] Bay leaf (1)
- [ ] Kosher salt, fine sea salt, and freshly ground black pepper
- [ ] Dried oregano (1 tablespoon)
- [ ] Ground cinnamon (1 tablespoon)
- [ ] Ground nutmeg (2 teaspoons)
- [ ] Ground ginger (2 teaspoons)
- [ ] Ground cumin (1 teaspoon)
- [ ] Dried tarragon (1 teaspoon)
- [ ] Onion powder (1 teaspoon)
- [ ] Paprika (½ teaspoon)

BAKERY:

- [ ] Corn tortillas (24)
- [ ] Fresh bread crumbs (5½ cups; about 1 loaf of French bread)

TO SAVE MORE TIME, PURCHASE:

- [ ] Broccoli florets in ready-to-steam packaging
- [ ] Chopped garlic
- [ ] Shredded cheese
- [ ] Fresh bread crumbs

Packaging

- [ ] Two 5-cup containers labeled Black Bean Soup with Jalapeño
- [ ] Five 2-cup containers labeled Tomato Sauce with Oregano and Kalamata Olives (3), Cream of Celery Soup (2)
- [ ] Two 3-quart baking dishes with lids or heavy-duty aluminum foil to cover, labeled Green Chile Rice Casserole
- [ ] Two quart-size zip-top freezer bags, labeled Tahini Vegetable Patties
- [ ] 4 gallon-size zip-top freezer bags, labeled Spiced Waffle Mix (2), Oatmeal–Chocolate Chip Pancake Mix (2)
- [ ] Four 9 × 13-inch pans with lids or heavy-duty aluminum foil to cover, labeled Cheese Enchiladas (2), Broccoli Gratin (2)
- [ ] Plastic wrap
- [ ] Waxed paper

Gadgets and Small Appliances

Food processor

Slow cooker

Rice cooker

Immersion blender

At least two large stockpots

Prep List

1. Assemble the storage containers and ingredients.
2. Chop the onions, pepper, celery, garlic, jalapeño, and scallions.
3. Shred the zucchini and carrot (shred the potato just before adding it to the soup).
4. Cook the rice and allow it to cool.
5. Cut the broccoli into florets if not purchased that way.
6. Make the bread crumbs in the blender or food processor.
7. Shred the cheese.
8. Zest the orange.
9. Juice the lemon.

Cooking Plan

1. Start the black bean soup, using canned black beans.
2. Prepare four batches of the cream of celery soup. Allow it to cool.
3. Prepare a double batch of the tahini veggie patties. Wrap and freeze. [VEGGIE PATTIES DONE]
4. Steam the broccoli. Assemble two batches of the broccoli gratin. Allow the casseroles to cool at room temperature. Chill them in the refrigerator before freezing. [BROCCOLI GRATINS DONE]
5. You should have 4 cups of the cream of celery soup left. Package this soup in 2-cup portions in plastic containers with lids and chill in the refrigerator before freezing. [CREAM OF CELERY SOUP DONE]
6. Wash out the pot and start the tomato sauce.
7. Assemble two batches of the green chile rice. Chill in the refrigerator before freezing. [GREEN CHILE RICE DONE]
8. Portion the black bean soup. Cool at room temperature. Chill the containers in the refrigerator before freezing. [BLACK BEAN SOUP DONE]
9. Fry the tortillas for the enchiladas. Assemble the enchiladas. Chill in the refrigerator before freezing. [CHEESE ENCHILADAS DONE]
10. Prepare pancake and waffle mixes assembly-line style. Divide among labeled bags. [PANCAKE MIXES AND WAFFLE MIXES DONE]
11. Portion the tomato sauce. Cool at room temperature. Chill the containers in the refrigerator before freezing. [TOMATO SAUCE DONE]
12. Clean up the workspace. Wipe down the counters. Once the items in the refrigerator have chilled for several hours, transfer them to the freezer.

Beef Plan: 2 Hours or Less

10-plus meals serving at least 4 people

Chipotle-Rubbed Tri-Tip, page 75, 2 batches
Seasoned taco meat, 2 pounds
Chipotle Taco Seasoning Mix, page 90, 1 batch
Soy-Balsamic Burgers, page 93, 2 batches
Herbed Meatballs (with meatloaf variation), page 97, 1 batch
Easy Make-Ahead Garlic Bread, page 322, 2 batches

Grocery List

FRESH PRODUCE:

- [ ] Onion (1 medium, for 1 cup chopped)
- [ ] Garlic (7 cloves)
- [ ] Basil (5 tablespoons chopped)
- [ ] Parsley (½ cup plus 1 tablespoon chopped)

DAIRY:

- [ ] Eggs (6)
- [ ] Butter (1 cup)

MEAT:

- [ ] Ground beef (10 pounds)
- [ ] Tri-tip roasts (2 roasts, 2 pounds each)

CANNED/BOTTLED/DRY GOODS:

- [ ] Balsamic vinegar (2 tablespoons)
- [ ] Soy sauce (2 tablespoons)

SEASONINGS:

- [ ] Dried parsley flakes (3 tablespoons), if not using fresh herb
- [ ] Ground chipotle chile powder (2 tablespoons plus 2 teaspoons)

- [ ] Kosher salt, fine sea salt, and freshly ground black pepper
- [ ] Onion flakes (2 tablespoons)
- [ ] Garlic powder (1 tablespoon plus 2 teaspoons)
- [ ] Dried basil (about 2 tablespoons), if not using fresh herb
- [ ] Ground cumin (1 tablespoon)
- [ ] Dried oregano (1 tablespoon)
- [ ] Dried thyme (1 teaspoon)

BAKERY:

- [ ] Fresh bread crumbs (3 cups, or about 9 slices of bread)
- [ ] French or Italian bread (2 large loaves)

TO SAVE MORE TIME, PURCHASE:

- [ ] Chopped onions
- [ ] Chopped garlic
- [ ] Fresh bread crumbs

Packaging

- ☐ 2 snack-size zip-top bags, labeled Chipotle Rub
- ☐ 1 pint-size zip-top freezer bag, labeled Chipotle Taco Seasoning
- ☐ 4 quart-size zip-top freezer bags, labeled Taco Meat (2), Meatballs (2)
- ☐ 5 gallon-size zip-top freezer bags, labeled Tri-tip (2), Burgers (2), Meatloaf (1)
- ☐ Heavy-duty aluminum foil
- ☐ Waxed paper
- ☐ Plastic wrap

Gadgets and Small Appliances

Food processor

Cookie scoop, quick release

Food scale

Prep List

1. Assemble the storage containers and ingredients.
2. Make the bread crumbs in the blender or food processor.
3. Chop the herbs.
4. Chop the onion.
5. Chop the garlic.
6. Soften the butter.

Cooking Plan

1. Preheat the oven to 350°F. In a large mixing bowl, prepare the meatball mixture. Using a quick-release cookie scoop, form half the prepared mixture into meatballs, arrange them on the prepared baking sheets, and place them in the oven.

2. Divide the remaining meatball mixture in half. Form each portion into a meatloaf. Wrap each loaf in aluminum foil, label, and bag. Two loaves should fit in 1 bag, but you can bag them separately if you prefer. Place in the freezer. [MEATLOAVES DONE]

3. Start cooking 2 pounds of ground beef, to make the seasoned taco meat, in a large skillet on the stovetop.

4. Prepare the chipotle taco seasoning mix (single batch) and the chipotle rub for the tri-tip (two batches) at the same time, since they share common ingredients. Pack the chipotle rub into two snack-size bags and seal. The taco seasoning can go in the pint-size bag.

5. Stir 2 to 4 tablespoons of the taco seasoning mix into the ground beef on the stove once it has started to brown; store the remainder of the taco

seasoning mix for another cooking session. Clean up and put away the spices while the taco meat cooks; leave the thyme, balsamic, parsley, soy sauce, and black pepper out for the hamburgers. Portion the cooked meat into two quart-size zip-top bags and allow it to cool to room temperature. Chill the cooked meat in the refrigerator before freezing. [SEASONED TACO MEAT DONE]

6. The meatballs should be done cooking. Remove them from the oven and loosen them from the foil, if they're sticking. Allow them to cool to room temperature and then bag them. Chill the meatballs in the refrigerator before storing in the freezer. [MEATBALLS DONE]

7. Package each tri-tip and its snack-size bag of chipotle rub together in a labeled freezer bag. Freeze. [TRI-TIPS DONE]

8. In a large mixing bowl, prepare the soy balsamic burgers, using the remaining 4 pounds of ground beef. Form the mixture into 16 patties. Stack the patties in groups of 4, separating them with waxed paper. Wrap with plastic wrap and place the bundles in the labeled freezer bags. Freeze. [HAMBURGERS DONE]

9. Prepare the garlic bread, wrap in foil, and freeze. [GARLIC BREAD DONE]

10. Clean up the workspace. Wipe down the counters. Once the items in the refrigerator have chilled for several hours, transfer them to the freezer.

Poultry and Seafood Plan: 2 Hours or Less

10-plus meals serving at least 4 people

Seasoned turkey taco meat, 2 pounds
Basic Taco Seasoning Mix, page 89, 1 batch
Tandoori Chicken, page 115, 2 batches
Spicy Taco Lasagna, page 138, 2 batches
Turkey Burgers with Scallions, page 139, 2 batches
Mahi Mahi with Almond-Lime Butter, page 142, 2 batches

Grocery List

FRESH PRODUCE:

- [ ] Lemon (1)
- [ ] Limes (2)
- [ ] Scallions (½ to 1 bunch, for ½ cup chopped)
- [ ] Ginger (1-inch piece for 2 teaspoons chopped)
- [ ] Dill (1 tablespoon chopped)
- [ ] Garlic (2 cloves)

DAIRY:

- [ ] Pepper Jack cheese (1 pound; 4 cups shredded)
- [ ] Cheddar cheese (1 pound; 4 cups shredded)
- [ ] Cream cheese (two 8-ounce packages)
- [ ] Plain yogurt or buttermilk (1½ cups)
- [ ] Butter (1 cup)

MEAT/POULTRY/SEAFOOD:

- [ ] Chicken pieces, such as boneless, skinless chicken breast (8 to 12 pieces)
- [ ] Ground turkey (6½ pounds)
- [ ] Mahi mahi or other fish fillets (8 fillets, 5 to 8 ounces each)

CANNED/BOTTLED/DRY GOODS:

- [ ] Olive oil (2 tablespoons)
- [ ] Sherry (2 tablespoons)
- [ ] Favorite purchased pasta sauce, or homemade (6 cups; 48 ounces)
- [ ] Favorite purchased salsa, or Easy Homemade Salsa, page 71 (16 ounces)
- [ ] Reduced-sodium chicken broth (2 cups)
- [ ] Lasagna noodles (12 to 16)
- [ ] Sliced almonds (½ cup)

SEASONINGS:

- [ ] Chili powder (¼ cup plus 1 teaspoon)
- [ ] Kosher salt, fine sea salt, and freshly ground black pepper
- [ ] Onion flakes (2 tablespoons)
- [ ] Dried oregano (2 tablespoons)
- [ ] Garlic powder (1 tablespoon)
- [ ] Paprika (2 teaspoons)
- [ ] Curry powder (2 teaspoons)
- [ ] Dried dill (1 teaspoon), if not using fresh herb

(continued)

Grocery List (continued)

BAKERY:

☐ Fresh bread crumbs (1 cup, or about 3 slices of bread)

TO SAVE MORE TIME, PURCHASE:

☐ Chopped ginger and garlic

☐ Shredded cheese

☐ Fresh bread crumbs

Packaging

☐ 2 quart-size zip-top freezer bags, labeled Seasoned Taco Meat

☐ 6 gallon-size zip-top freezer bags, labeled Tandoori Chicken (2), Mahi Mahi with Almond-Lime Butter (2), Turkey Burgers with Scallions (2)

☐ Two 9 × 13-inch pans with lids or heavy-duty aluminum foil to cover, labeled Spicy Taco Lasagna

☐ 1 pint-size zip-top freezer bag, labeled Taco Seasoning Mix

☐ Freezer paper for wrapping fish, if not already wrapped

☐ Plastic wrap

☐ Waxed paper

Gadgets and Small Appliances

Food processor

Prep List

1. Assemble the storage containers and ingredients.

2. Make the bread crumbs in the blender or food processor. Toast the almonds.

3. Soften the butter.

4. Chop the scallions.

5. Shred the cheeses for the lasagna.

6. Juice the lemons.

7. Chop the garlic and ginger.

8. Zest the lime.

Cooking Plan

1. Mix up a batch of taco seasoning mix.

2. Brown 4 pounds of the ground turkey and season it with 1 to 2 tablespoons of the taco seasoning mix. Reserve the remaining seasoning mix for another time. It can be stored in the labeled bag in the pantry or in the freezer for longer keeping.

3. Portion out half of the cooked taco meat and set it aside to use in the lasagna. Divide the remaining taco meat between the labeled zip-top freezer bags. Allow the meat to cool to room temperature and then chill it in the refrigerator before freezing. [SEASONED TACO MEAT DONE]

4. Assemble the spicy taco lasagna. Chill and freeze. [LASAGNA DONE]

5. Using the remaining 2½ pounds of ground turkey, make the turkey burgers. Wrap and freeze. [TURKEY BURGERS DONE]

6. Prepare the almond-lime butter. Assemble the mahi mahi kits as directed in the recipe. Freeze. [MAHI MAHI DONE]

7. Prepare two batches of the tandoori chicken. Pack into labeled bags and freeze. [TANDOORI CHICKEN DONE]

8. Clean up the workspace. Wipe down the counters. Once the items in the refrigerator have chilled for several hours, transfer them to the freezer.

Meat and Poultry Plan: 3 to 4 Hours

28 meals serving at least 4 people

Not Your Convenience Store's Frozen Burritos, page 87, 4 batches
Taco kit, using ground turkey, page 89, 2 kits, using 2 pounds meat
Basic Taco Seasoning Mix, page 89, 2 batches
Outside-In Cheeseburgers, page 96, 2 batches
Herbed Meatballs, page 97, 1 batch
Spicy Taco Lasagna, page 138, 2 batches
Southwest Seasoned Pork Chops, page 153, 2 batches
Easy Slow Cooker Red Sauce, page 205, 1 batch
Basic pizza kits, page 238, 1 batch dough to make kits for 4 pizzas
Eggs Florentine Casserole, page 275, 2 batches

Grocery List

FRESH PRODUCE:

- [ ] Onions (6 medium, for 6 cups chopped)
- [ ] 1 head garlic
- [ ] Basil (about ½ cup chopped)
- [ ] Parsley (about ½ cup chopped)
- [ ] Dill (1 tablespoon chopped)

DAIRY:

- [ ] Cheddar cheese (a little over 4 pounds; 17 cups shredded)
- [ ] Mozzarella cheese (1½ pounds; 6 cups shredded)
- [ ] Pepper Jack or Monterey Jack cheese (1 pound; 4 cups shredded)
- [ ] Swiss cheese (1 pound; 4 cups shredded)
- [ ] Feta cheese (4 cups crumbled)
- [ ] Cottage cheese (2 pints)
- [ ] Cream cheese (two 8-ounce packages)
- [ ] Eggs (2 dozen)

MEAT:

- [ ] Ground beef (12 pounds)
- [ ] Ground turkey (4 pounds)
- [ ] Pork chops (8 chops, ½ inch thick)

FROZEN:

- [ ] Frozen chopped spinach (two 10-ounce packages)

CANNED/BOTTLED/DRY GOODS:

- [ ] Refried beans or cooked pinto beans (12 cups, 96 ounces, about seven 15-ounce cans)
- [ ] Enchilada sauce (32 ounces)
- [ ] Reduced-sodium chicken broth (2 cups)
- [ ] Diced green chiles (four 4-ounce cans)
- [ ] Favorite purchased salsa, or Easy Homemade Salsa, page 71 (16 ounces)
- [ ] Lasagna noodles (12 to 16 noodles)
- [ ] Crushed tomatoes (four 28-ounce cans)
- [ ] Unbleached all-purpose flour (4½ cups)

Grocery List (continued)

- ☐ Vegetable oil (½ cup)
- ☐ Olive oil (½ cup)
- ☐ Red wine vinegar (½ cup)
- ☐ Honey or granulated sugar (2 tablespoons)
- ☐ Active dry yeast (1 tablespoon)

SEASONINGS:

- ☐ Chile powder (½ cup)
- ☐ Dried basil (3 tablespoons), if not using fresh herb
- ☐ Dried parsley flakes (about 3 tablespoons), if not using fresh herb
- ☐ Kosher salt, fine sea salt, and freshly ground black pepper
- ☐ Dried oregano (¼ cup)
- ☐ Garlic powder (2 tablespoons)

- ☐ Onion flakes (¼ cup)
- ☐ Dried dill (1 teaspoon), if not using fresh herb
- ☐ Crushed red pepper flakes (½ teaspoon)

BAKERY:

- ☐ Soft taco-size flour tortillas (two 12-count packages)
- ☐ Burrito-size flour tortillas (48)
- ☐ Fresh bread crumbs (3 cups, or about 9 slices of bread)

TO SAVE MORE TIME, PURCHASE:

- ☐ Chopped garlic
- ☐ Chopped onions
- ☐ Shredded cheese
- ☐ Fresh bread crumbs

Packaging

- ☐ 4 sandwich-size bags, labeled Pizza Dough
- ☐ 1 pint-size freezer bag, labeled Taco Seasoning Mix
- ☐ 12 quart-size zip-top freezer bags, labeled Seasoned Taco Meat (2), Taco Cheese if not prepackaged in 2-cup portions (2), Meatballs (4), Pizza Cheese (4)
- ☐ 18 gallon-size zip-top freezer bags, labeled Taco Kit (2), Burritos (8),

Southwest Pork Chops (2), Pizza Kit (4), Outside-In Cheeseburgers (2)

- ☐ Four 9 × 13-inch pans with lids or heavy-duty aluminum foil for covering, labeled Eggs Florentine (2), Taco Lasagna (2)
- ☐ Three or four 2-cup plastic containers with lids, labeled Red Sauce
- ☐ Four ½-cup plastic containers with lids for Red Sauce for pizza kits
- ☐ Heavy-duty aluminum foil

Gadgets and Small Appliances

Food processor

Bread machine

Prep List

1. Assemble the storage containers and ingredients.
2. Make the bread crumbs in the food processor or blender.
3. Chop the onions and garlic.
4. Chop the herbs.
5. Make the salsa, if using homemade.
6. Shred the cheese.
7. Thaw the spinach.

Cooking Plan

1. Start cooking the red sauce on the stovetop. It will simmer for 2 hours.
2. Begin the pizza dough in the bread machine. After it's been mixing for a few minutes, make sure all the ingredients are incorporated by scraping the sides of the bread pan with a rubber scraper. Allow the kneading cycle to run.
3. Meanwhile, season and form the cheeseburgers, using 4 pounds of the ground beef. Lay the patties on a tray or trays and freeze.
4. Once the bread machine is done kneading the dough, set the timer for a 30-minute rise.
5. Mix up two batches of taco seasoning mix.
6. Brown 4 pounds of the ground beef in a large skillet or pot. Season it with the taco seasoning mix to taste, using 1 to 2 tablespoons per pound. Drain and transfer the meat to a large bowl. Allow the meat to cool. Wash the pot.
7. The pizza dough is done with the first rise. Turn the dough out onto a lightly oiled surface. Divide the dough ball into 4 sections. Form each section into a tight ball and place in a labeled sandwich-size bag. Place 1 dough ball into each pizza kit bag and place in the freezer immediately. The dough will continue to rise, so move quickly.
8. Portion the mozzarella cheese into the 4 bags labeled Pizza Cheese, 1½ cups of cheese per bag. Slip the bags into the pizza kit bags in the freezer.
9. Assemble the burritos with the 4 pounds of cooled cooked beef. Place 6 in each labeled freezer bag. Seal the bags, removing as much air as possible before sealing. Place the bags in the freezer. [BURRITOS DONE]
10. Cook the ground turkey in a large pot. Season the meat with the remaining taco seasoning mix according to taste. Remove half of the meat to a large mixing bowl for the lasagna. Spoon the remaining meat into the two bags labeled Taco Meat. Allow the meat to cool slightly on the counter and then chill it in the refrigerator.
11. Remove 6 cups of the red sauce to prepare the spicy taco lasagna. Cool the lasagna, cover, and chill in the refrigerator. [LASAGNA DONE]
12. Preheat the oven to 350°F. Use the remaining 4 pounds of ground beef

to prepare the meatballs. Place the meatballs on a foil-lined rimmed baking sheet and place in the oven.

13. Divide 2 cups of the red sauce among the four ½-cup plastic containers. These will be added to the pizza kits. Allow the sauce to cool slightly before securing the lids. Chill the sauce in the refrigerator. [PIZZA KITS DONE]

14. Portion the remaining red sauce into the labeled 2-cup containers.

15. Remove the hamburgers from the trays in the freezer and place them in the labeled bags. Seal the bags and return the burgers to freezer. [BURGERS DONE]

16. Portion the remaining cheddar cheese into bags labeled Taco Cheese. Place one cheese bag in each taco kit bag. Add a chilled bag of taco meat and a package of taco-size tortillas to each bag. [TACO KITS DONE]

17. When the meatballs are done, remove from the oven and allow to cool.

18. Assemble the egg casseroles. Wrap and freeze. [EGG CASSEROLES DONE]

19. Prepare the marinade for the pork chops and divide it between the labeled bags. Add the chops to the bags, putting 4 pork chops in each bag. Seal the bags and freeze. [PORK CHOPS DONE]

20. Package the meatballs in the labeled freezer bags. Chill the meatballs in the refrigerator before freezing. [MEATBALLS DONE]

21. Package any remaining taco seasoning mix in the labeled bag and store in the pantry or freezer for later use.

22. Clean up the workspace. Wipe down the counters. Once the items in the refrigerator have chilled for several hours, transfer the packages to the freezer.

25-plus meals serving at least 4 people

Beefy Mushroom Gravy, page 81, 4 batches
Vegetable Bolognese, page 83, 2 batches
Jamie's Spice Mix, page 90, 1 batch
Sweet and Spicy Joes, page 91, 2 batches
Swedish Meatballs with Dill, page 100, 1 batch
Simply Poached Chicken, page 107, 2 batches
Spicy Southwest Chicken, page 111, 2 batches
Spicy Dijon Chicken, page 114, 2 batches
Garlicky Italian Chicken Breasts, page 117, 2 batches
Garlic Butter Chicken with Lemon Sauce, page 127, 2 batches
Crumb-Topped Cod Fillets, page 145, 2 batches
Tarragon-and-Lemon-Rubbed Fish, page 146, 2 batches
Shrimp Tacos, page 147, 2 batches
Potatoes Stuffed with Caramelized Onions and Dubliner Cheese, page 193, 1 batch

Grocery List

FRESH PRODUCE:

- [ ] Onions (5 or 6 medium, for about 5½ cups chopped)
- [ ] 8 baking potatoes
- [ ] Red bell peppers (2)
- [ ] Carrots (2)
- [ ] Eggplants (2 medium)
- [ ] Zucchini (2)
- [ ] Tomatoes (2 medium)
- [ ] Mushrooms (8 ounces)
- [ ] Garlic (3 heads)
- [ ] Jalapeño pepper (1)
- [ ] Lime (1)
- [ ] Lemons (3)
- [ ] Parsley (1 bunch chopped)
- [ ] Basil (about ¾ cup chopped)
- [ ] Dill (about ½ cup chopped)
- [ ] Cilantro (1 bunch)

MEAT:

- [ ] Ground beef (9 pounds)
- [ ] Chicken pieces for marinating (24 to 36 pieces)
- [ ] Boneless, skinless chicken breasts (8)
- [ ] Boneless, skinless chicken tenders (4 pounds)
- [ ] Medium-size shrimp, peeled and deveined (2 pounds)
- [ ] Cod fillets (8 fillets, 5 to 8 ounces each)
- [ ] Fish fillets, such as salmon (8 fillets, 5 to 8 ounces each)
- [ ] Ground pork (1 pound)

Grocery List *(continued)*

DAIRY:
- [ ] Eggs (6)
- [ ] Butter (about 1½ pounds)
- [ ] Dubliner cheese (4 ounces; 1 cup shredded)
- [ ] Sour cream (8 ounces)

CANNED/BOTTLED/DRY GOODS:
- [ ] Tomato sauce (six 15-ounce cans)
- [ ] Reduced-sodium beef broth (64 ounces)
- [ ] Petite diced tomatoes (two 14.5-ounce cans)
- [ ] Vegetable oil (½ cup)
- [ ] Olive oil (about 2 cups)
- [ ] Panko bread crumbs (1 cup)
- [ ] Unbleached all-purpose flour (1 cup)
- [ ] Red wine vinegar (¾ cup)
- [ ] Dijon mustard (⅔ cup)
- [ ] Red wine (½ cup), optional
- [ ] White wine or sherry (½ cup)
- [ ] Soy sauce (½ cup)
- [ ] Light or dark brown sugar (2 tablespoons)
- [ ] Granulated sugar (2 pinches)

SEASONINGS:
- [ ] Dried parsley flakes (about ⅓ cup), if not using fresh herb
- [ ] Kosher salt, fine sea salt, and freshly ground pepper
- [ ] Paprika (about ¼ cup)
- [ ] Dried basil (about ¼ cup), if not using fresh herb
- [ ] Onion powder (2 tablespoons)
- [ ] Dried dill (2 to 3 tablespoons), if not using fresh herb
- [ ] Garlic powder (3 tablespoons plus 1 teaspoon)
- [ ] Dried oregano (1 tablespoon plus 1 teaspoon)
- [ ] Cayenne pepper (1 tablespoon)
- [ ] Sesame seeds (1 tablespoon)
- [ ] Celery seeds (2 teaspoons)
- [ ] Dried tarragon (2 teaspoons)
- [ ] Dried thyme (2 teaspoons)
- [ ] Ground ginger (1 teaspoon)
- [ ] Ground allspice (¼ teaspoon)
- [ ] Bay leaves (4)
- [ ] Peppercorns (8)

BAKERY:
- [ ] Fresh bread crumbs (6 cups, or about 18 slices of bread)

TO SAVE MORE TIME, PURCHASE:
- [ ] Shredded cheeses
- [ ] Chopped onion
- [ ] Chopped garlic
- [ ] Fresh bread crumbs

Packaging

- ☐ 6 snack-size zip-top bags, labeled Shrimp Taco Spice (2), Crumb Topping for Fish (2), Tarragon-Lemon Rub (2), Jamie's Spice Mix (1)
- ☐ 5 pint-size zip-top freezer bags, labeled Gravy for Swedish Meatballs (4), Jaime's Spice Mix (1)
- ☐ 6 quart-size zip-top freezer bags, labeled Swedish Meatballs (4), Poached Chicken (2)
- ☐ 14 gallon-size zip-top freezer bags, labeled Stuffed Potatoes with Caramelized Onions and Dubliner
- Cheese (2), Spicy Southwest Chicken (2), Dijon Chicken (2), Garlicky Italian Chicken (2), Shrimp Taco Kit (2), Crumb-Topped Cod Kit (2), Tarragon-Lemon Fish (2)
- ☐ Two 9 × 13-inch pans with lids or heavy-duty aluminum foil to cover, labeled Garlic Butter Chicken with Lemon Sauce
- ☐ 7 quart-size plastic containers with lids, labeled Vegetable Bolognese (3) and Sweet and Spicy Joes (4)
- ☐ Plastic wrap

Gadgets and Small Appliances

Food processor and/or blender

At least 2 large stockpots

Prep List

1. Assemble the storage containers and ingredients.
2. Shred the cheese.
3. Chop the onion and garlic.
4. Chop the herbs.
5. Make the bread crumbs in the blender or food processor.
6. Soften the butter.
7. Make the garlic butter for the stuffed chicken.
8. Bake the baking potatoes.
9. Chop the mushrooms, carrots, red bell peppers, and zucchini.
10. Core and halve the tomatoes.
11. Peel and chop the eggplants.
12. Halve the chicken breasts for stuffing.

Cooking Plan

1. Make an 8-cup batch of the beefy mushroom gravy. Add 2 tablespoons of the fresh dill. Place 4 pint-size bags marked Gravy for Swedish Meatballs inside a bowl, so that the bags are stabilized to hold liquids. Divide the gravy among the pint-size bags. Allow the bags to cool to room temperature and then chill the bags in the refrigerator before freezing them.

2. Wash the pot.

3. Mix one batch of Jamie's spice mix, placing it in the labeled pint-size bag.

4. Brown 4 pounds of meat for the sweet and spicy Joes. Add the remaining ingredients to the stockpot and allow the mixture to simmer.

5. Start cooking the Bolognese in a second pot, using 2 pounds of the ground beef.

6. Stuff the baked potatoes. Place in labeled bags and freeze. [STUFFED POTATOES DONE]

7. Portion out the sweet and spicy Joes in the labeled containers. Allow to cool on the counter before covering the containers and chilling them in the refrigerator. [SWEET AND SPICY JOES DONE]

8. Preheat the oven to 350°F. Prepare the meatballs using the remaining 3 pounds of ground beef and the ground pork. Place the meatballs on a foil-lined rimmed baking sheet and place them in the oven.

9. Start poaching the 4 pounds of chicken tenders. Be sure to set a timer, according to the recipe instructions.

10. Portion out the Bolognese in the labeled containers. Allow it to cool on the counter before covering the containers and chilling them in the refrigerator. [BOLOGNESE DONE]

11. The meatballs should be done. Remove them from the oven. Loosen the meatballs from the aluminum foil, if they are sticking. Allow them to cool.

12. Wash the pots.

13. Prepare the garlic butter chicken breasts, using the 8 boneless chicken breasts. Wrap and freeze. [GARLIC BUTTER CHICKEN DONE]

14. Portion the meatballs into the labeled bags. Allow them to cool on the counter before chilling them in the refrigerator. [MEATBALLS DONE]

15. Prepare the marinades for the spicy Southwest chicken, Dijon chicken, and garlicky Italian chicken. Distribute the marinades and chicken pieces among the labeled bags, seal, and freeze. [SOUTHWEST CHICKEN, DIJON CHICKEN, AND ITALIAN CHICKEN DONE.]

16. Check the poached chicken. If the water is cool, remove the chicken tenders and portion them, whole or chopped, into the labeled bags and chill before freezing. [POACHED CHICKEN DONE]

17. Prepare the rubs and crumb toppings for the shrimp and fish dishes and assemble the shrimp and fish kits. [SHRIMP TACOS, CRUMB-TOPPED COD FILLET, AND TARRAGON-AND-LEMON-RUBBED FISH KITS DONE]

18. Clean up the workspace. Wipe down the counters. Once the items in the refrigerator have chilled for several hours, transfer them to the freezer.

25-plus meals serving at least 4 people

Basic Herb-Baked Chicken, page 104, 2 batches
Chicken Enchilada Bake with Green Chiles and Jalapeños, page 120, 2 batches
Chicken-Bacon Subs, page 135, 2 batches
Make-Ahead Baked Bacon, page 169, 2 batches
Queso Fundido, page 172, made with mild Italian sausage, 2 batches
Red Sauce with Sausage, page 174, 1 batch
Bean and Cheese Nacho Bake, page 182, 2 batches
Cozy Cheese and Potato Casserole, page 184, 2 batches
Homemade Cream of Celery Soup for Cooking, page 223, 4 batches
Cinnamon French Toast Dippers, page 265, 1 batch
Bacon-Cheddar Egg Bake for a crowd, page 273, 2 batches
Chile and Sausage Oven Frittata, page 278, 2 batches
Easy Make-Ahead Garlic Bread, page 322, 2 batches

Grocery List

FRESH PRODUCE:

- [ ] Onions (5 medium, for 4⅔ cups chopped)
- [ ] Jalapeño peppers (2)
- [ ] Garlic (1 to 2 heads)
- [ ] Celery (2 to 3 ribs, for ½ cup chopped)
- [ ] Parsley (about ⅓ cup chopped)
- [ ] Basil (about ⅓ cup chopped)
- [ ] Cilantro (2 tablespoons chopped)
- [ ] Orange (1)

DAIRY:

- [ ] Eggs (35)
- [ ] Cheddar cheese (about 3 pounds; 11⅔ cups shredded)
- [ ] Milk (9 cups)
- [ ] Pepper Jack cheese (2 pounds; 8 cups shredded)

- [ ] Monterey Jack cheese (6 ounces; 1½ cups shredded)
- [ ] Mozzarella or additional Monterey Jack cheese (10 ounces sliced)
- [ ] Sour cream (5⅓ cups)
- [ ] Ricotta cheese (16 ounces)
- [ ] Butter (1½ pounds)
- [ ] Parmesan cheese (¼ cup shredded)

FROZEN:

- [ ] Frozen shredded potatoes (two 32-ounce bags)

MEAT:

- [ ] Bone-in split chicken breasts (12)
- [ ] Mild Italian sausage (4½ pounds)
- [ ] Bacon (3 pounds)

Grocery List *(continued)*

CANNED/BOTTLED/DRY GOODS:

- [ ] Olive oil (2 tablespoons)
- [ ] Tomato puree (four 28-ounce cans)
- [ ] Refried beans (48 ounces)
- [ ] Tomato sauce (two 8-ounce cans)
- [ ] Favorite purchased salsa, or Easy Homemade Salsa, page 71 (16 ounces)
- [ ] Chopped green chiles (four 4-ounce cans)
- [ ] Tortilla chips (13 ounces)
- [ ] Sliced black olives (about 1⅓ cups)
- [ ] Unbleached all-purpose flour (1 cup plus 2 tablespoons)
- [ ] Light or dark brown sugar (1½ tablespoons)

SEASONINGS:

- [ ] Kosher salt, fine sea salt, and freshly ground black pepper
- [ ] Dried parsley flakes (about 2 tablespoons), if not using fresh herb
- [ ] Dried basil (about 2 tablespoons), if not using fresh herb

- [ ] Garlic powder (2 teaspoons)
- [ ] Ground cumin (2 teaspoons)
- [ ] Paprika (2½ teaspoons)
- [ ] Chili powder (4 teaspoons)
- [ ] Dried oregano (1½ teaspoons)
- [ ] Onion powder (1 teaspoon)
- [ ] Ground cinnamon (½ teaspoon)
- [ ] Crushed red pepper flakes (¼ teaspoon)
- [ ] *Herbes de Provence*, chili powder, or Italian herbs (optional; 2 teaspoons)
- [ ] Vanilla extract (1 teaspoon)

BAKERY:

- [ ] Italian bread (4 large loaves)
- [ ] Bread cubes (12 cups)
- [ ] French bread or sub rolls (three 8-inch)
- [ ] Corn tortillas (24)

TO SAVE MORE TIME, PURCHASE:

- [ ] Shredded cheeses
- [ ] Chopped onions
- [ ] Chopped garlic

Packaging

- [ ] 3 quart-size zip-top freezer bags, labeled Cooked Sausage (2), Cooked Chicken (1)
- [ ] 8 gallon-size zip-top freezer bags, labeled Queso Fundido (2), Bacon (2), French Toast Dippers (2), Sausage and Chile Frittata (2)
- [ ] Four 8-inch pie plates, labeled Queso Fundido (2), Sausage and Chile Frittata (2)

- [ ] 6 or 7 pint-size plastic containers with lids, labeled Red Sauce
- [ ] Eight 9 × 13-inch baking pans with lids, labeled Enchilada Bake (2), Bean and Cheese Nacho Bake (2), Potato Casserole (2), Bacon-Cheddar Egg Bake (2)
- [ ] Heavy-duty aluminum foil

Gadgets and Small Appliances

Slow cooker

2 large stockpots

Food processor

Prep List

1. Assemble the storage containers and ingredients.

2. Soften the butter.

3. Shred the cheeses.

4. Slice the French bread or sub rolls for French toast.

5. Slice the 4 loaves of Italian bread horizontally.

6. Chop the herbs.

7. Make the garlic butter for the Easy Make-Ahead Garlic Bread and Chicken Bacon Subs.

Cooking Plan

1. Preheat the oven to 375°F. Bake the chicken and the bacon. Be sure to set a timer and check on the pans in between the other steps. If your oven is not large enough, bake in stages.

2. Start the red sauce in the slow cooker or on the stovetop.

3. Make an 8-cup batch of cream of celery soup. Allow to cool. Once cool, use in recipes or chill in refrigerator until needed.

4. Remove the casings from 2½ pounds of the sausage and cook the meat in a skillet on the stovetop, breaking up any chunks with the back of a spoon. Drain. Remove about one-fifth of the meat to use in the frittatas. Use the remaining cooked sausage for the queso fundido.

5. Assemble the queso fundido in the labeled pie plates. Allow the plates to cool slightly on the counter before chilling them in the refrigerator. [QUESO FUNDIDO DONE]

6. Assemble the 2 frittatas in the labeled pie plates, using the reserved cooked and cooled sausage. [FRITTATAS DONE]

7. The bacon should be cooked and cooled by now. Reserve 12 slices and package the rest for later use, dividing it between the two labeled bags. [BACON DONE]

8. Add the remaining 2 pounds sausage links to the red sauce.

9. The chicken should be baked and at least partially cooled by now. Shred or chop the chicken, according to your preference. Reserve 6 cups for the enchilada bakes and 4 cups for the chicken-bacon subs. Package the remaining chicken into the bag labeled Cooked Chicken for later use. [COOKED CHICKEN DONE]

10. Make the chicken-bacon subs using 4 cups of chicken and 4 slices of bacon. At the same time, make 2 loaves of garlic bread. Wrap both bread and subs

in heavy-duty foil and freeze. [SUBS AND GARLIC BREAD DONE]

11. Use the remaining 6 cups of cooked chicken to make the enchilada bakes. Cover and chill in the refrigerator before freezing. [ENCHILADA BAKES DONE]

12. Turn the oven up to 500°F. Make the French toast dippers and bake them in batches. As each batch is done, cool the dippers on a rack.

13. Assemble the bacon-cheddar egg bakes. Wrap and freeze. [EGG BAKES DONE]

14. Assemble the bean and cheese nacho bakes. Cover and chill in the refrigerator before freezing. [NACHO BAKES DONE]

15. Package the cooled French toast dippers in the labeled bags and freeze. [FRENCH TOAST DONE]

16. Remove the cooked sausages from the red sauce and package them in the labeled bags. Portion the red sauce into the labeled plastic containers. Allow the sausages and sauce to cool to room temperature before chilling in the refrigerator. [RED SAUCE WITH SAUSAGE DONE]

17. Assemble the cheese and potato casserole. Freeze immediately. [POTATO CASSEROLE DONE]

18. Clean up the workspace. Wipe down the counters. Once the items in the refrigerator have chilled for several hours, transfer them to the freezer.

25-plus meals serving at least 4 people

Mexican Beef Tortas, page 71, 1 batch
Mediterranean-Style Steak, page 76, 2 batches
Seasoned Steak with Gorgonzola-Herb Butter, page 78, 2 batches
Jamie's Spice Mix, page 90, 1 batch
Herb Butter Chicken Tenders, page 118, 2 batches
Teriyaki Chicken Skewers, page 119, 2 batches
Spicy Shrimp and Tomatoes, page 149, 1 batch
Soy-Ginger Pork Tenderloin, page 159, 2 batches
Grilled Caribbean Pork Tenderloin, page 163, 2 batches
Herb-Crusted Pork Roast, page 165, 2 batches
Ham and Swiss Potato Gratin, page 170, 1 batch
Quick and Spicy Marinara Sauce, page 202, 1 batch
Fish Chowder with Red Potatoes and Corn, page 220, 1 batch
Tortilla Soup with Shrimp, page 221, 1 batch
Homemade Cream of Celery Soup for Cooking, page 223, 4 batches

Grocery List

FRESH PRODUCE:

☐ Limes (2)

☐ Lemons (2)

☐ Onions (5 to 6 medium, for 5½ cups chopped)

☐ Jalapeño pepper (1)

☐ Garlic (1 to 2 heads)

☐ Carrots (3 or 4, for 2 cups chopped)

☐ Red, green, or mixed bell peppers (about 3, for 3 cups chopped)

☐ Celery (about 4 ribs, for 2 cups chopped)

☐ Red potatoes (2 pounds)

☐ Ginger (2-inch piece)

☐ Basil (3 tablespoons chopped)

☐ Dill (2 tablespoons chopped)

☐ Parsley (1 tablespoon chopped)

MEAT:

☐ Boneless chicken tenders (8 pounds)

☐ Boneless chuck roast (4 pounds)

☐ Top sirloin steaks (2 large, about 2 pounds each)

☐ Tri-tip roasts (2, about 2 pounds each)

☐ Pork tenderloins (4 tenderloins, 1 pound each)

☐ Pork roasts (two 2-pound roasts)

☐ Diced ham (8 ounces)

FROZEN FOODS:

☐ Frozen shredded potatoes (one 32-ounce package)

☐ Frozen (or canned) corn (12 ounces)

Grocery List *(continued)*

DAIRY:

- [ ] Swiss cheese (8 ounces; 2 cups shredded)
- [ ] Gorgonzola cheese (½ cup crumbled)
- [ ] Parmesan cheese (1 ounce; ¼ cup shredded)
- [ ] Heavy cream (½ cup)
- [ ] Milk (1 quart)
- [ ] Butter (about 1½ pounds)

CANNED/BOTTLED/DRY GOODS:

- [ ] Crushed tomatoes (four 28-ounce cans)
- [ ] Reduced-sodium chicken broth (7 cups)
- [ ] Petite diced tomatoes (two 14.5-ounce cans)
- [ ] Black beans (one 15-ounce can)
- [ ] Hominy (one 15.5-ounce can)
- [ ] Tomato sauce (one 15-ounce can)
- [ ] Olive oil (about 1 cup)
- [ ] Soy sauce (about 1 cup)
- [ ] Unbleached all-purpose flour (1 cup)
- [ ] Vegetable oil
- [ ] Sherry (¾ cup)
- [ ] Tomato paste (one 6-ounce can plus 1 tablespoon)
- [ ] Chopped green chiles (one 4-ounce can)
- [ ] Rice vinegar (½ cup)
- [ ] Red wine vinegar (½ cup)
- [ ] Dijon mustard (3 tablespoons)
- [ ] Apple cider vinegar (3 tablespoons)
- [ ] Sesame oil (2 tablespoons)
- [ ] Light or dark brown sugar (2 teaspoons)

SEASONINGS:

- [ ] Garlic powder (¼ cup plus 2 teaspoons)
- [ ] Kosher salt, fine sea salt, and freshly ground black pepper
- [ ] Onion powder (2 tablespoons plus 1 teaspoon)
- [ ] Paprika (2 tablespoons plus 1 teaspoon)
- [ ] Dried thyme (2 tablespoons)
- [ ] Dried oregano (about 3 tablespoons)
- [ ] Dried basil (1 tablespoon), if not using fresh herb
- [ ] Dried dill (1 tablespoon), if not using fresh herb
- [ ] Chili powder (1 tablespoon)
- [ ] Dried parsley flakes (1 teaspoon), if not using fresh herb
- [ ] Red pepper flakes (⅝ teaspoon)
- [ ] Rubbed sage (2 teaspoons)
- [ ] Ground ginger (2 teaspoons)
- [ ] Dried rosemary (1½ teaspoons)
- [ ] Ground allspice (1 teaspoon)
- [ ] Celery seeds (1 teaspoon)
- [ ] Ground nutmeg (1 teaspoon)
- [ ] Smoked paprika (1 teaspoon)
- [ ] Cayenne pepper (1 teaspoon)
- [ ] Ground cinnamon (1½ teaspoons)
- [ ] Chipotle chile powder (½ teaspoon)
- [ ] Dried tarragon (½ teaspoon)
- [ ] Bay leaf (1)

BAKERY:

- [ ] Fresh bread crumbs (1 cup, or about 3 slices of bread)

(continued)

Grocery List *(continued)*

TO SAVE MORE TIME, PURCHASE:

- ☐ Shredded cheese
- ☐ Chopped onions
- ☐ Chopped garlic
- ☐ Fresh bread crumbs

Packaging

- ☐ Plastic wrap
- ☐ 4 snack-size bags, labeled Steak Rub (2), Caribbean Rub (2)
- ☐ 2 sandwich-size bags, labeled Gorgonzola Butter
- ☐ 1 pint-size zip-top freezer bag, labeled Jamie's Spice Mix
- ☐ 2 to 4 quart-size zip-top freezer bags, labeled Mexican Tortas
- ☐ 14 gallon-size zip-top freezer bags, labeled Soy-Ginger Pork Tenderloin (2), Caribbean Pork Tenderloin (2), Herb-Crusted Pork Roast (2), Mediterranean-Style Steak (2), Seasoned Steak with Gorgonzola-Herb Butter (2), Teriyaki Chicken Skewers (2), Herb Butter Chicken Tenders (2)
- ☐ Four 6-cup plastic containers with lids, labeled Tortilla Soup (2), Fish Chowder (2)
- ☐ Six or seven 2-cup plastic containers with lids, labeled Marinara Sauce
- ☐ Two 3-cup plastic containers with lids, labeled Shrimp Sauce
- ☐ One 9 × 13-inch baking pan, labeled Ham and Swiss Gratin

Gadgets and Small Appliances

Slow cooker

Immersion blender

2 or 3 stockpots

Prep List

1. Assemble the storage containers and ingredients.
2. Shred the cheese.
3. Grate the lime and lemon zests.
4. Chop the herbs.
5. Chop the garlic, onions, carrots, bell peppers, celery, and jalapeños.
6. Make the bread crumbs in a blender or food processor.
7. Cook the red potatoes.

Cooking Plan

1. Start the meat for the Mexican tortas in the slow cooker.

2. Make the cream of celery soup in a stockpot on the stove. Remove 2 cups for the ham and Swiss gratin and chill in the refrigerator.

3. Prepare the chowder using the remaining 6 cups of cream of celery soup. Instead of sautéing the vegetables in the stockpot, cook them in a small sauté pan and then add them to the cream of celery soup already in the pot. Divide the soup between the two labeled 6-cup plastic containers. Allow the soup to cool to room temperature and then chill it in the refrigerator before freezing. [CHOWDER DONE] Wash the pot.

4. Prepare Jaime's Spice Mix and place it in the labeled bag.

5. Start the marinara sauce on the stovetop.

6. If the reserved 2 cups of celery soup have cooled, assemble the ham and Swiss gratin and freeze it immediately. If not, complete the next step and then come back to this one. [HAM AND SWISS POTATO GRATIN DONE]

7. Prepare the rubs for the seasoned steak, herb-crusted pork roasts, and Caribbean pork tenderloins. Make the Gorgonzola butter to go with the steaks. Assemble these meal kits by placing each piece of meat with the appropriate seasoning or condiment in the labeled bags. Freeze. [SEASONED STEAK, PORK ROASTS, AND CARIBBEAN PORK TENDERLOINS DONE]

8. Cook the sauce for the shrimp and tomatoes.

9. While the sauce is simmering, revisit previous steps, putting containers in the refrigerator to chill or cleaning up the kitchen as needed.

10. Once the shrimp sauce is done, portion the sauce into the labeled 6-cup containers. Allow the sauce to cool to room temperature, then chill it in the refrigerator before freezing. [SAUCE FOR SHRIMP AND TOMATOES DONE]

11. Wash the pot.

12. Prepare the tortilla soup.

13. While the tortilla soup is simmering, prepare the marinades for the teriyaki chicken, herb butter chicken, Mediterranean-style steak, and soy-ginger tenderloin. Assemble and freeze these meals. [TERIYAKI CHICKEN, HERB BUTTER CHICKEN, MEDITERRANEAN STEAK, AND SOY-GINGER TENDERLOIN DONE]

14. Divide the tortilla soup between the two labeled 6-cup plastic containers. Allow the soup to cool to room temperature, then chill it in the refrigerator before freezing. [TORTILLA SOUP DONE]

15. Portion the cooked meat for the tortas into the labeled quart-size freezer bags. Allow the meat to cool to room temperature with the bag open, then chill it in the refrigerator before freezing. [TORTAS DONE]

(continued)

Cooking Plan *(continued)*

16. Divide the marinara sauce among the labeled 2-cup plastic containers. Allow the sauce to cool to room temperature, then chill it in the refrigerator before freezing. [MARINARA SAUCE DONE]

17. Clean up the workspace. Wipe down the counters. Once the items in the refrigerator have chilled for several hours, transfer them to the freezer.

Creating Your Own
Cooking Plan

In the Quick-Start Guide on page 1, I explained the basic steps to developing a bulk cooking plan. The previous chapter provides a number of specific cooking plans for you to follow, and those will serve you well. However, if you want to make "freezer cooking" your new regular mode of operation, you may want to bust out and create your own plans, using your own recipes. Here are the basic tenets from the Quick-Start Guide explained in greater detail, to help you create great cooking plans all your own.

1. Choose recipes you know your family likes.

Visit your freezer and pantry to see what ingredients you already have. Build your list from your supplies on hand first, and then consult the grocery ads to see what might be a good deal this week. Varying the types of protein (beef, pork, poultry, and so on) will help keep you from getting bored by week three. At the same time, though, you'll want to choose some dishes that have similar ingredients, so you can take advantage of bulk-buying savings. For instance, if ground beef is on sale, you might choose to make meatloaf, meatballs, and tacos, so you can buy several pounds of ground beef at a low price. It's also a time-saver: You can mix all of the meat with onions at once and then divide it up to complete the individual recipes.

Consult the list of what freezes well on pages 4 to 7. Once you've chosen your recipes, jot the recipe names down on a list (use the Freezer Cooking Master Plan sheet, page 61). As you do so, group them according to the protein or main ingredient featured. When you get cooking, you will prepare all the chicken recipes or all the beef recipes at one time, making use of common ingredients and reducing your work time. Remember the magic of the assembly line.

2. Create a grocery list, keeping multiplication in mind.

The reason freezer cooking can save you time and money is that you're going to prepare multiple batches at one time, creating possibly several weeks' or a month's worth of food in one cooking session. You're also going to do a lot of grocery shopping at one time. And fewer trips to the grocery store means fewer impulse buys and even more grocery savings.

With paper and pencil in hand, go through each recipe and create a shopping list. For duplicate items, like the aforementioned ground beef, just write tally marks next to the item until you get through the recipes and can calculate the totals for each item. Consult the contents of your pantry to make sure you don't overbuy.

Make your grocery list reflect the multiple batches you're preparing. Use the Freezer Cooking Master Plan sheet (page 61) to keep track of your list.

3. Consider how you will package your meals.

There are lots of options: freezer bags, reusable foil containers, plastic containers, and baking dishes. Make sure you have enough supplies for each recipe you are preparing. If you need additional dishes or packaging, add those to your grocery list.

4. Plan your Prep Chef List.

In higher-end restaurants, the chef doesn't usually do all his or her own chopping and slicing; the prep chef does this. At home, you can be your own prep chef. Having the ingredients ready will make the cooking smoother, faster, and more enjoyable. Read each recipe and create a list of all the items that need to be sliced, grated, chopped, or precooked. As a shortcut, consider buying ingredients that are already prepped, like shredded cheese, chopped vegetables, and toasted nuts.

Group each family of recipes, according to core ingredient. (You can use the Freezer Cooking Planning Worksheet on page 63.) For example, one list might read "Freezer Cooking Planning Worksheet: Chicken" across the top. Then walk through each of your chicken recipes, jotting down in the appropriate spaces the ingredients needed as well as how those ingredients need to be prepped.

At the bottom, you can tally all the items that you need to prep ahead of time. Make sure that you double-check that needed ingredients and packaging items are on your grocery list. As you make your tallies, move those items to the Prep Chef List and Timeline (page 62). Here you'll jot down the total ingredients that need to be prepped, giving you a working to-do list.

5. Plan out the order in which you will cook your meals.

Use the Prep Chef List and Timeline form (page 62) to map out an order of meal assembly. Consider how long something takes to cook, whether you can multitask while it's cooking, and which recipes build on one another. For instance, if you're going to make a big pot of red sauce as well as several pans of lasagna, then you need to make the sauce recipe first. The sauce will take several hours to simmer, so plan to prepare other meals while that happens. The lasagna makes use of the red sauce, so you can assemble those when the sauce is done.

Many of the recipes in this book utilize a common cooking sauce or core protein. Those basic components will always need to be prepared first so that you can use them in later recipes. If you're making Best-Ever Chicken Pot Pie (page 121), Not Your Mother's Chicken Noodle Soup (page 210), and Green Chile Chicken Taquitos (page 133), you'll obviously need cooked chicken to prepare those meals. You work out what fits you best and then write out a plan.

6. Shop.

Consult your Freezer Cooking Master Plan sheet. Make sure that you clean out the fridge before you go shopping. You'll be amazed at how quickly it will fill up again. And if you can stand it, just leave the nonperishables in the bags when you return from the store. Why waste time putting them away just to get them back out again?

7. Prep.

Consult your Prep Chef List and Timeline. Before cooking, prep as many of the ingredients as you can. Do all your slicing, dicing, and chopping. Precook meats for casseroles or enchiladas.

8. Get cooking.

Refer to both your Prep Chef List and Timeline and your Freezer Cooking Planning Worksheet to walk you through these steps. Pick some music you like, supply yourself with beverages and snacks, make sure the kids are safe and happy, and go to it. For ideas on how to include a friend, see page 272.

9. Chill out.

Remember that food will freeze better and more quickly if it is really cold to begin with. You can cool the foods to room temperature, wrap them well, and then chill them in the refrigerator before freezing. Food should not sit at room temperature for more than 2 hours, so be mindful of this timeline. Once the food is very cold, it's ready for the freezer.

Adapting Your Own Recipes

If you cook regularly, chances are you already have an arsenal of recipes. Some—think soups, stews, and casseroles—will do quite well as make-ahead and freeze dishes, provided you cool and package them appropriately for the freezer. Others may need some tweaking to render them freezer friendly. Risotto, for example, doesn't freeze well, but you *could* precook or marinate the chicken that you'll add to it.

If you're not sure whether a family recipe is freezer friendly, then test it.

The next time you prepare it, set aside a small portion. Cool it completely and wrap it well for freezing, then freeze, thaw, and reheat it. If you still like the taste and texture, you know you've got a winner.

There are bound to be a few favorite recipes that cannot be frozen either in part or in full; those will need to be relegated to days when you don't mind making everything on the spot. (A cheese soufflé would fall into this category.) And if you don't have a cache of go-to recipes, well, this book has got you covered!

Covering the Bases: Sauces and Spice Mixes

Traditional recipes for freezing usually feature canned soups, prepared sauces, and foil packets of seasoning mixes. While these products are certainly quick and easy to use, they can be expensive and contain dubious ingredients. Creating your own cooking sauces and spice mixes is a great way to have flavor at your fingertips without a lot of fuss—or a lot of fake food.

The following sauces and spice blends are featured in recipes throughout this book. By preparing a bulk batch at the beginning of a cooking session, you can save yourself a great deal of time and ensure that delicious, quality ingredients are incorporated into your meals.

- Beefy Mushroom Gravy, page 81
- Basic Taco Seasoning Mix, page 89
- Chipotle Taco Seasoning Mix, page 90
- Jamie's Spice Mix, page 90
- Easy Chicken (or Turkey) Gravy, page 110
- Easy Slow Cooker Red Sauce, page 205
- Homemade Cream of Celery Soup for Cooking, page 223
- Parmesan Herb Blend, page 240

Freezer Cooking Master Plan

Main Ingredient / Protein	Recipe	Groceries

Prep Chef List and Timeline

Prep Chef List	Cooking Timeline	X
Grate/Shred		
Chop/Slice		
Prepare		
Cook		
Other		

Freezer Cooking Planning Worksheet

Recipe Name / Packaging	Ingredients Needed	Pre-Prep List		
		Cook/Prepare	Chop/Slice	Grate/Shred
		Cook	Chop/Slice	Grate/Shred

{ Prep-Chef List }

Bountiful Beef

Versatile Shredded Beef Filling

SEASONED, SHREDDED BEEF is a wonderful filling for all sorts of sandwiches, as well as a variety of Mexican dishes like taquitos, tacos, and tostadas. It's also delicious on barbecue beef sandwiches. It's economical because beef chuck roast often goes on sale for a low price, and it's super easy to make because the slow cooker does most of the work. You can change the flavor profile of this shredded beef filling by varying the spices and aromatics used (see the variations that follow). With a few bags waiting in the freezer, you'll be able to pull a variety of meals together in just minutes. ○ *Serves 10 to 12*

Packaging: Large plastic containers or quart-size zip-top freezer bags

1 tablespoon olive oil
One 4-pound boneless chuck roast or chuck steak
Salt and freshly ground black pepper
1 medium-size onion, chopped
1 tablespoon chili powder
1 teaspoon dried oregano
¼ cup water

1. In a large skillet, heat the olive oil over medium-high heat until shimmering. Generously season the chuck roast with salt and pepper. Add the meat to the hot pan and brown it well on all sides. Transfer the roast to a 5-quart slow cooker.

2. Add the onion to the drippings in the skillet and sauté, scraping up any browned bits. Cook until the onion is translucent. Add the chili powder and the oregano, stirring to combine well.

3. Add the water, stirring and scraping up any remaining browned bits. Scrape the onion mixture into the slow cooker.

4. Cook the roast on LOW for 6 to 8 hours or on HIGH for about 4 hours. The meat should be extremely tender and shred easily.

5. Remove the meat from the slow cooker and allow it to cool slightly. Shred the meat by chopping it into chunks and pulling it apart with two forks or small tongs.

6. Adjust the seasonings to taste. Add some of the drippings to moisten the meat, if necessary. Otherwise, strain the drippings and save them for another dish, such as soup or gravy.

Freezing instructions:

Divide the shredded beef and juices into meal-size portions in plastic containers or freezer bags. Chill the beef in the refrigerator before freezing.

To thaw and serve:

Thaw the meat in the refrigerator. Use this shredded beef for tostadas, chimichangas, burritos, tacos, enchiladas, and sandwiches. Reheat the meat in a pan on the stovetop, stirring frequently, or in a microwave-safe dish in the microwave on HIGH for 2 to 3 minutes, stirring once.

VARIATIONS

Italian Shredded Beef Filling

This variation of shredded beef is great mixed into Easy Slow Cooker Red Sauce (page 205) or used in hot Italian sandwiches. For sandwiches, spoon reheated meat and some of the juices into a crusty sub roll. Add spicy peppers and shredded Italian-blend cheese if you desire. **o** *Serves 10 to 12*

Packaging: Large plastic containers or quart-size zip-top freezer bags

1 tablespoon olive oil
One 4-pound boneless chuck roast or chuck steak
Salt and freshly ground black pepper
3 cloves garlic, crushed
1 tablespoon finely shredded fresh basil or 1 teaspoon dried basil
1 teaspoon dried oregano
½ teaspoon freshly ground black pepper
¼ teaspoon crushed red pepper flakes
¼ cup water

Follow the method for Versatile Shredded Beef Filling, substituting the garlic, herbs, and spices for the onion, chili powder, and oregano in step 2.

Provençal Shredded Beef Filling

This variation on shredded beef goes well with Beefy Mushroom Gravy (page 81); you can also use it in French dip sandwiches. Save the drippings for the dipping *jus*. ○ *Serves 10 to 12*

Packaging: Large plastic containers or quart-size zip-top freezer bags

1 tablespoon olive oil
One 4-pound boneless chuck roast or chuck steak
Salt and freshly ground black pepper
3 shallots, finely chopped
1 tablespoon *herbes de Provence*
¼ cup red wine

Follow the method for Versatile Shredded Beef Filling, substituting the shallots and herbs for the onion, chili powder, and oregano in step 2. Use the wine instead of water in step 3.

Salsa Verde Beef

AFTER YOU SERVE THIS DISH ONCE, eyes will light up at the mere mention of it. It's hearty and filling and has a little kick—and there is rarely any left over. I love it for its versatility. Serve it simply over rice or use it as a taco or burrito filling. You can also add 5 cups of cooked pinto beans to the slow cooker near the end of the cooking time to make a delicious chili. ○ *Serves 6 to 8*

Packaging: Large plastic containers with lids

1 tablespoon olive oil
One 3-pound boneless rump or chuck roast, cut into 1½-inch cubes
½ cup chopped onion
2 tablespoons Basic Taco Seasoning Mix (page 89)
1 cup salsa verde

When ready to serve, you will need:

Cooked rice or flour tortillas
Shredded cheddar, Monterey Jack, or Mexican-blend cheese
Easy Homemade Salsa (page 71)
Super-Simple Guacamole (page 71)
Sour cream

1. Heat the oil in a large skillet. Add the beef cubes and brown on all sides, working in batches if necessary.

2. Transfer the meat to a 5-quart slow cooker. Add the onion to the drippings in the pan and sauté until lightly browned, 3 to 4 minutes. Stir in the taco seasoning and cook for about 1 minute. Add the salsa and stir, scraping up any browned bits.

3. Add the salsa mixture to the beef. Stir to combine. Cook on LOW for 6 to 8 hours or on HIGH for about 4 hours. The meat should be very tender and shred easily when stirred.

Freezing instructions:

Divide the beef into meal-size portions in plastic containers. Chill in the refrigerator before freezing.

To thaw and serve:

Thaw the container in the refrigerator. Reheat the meat in a pan on the stovetop, stirring frequently, or in a microwave-safe dish in the microwave on HIGH for 2 to 3 minutes, stirring once. Serve with guacamole and sour cream.

Oven-Baked Beef Taquitos

HAVE GREAT MEMORIES of visiting the little taco stand in my hometown. I loved going there with my dad; he'd order me two taquitos and a side of their very cold, probably-had-been-frozen guacamole. It is a precious memory of a special time with my pop. These taquitos are reminiscent of that era, only better. They're filled with a delicious beef-and-green-chile mixture. They freeze easily and bake quickly in the oven, making them the ideal quick-fix dinner. Accompany them with your own fresh, homemade guacamole. ○ *Serves 4 to 6*

Packaging: Zip-top freezer bag or large plastic container with lid

Vegetable oil for frying the tortillas
24 corn tortillas
3 cups Versatile Shredded Beef Filling (page 66)
One 4-ounce can diced green chiles
2 scallions, finely chopped
Salt and freshly ground black pepper

When ready to serve, you will need:

Easy Homemade Salsa (page 71)
Super-Simple Guacamole (page 71)
Sour cream

1. Fill a skillet with vegetable oil to a depth of 1 inch. Heat over medium heat until the oil shimmers. Fry the tortillas in the hot oil for 30 to 45 seconds each, turning once with tongs. Drain the tortillas on paper towels. Allow the tortillas to cool enough to be easily handled.

2. In a large bowl, combine the shredded beef, green chiles, and scallions. Season the mixture to taste with salt and pepper.

3. To assemble the taquitos, roll about 2 tablespoons of filling tightly into each tortilla. Secure the taquitos with toothpicks and set them on a baking sheet.

Freezing instructions:

Place the baking sheet in the freezer for about 20 minutes, or until the taquitos are partially frozen but not so firm that you can't remove the toothpicks. If the toothpicks get frozen stuck, that's fine; you can store them with the toothpicks, though you may not be able to pack them as compactly. Once frozen, pack the taquitos into freezer bags or containers and store them in the freezer.

To serve:

Preheat the oven to 475°F. Place the frozen taquitos, seam side down, on a baking sheet and bake for 15 to 25 minutes, turning once. Check for crispness after 15 minutes. Serve with salsa, guacamole, and sour cream.

Easy Homemade Salsa

○ *Makes about 4 cups*

One 14.5-ounce can diced tomatoes with juices
One 14.5-ounce can fire-roasted diced tomatoes with juices
1 large handful chopped fresh cilantro
¼ cup sliced fresh jalapeño pepper
¼ cup chopped scallion
Juice of ½ lime
1 clove garlic
Salt

Combine all of the ingredients in the bowl of a food processor. Pulse until smooth. Season to taste with salt.

Super-Simple Guacamole

○ *Makes about 1 cup*

2 ripe avocados, halved and pitted
Juice of ½ lemon or 1 lime
2 tablespoons salsa
1 tablespoon finely chopped fresh jalapeño pepper (optional)
Salt

Scoop the flesh of the avocados into a small bowl. Sprinkle the juice over the avocados. Mash with a fork, allowing a few chunks to remain. Stir in the salsa and jalapeño, if using. Season to taste with salt.

Mexican Beef Tortas

A MEXICAN TORTA is a sandwich served on either a crisp, torpedo-shaped *bolillo* roll or a soft, round *telera* roll. It is served cold or hot, often toasted in a press like a panini or Cuban sandwich. This meat mixture is very freezer-friendly and can do double duty as a taco or burrito filling. ○ *Serves 10 to 12*

Using Batch Cooking as a Way to Help Others

If your freezer is stocked with healthy, home-cooked meals, it's easier to be hospitable. Having folks over for dinner isn't so much of a hassle if you can pull two dozen enchiladas from the freezer and spend extra time on side dishes and a pretty presentation.

Batch cooking also enables you to serve others in different ways. When we have a stockpile, it's easier to share. And sharing is always a good thing.

Help out the new parents

Fill the freezer of a new mom and dad with a few meals. Not only will this be a gift that outlasts that first pack of diapers, it is also one that is desperately needed during those early weeks with a baby at home. New moms are ravenous—and busy with the babe in arms. So a few home-cooked meals, whether in family-size pans or individual-serving containers, are an ideal gift. You can even organize a "meal shower" by inviting other friends to bring a few frozen meals as gifts. Just coordinate a little with the others so that the new parents don't end up with a dozen pans of baked manicotti. And be sure to include cooking directions. Also, check to make sure there's room in their freezer!

Feed the hungry

There are numerous homeless shelters that would gratefully accept meals that you've prepared and frozen. Contact your local church, synagogue, or other charitable organization to see where you can donate food to those who are less fortunate.

Serve your elders

Elderly family, friends, and neighbors are also among those who could benefit from ready-made meals. If you make the meals yourself, you can ensure that the foods fit any dietary restrictions they might have and portion the food in single-serving containers. If you can stick around and keep the recipients company for a while when you drop off the meals, it will be a double kindness.

Be a good neighbor

Chances are you know someone who's struggling. Military deployments, divorce, illnesses, and unemployment can make it hard for people to have regular mealtimes. There may be too much to do, too much on one's mind, or a shortage of food. Reach out to those around you with a helping hand. Some churches even stockpile meals in the church freezer to be able to share at will with those in need.

Packaging: Plastic containers with lids or zip-top freezer bags

1 tablespoon vegetable oil
One 4-pound boneless chuck roast
Salt and freshly ground black pepper
1 cup chopped onion
One 4-ounce can chopped green chiles
1 tablespoon chili powder
1 tablespoon tomato paste
1 clove garlic, minced
1 teaspoon chipotle chile powder
1 teaspoon dried oregano

When ready to serve, you will need:

Telera or *bolillo* rolls, or other soft sandwich rolls
Sliced cheddar cheese
Shredded lettuce
Sliced tomatoes and avocado

1. In a large skillet, heat the oil over medium-high heat until shimmering. Season the meat to taste with salt and pepper. Brown the roast on all sides. Transfer the roast to a 5-quart slow cooker.

2. Add the onion to the drippings in the skillet, scraping up any browned bits. Cook until the onion is translucent, about 5 minutes, stirring occasionally. Add the green chiles, chili powder, tomato paste, garlic, chipotle chile powder, and oregano. Stir to combine.

3. Add this mixture to the slow cooker. Cook the roast on LOW for 6 to 8 hours or on HIGH for about 4 hours. The meat should be very tender and shred easily.

4. Remove the roast from the slow cooker. Shred the meat. Adjust the seasoning with salt and pepper. Moisten the meat with some of the drippings.

5. Discard the drippings or strain them and save for another dish, such as a soup or stew.

Freezing instructions:

Divide the meat filling into meal-size portions in containers or freezer bags. Chill in the refrigerator before freezing.

To thaw and serve:

Thaw the meat in the refrigerator. Reheat the meat in a pan on the stovetop, stirring frequently, or in a microwave-safe dish in the microwave on HIGH for 2 to 3 minutes, stirring once. Serve on rolls with cheese, lettuce, tomatoes, and avocado slices. If you wish, heat the sandwich in a panini press before serving.

Red and Green Beef Enchiladas

A FRIEND BROUGHT US THIS DINNER shortly after we welcomed a new baby into our family. Not only did she lighten the load, she also completely wowed us with this delicious supper. Many kids and a few tweaks later, it is one of our favorite meals, especially when it's ready and waiting in the freezer. I like to cook the meat overnight in the slow cooker. That way, it's ready for shredding in the morning. ○ *Serves 8*

Packaging: Two 9 × 13-inch baking dishes with lids

One 4-pound boneless chuck roast
1 medium-size onion, chopped
Salt and freshly ground black pepper
1 cup warm water
1 bunch scallions, chopped
One 7-ounce can diced green chiles
Vegetable oil, for frying the tortillas
24 corn tortillas
Two 28-ounce cans red enchilada sauce
4 cups shredded cheese (cheddar, Monterey Jack, or a mixture)
Sliced black olives

1. Place the chuck roast in a 5-quart slow cooker along with the onion, salt, pepper, and water. Cook on LOW for 6 to 8 hours or on HIGH for about 4 hours. The meat should be tender and shred easily.

2. Remove the meat from the slow cooker. Remove the fat and shred the meat. Save the drippings for soup or simply discard them.

3. In a large bowl, combine the shredded beef, scallions, and green chiles. Add salt and pepper to taste. Set the mixture aside.

4. Fill a skillet with vegetable oil to a depth of 1 inch. Heat over medium heat until the oil shimmers. Fry the tortillas in the hot oil for 30 to 45 seconds each, turning once with tongs. Drain the tortillas on paper towels. Allow the tortillas to cool enough to be easily handled.

5. Grease the baking dishes. Spread 1 cup of the enchilada sauce on the bottom of each dish.

6. To assemble, place 2 tablespoons beef filling and 2 tablespoons cheese on a tortilla. Roll the tortilla around the filling and place the enchilada, seam side down, in a prepared baking pan. Continue until all the enchiladas are rolled and arranged in the pans.

7. Pour the remaining sauce over the enchiladas and sprinkle them with the remaining cheese and the black olives.

Freezing instructions:

Cover the pans and chill in the refrigerator before freezing.

To thaw and serve:

Thaw the enchiladas in the refrigerator. Preheat the oven to 350°F. Bake the enchiladas, uncovered, for 20 minutes, or until heated through. Serve immediately.

Chipotle-Rubbed Tri-Tip

FOR DECADES ON THE WEST COAST, tri-tip has been a favorite grilling cut. It's meaty and full of flavor. Thankfully, meat cutters throughout the country are finally catching on to what California butchers have long known: The tri-tip is a delicious cut of beef. If you don't see it in the meat case, ask your butcher. You can also use your favorite grilling cut of beef instead. Having the meat and spice rub ready to throw on the grill will help you pull off a great cookout. Serve the roast, sliced, with fresh salsa. ○ *Serves 4 to 8*

Packaging: Snack-size zip-top bag, gallon-size zip-top freezer bag

1 teaspoon chipotle chile powder
½ teaspoon ground cumin
¼ teaspoon freshly ground black pepper
1 teaspoon fine sea salt
1 teaspoon garlic powder
One 2-pound tri-tip roast, in its original wrapper

When ready to serve, you will need:

1 tablespoon grapeseed oil or olive oil
Easy Homemade Salsa (page 71)

Combine all the spices in the snack-size bag. Place the tri-tip roast and the bag of spices in the freezer bag.

Freezing instructions:

Store the roast and spice packet in the freezer until a day or two before serving.

To thaw and serve:

Thaw the roast completely on a tray in the refrigerator. Rub the tri-tip with the oil. Rub the seasoning mix into the meat, coating it thoroughly. Cook the roast on a hot grill, turning once, for 40 minutes, or until it reaches the desired doneness; the internal temperature should be 135°F for medium-rare or 160°F for well done. Allow the roast to rest, tented with foil, for 10 minutes. Slice the meat against the grain and serve with salsa.

Mediterranean-Style Steak

MARINATED MEATS are quick freezer meals to put together. The meat marinates while it thaws, reducing prep time. Serve this flavorful steak as a main dish, in pita sandwiches, or atop Mediterranean Steak Salad (page 77). ○ *Serves 4 to 8*

Mediterranean Steak Salad

I love a good salad. And this one is a winner, with grilled beef, dark leafy greens, couscous, onions, tomatoes, and garbanzo beans, all drizzled with a yogurt-dill dressing. Yum! Taste-wise, this is fantastic. But work-wise, it is even better. While salads generally cannot be frozen, many of the components that make a great salad can be prepared ahead and stored in the freezer. And the other ingredients here come together in a snap. ○ *Serves 6*

1 recipe Mediterranean-Style Steak (page 76), thawed
1 cup couscous
9 cups spinach and mixed salad greens (about 1½ cups per person)
1 small red onion, sliced
3 cups chopped tomatoes
1 cup canned garbanzo beans
1 cup crumbled feta cheese
1 recipe Yogurt-Dill Dressing (recipe follows)

1. Cook the steak on a hot grill until it has reached the desired doneness.

2. Prepare the couscous according to the package directions.

3. While the steak rests, assemble the salads on individual plates, layering greens, sliced onion, tomatoes, garbanzo beans, and feta cheese. Spoon the couscous on the side.

4. Place the sliced steak atop the salads. Serve the dressing on the side.

Yogurt-Dill Dressing ○ *Makes about 1¼ cups*

½ cup plain yogurt
½ cup mayonnaise
1 tablespoon chopped fresh dill or 1 teaspoon dried dill
2 cloves garlic, minced
¼ teaspoon cayenne pepper
¼ cup freshly squeezed lemon juice
½ teaspoon ground cumin

In a small bowl, combine all of the ingredients. Chill the dressing until ready to serve.

Packaging: Gallon-size zip-top freezer bag

¼ cup olive oil
¼ cup red wine vinegar
1 tablespoon apple cider vinegar
1 teaspoon dried oregano
2 cloves garlic, chopped
½ teaspoon freshly ground black pepper
Large top-sirloin steak, about 2 pounds

1. Place the freezer bag in a medium bowl, folding the top over the edges.

2. Add the olive oil, vinegars, oregano, garlic, and pepper to the bag. Seal and massage the bag to combine the marinade ingredients.

3. Add the steak to the bag. Seal the bag carefully, squeezing out as much air as possible. Massage the bag to distribute the marinade evenly.

Freezing instructions:

Lay the bag flat to freeze.

To thaw and serve:

Place the bag on a tray or dish and thaw it in the refrigerator. Cook the thawed steak, turning once, on a hot grill until cooked through, 15 to 20 minutes.

Seasoned Steak with Gorgonzola-Herb Butter

GRILLED STEAK is simple enough to prepare. It's delicious on its own with a little salt and pepper. However, it improves in taste and elegance when you add a custom spice rub before grilling and top the cooked meat with a compound butter laden with rich Gorgonzola and fragrant herbs. If you can't find tri-tip, use your favorite grilling cut of beef instead. ● *Serves 4 to 8*

Packaging: Gallon-size zip-top freezer bag, snack-size zip-top bag, plastic wrap, sandwich-size zip-top bag

One 2-pound tri-tip roast, in its original wrapper
1 tablespoon garlic powder
1 teaspoon salt
1 teaspoon paprika
½ teaspoon plus ⅛ teaspoon freshly ground black pepper
½ cup (1 stick) unsalted butter, softened
¼ cup crumbled Gorgonzola or other blue cheese
1½ teaspoons chopped fresh parsley or ½ teaspoon dried parsley flakes
½ teaspoon dried thyme

When ready to serve, you will need:

1 tablespoon grapeseed oil or olive oil

1. Place the packaged tri-tip in the gallon-size freezer bag. Set aside.

2. In the snack-size bag, combine the garlic powder, salt, paprika, and ½ teaspoon of the pepper. Seal the bag and place it inside the large bag next to the tri-tip.

3. In a small bowl, combine the butter, cheese, parsley, thyme, and remaining ⅛ teaspoon black pepper. Mash together until well combined.

4. Spoon the butter mixture onto a small sheet of plastic wrap. Wrap the plastic wrap around the butter mixture, forming a small log about 1 inch in diameter. Wrap the butter log tightly and place it in the sandwich bag. Seal the bag. Place this bag in the larger bag with the roast and the seasoning packet.

Freezing instructions:

Store the large bag containing the tri-tip, seasoning packet, and Gorgonzola butter in the freezer.

To thaw and serve:

A day or two before serving, pull the bag from the freezer. Remove the tri-tip package from the bag and thaw it in the refrigerator on a tray. Thaw the butter in the refrigerator as well. About an hour before serving, brush the thawed tri-tip with the oil. Rub the spice mixture all over the meat. Cook the meat on a hot grill, turning once, for 40 minutes, or until it reaches the desired doneness; the internal temperature should be 135°F for medium-rare or 160°F for well done. Allow the meat to rest, tented with foil, for 10 minutes before slicing. Serve topped with slices of Gorgonzola butter.

Quick and Easy Pepper Steak

THIS DELECTABLE ASIAN CONCOCTION features seasoned beef strips in a flavorful sauce with crisp-tender bell peppers. Get a head start on it by preparing the beef and sauce ahead of time. Add the bell peppers right before serving. This is delicious served over steamed rice. You can also make this with strips of chicken breast and chicken broth instead of beef. ○ *Serves 4 to 6*

Packaging: Plastic container with lid

One 1-pound beef round steak, ½ inch thick, cut into ¼-inch strips
1 tablespoon paprika
2 tablespoons vegetable oil
2 cloves garlic, minced
1½ cups beef broth
½ cup chopped scallions
2 tablespoons cornstarch
¼ cup water
¼ cup soy sauce

When ready to serve, you will need:

2 green bell peppers, cut into strips
1 red bell pepper, cut into strips
Hot cooked rice

1. Place the beef strips in a medium bowl and sprinkle them with the paprika. Allow the mixture to stand for 10 minutes.

2. In a large skillet, heat the oil over medium heat. Add the meat and cook until browned. Stir in the garlic and broth. Cover and simmer for 10 minutes. Stir in the scallions and cook 5 minutes more.

3. In a small bowl, combine the cornstarch, water, and soy sauce. Stir this mixture into the meat mixture and cook until smooth and thickened, 5 to 10 minutes more.

Freezing instructions:

Spoon the meat mixture into a plastic container. Chill in the refrigerator before freezing.

To thaw and serve:

Thaw the meat completely in the refrigerator. Heat through in a large saucepan over medium heat. Add the bell peppers and cook until the peppers are just crisp-tender, about 5 minutes. Serve over hot cooked rice.

Beefy Mushroom Gravy

P RECEDING GENERATIONS may have relied on canned cream soups and gravies to pull together quick meals. But these soups, chock full of sodium and additives, don't do a lot for us except save some time. Actually, it doesn't take very long to make up a batch of this beef and mushroom gravy. Use it as a simple sauce, in place of cream of mushroom soup, and in recipes like Shepherd's Pie with Green Chile Mashed Potatoes (page 86) and Swedish Meatballs with Dill (page 100). If you are using commercial beef broth, taste the gravy before adding salt, since such broths can vary greatly in their levels of saltiness. ○ *Makes about 2 cups*

Packaging: Plastic container with lid or pint-size zip-top freezer bag

4½ tablespoons unsalted butter
¼ cup finely chopped fresh mushrooms
2 tablespoons finely chopped onion
¼ cup unbleached all-purpose flour
2 cups beef broth
2 teaspoons fresh chopped parsley or ¾ teaspoon dried parsley flakes
¾ teaspoon salt
⅛ teaspoon freshly ground black pepper
⅛ teaspoon paprika

Cream Cheese Mashed Potatoes

Mashed potatoes can be time-intensive to make, but they are such a comforting, ideal side dish that one doesn't want to leave them off the menu. So make a bulk batch! These freezer-friendly spuds owe their richness and flavor to the addition of cream cheese. Feel free to leave the skins on, if you prefer. ○ *Serves 8*

Packaging: Two 8-inch round baking dishes with lids or one 9 × 13-inch baking dish with lid

5 pounds russet or red potatoes, peeled and quartered
8 ounces cream cheese
1 teaspoon salt
¼ teaspoon freshly ground black pepper
1 cup half-and-half
2 tablespoons butter

1. In a large pot of salted boiling water, cook the potatoes until very tender when pierced with a fork. Drain the potatoes and transfer them to the bowl of a stand mixer. Blend the potatoes until smooth.

2. Add the cream cheese and blend to combine. Stir in the salt, pepper, and half-and-half. Blend well.

3. Grease the baking dish or dishes. Spoon in the mashed potatoes. Dot the potatoes with the butter.

Freezing instructions:

Cool slightly. Cover the potatoes. Chill in the refrigerator before freezing.

To thaw and serve:

Thaw the potatoes in the refrigerator. Preheat the oven to 375°F. Bake the mashed potatoes, covered, for 30 to 45 minutes or until hot. Stir the potatoes before serving.

1. In a medium skillet, melt ½ tablespoon of the butter over medium heat. Add the mushrooms and onion. Sauté the vegetables, stirring occasionally, until the mushrooms start to brown and the onion becomes translucent. Set aside.

2. In a heavy stockpot, melt the remaining 4 tablespoons butter over medium heat. Stir in the flour and cook, stirring, until the mixture bubbles. Cook 1 minute more.

3. Whisk in the beef broth, stirring constantly, until the mixture thickens to a gravy consistency.

4. Stir in the mushroom and onion mixture, parsley, salt, pepper, and paprika. Adjust the seasonings to taste.

Freezing instructions:

Divide the gravy into desired portions in plastic containers. Chill the gravy in the refrigerator before freezing.

To thaw and serve:

Thaw the gravy in the refrigerator. Reheat in a saucepan over medium heat, whisking to recombine.

NOTE: To make a big batch of this gravy, simply multiply all the ingredients by four. The cooking method remains the same.

Vegetable Bolognese

ONE SUMMER our CSA provided an abundance of eggplant. This Bolognese was the delicious result of my efforts to use it! Packed with vegetables, it goes nicely over hot cooked noodles or rice and makes the base for a fantastic lasagna. ○ *Serves 6 to 8*

Packaging: Plastic containers with lids

¼ cup olive oil

1 carrot, peeled and finely chopped

1 eggplant, peeled and chopped into ½-inch cubes

1 medium-size onion, coarsely chopped

1 red bell pepper, coarsely chopped

1 medium-size zucchini, coarsely chopped

2 cloves garlic, minced

Salt and freshly ground black pepper

1 pound ground beef

3½ cups tomato sauce

One 14.5-ounce can diced tomatoes with juices

¼ cup red wine (optional)

3 tablespoons chopped fresh basil or 1 tablespoon dried basil

1. In a large stockpot, heat the olive oil over medium heat until shimmering. Add the carrot and eggplant and cook, stirring to prevent the eggplant from sticking, for 10 minutes.

2. Add the onion, bell pepper, zucchini, and garlic. Cook 5 minutes more. Add salt and pepper to taste.

3. Add the ground beef and cook, stirring often, until the meat is cooked through, about 10 minutes. Add the tomato sauce, tomatoes, red wine (if using), and basil. Add a bit of water if the mixture is too thick.

4. Adjust the seasonings to taste and bring to a bubble. Reduce the heat, cover, and simmer for 25 minutes.

Freezing instructions:

Divide the sauce into meal-size portions in plastic containers. Chill the sauce in the refrigerator before freezing.

To thaw and serve:

Thaw the sauce in the refrigerator and reheat it in a saucepan.

Vegetable-Beef Lasagna

LASAGNA IS A FAITHFUL FRIEND to a freezer cook. This delicious version features cream cheese in the filling, inspired by a recipe by cookbook author Ann Hodgman. Use uncooked noodles for even quicker prep time. With an adequate amount of sauce, the uncooked noodles will soften during freezing and cook during baking. ○ *Serves 6 to 8*

Packaging: 9 × 13-inch baking dish with lid

3 cups Vegetable Bolognese (page 83) or other favorite sauce
3 cups shredded mozzarella cheese
8 regular (not no-boil) lasagna noodles, uncooked
8 ounces Neufchâtel cheese
1 cup chicken broth

1. Grease the baking dish. Spread 1½ cups of the Bolognese sauce across the bottom of the pan. Sprinkle 1 cup of the mozzarella cheese over the sauce. Lay 4 lasagna noodles across the cheese, overlapping slightly.

2. In a medium saucepan, heat the cream cheese and chicken broth over low heat. As the cream cheese begins to warm and soften, whisk it into the chicken broth until well blended. Pour this mixture over the noodle layer. Sprinkle 1 cup of the mozzarella cheese over the white sauce. Lay the remaining 4 lasagna noodles across the layer of cheese.

3. Spoon the remaining Bolognese over the noodles and spread evenly. Top the sauce with the remaining 1 cup mozzarella cheese.

Freezing instructions:

Cover the pan and chill completely in the refrigerator before freezing.

To thaw and serve:

Thaw the lasagna in the refrigerator overnight for best results. Preheat the oven to 400°F. Bake for 45 minutes or until the sauce is bubbly and the cheese is melted. Allow the lasagna to rest for 10 minutes before cutting and serving.

Shepherd's Pie with
Green Chile Mashed Potatoes

SHEPHERD'S PIE is a ground meat-and-vegetable mixture that's topped with mashed potatoes. This one is spiced up with jalapeños, cilantro, and cheddar cheese, giving it a little South of the Border flavor. ● *Serves 6 to 8*

Packaging: 9 × 13-inch baking dish with lid

8 medium-size red potatoes (about 2 pounds), scrubbed and quartered (no need to peel, unless you prefer them that way)
1 pound ground beef
1 cup chopped onion
½ cup chopped red bell pepper
1 tablespoon finely chopped fresh jalapeño pepper
2 cups Beefy Mushroom Gravy (page 81)
1 cup fresh or frozen green peas
⅓ cup chopped fresh cilantro
1 teaspoon ground cumin
¼ cup (½ stick) salted butter
2 tablespoons half-and-half
½ cup shredded cheddar cheese
1 tablespoon canned green chiles

1. Grease the baking dish. In a large pot of boiling salted water, cook the potatoes until tender, then drain. Set aside.

2. Meanwhile, in a large skillet, cook the beef, onion, bell pepper, and jalapeño over medium-high heat until the meat is cooked and the vegetables are tender. Drain the meat and vegetables and transfer the mixture to a large bowl.

3. Add the gravy, peas, cilantro, and cumin. Stir gently to combine. Spread the meat mixture in the prepared pan.

4. Mash the potatoes with a potato masher until smooth. Blend in the butter. Stir in the half-and-half until smooth. Add the cheddar cheese and green chiles, and stir until well combined.

5. Spoon the mashed potatoes over the meat mixture, spreading to cover evenly.

Freezing instructions:

Cover the dish and chill in the refrigerator before freezing.

To thaw and serve:

Thaw the casserole in the refrigerator. Preheat the oven to 350°F. Bake for 1 hour, until the filling is bubbly and the mashed potatoes are golden brown.

Not Your Convenience Store's Frozen Burritos

ONCE TURNED MY NOSE UP at frozen burritos, assuming they were mushy and blah-tasting. But friends raved about making their own, so I had to try it out. And we loved them! Snacks and dinners come together so easily when the burritos are premade. Crisping them on the griddle takes them to a new level, and you'd never know they'd been frozen. o *Serves 6 to 12*

Packaging: Gallon-size zip-top freezer bags

1 pound ground beef
1 to 2 tablespoons Basic Taco Seasoning Mix (page 89)
3 cups refried beans or Seasoned Versatile Pinto Beans (page 180)
2 cups shredded cheddar cheese
1 cup enchilada sauce
½ cup diced onion
One 4-ounce can chopped green chiles
12 burrito-size flour tortillas

1. In a large skillet, cook the meat over medium-high heat, stirring frequently, until no pink remains. Stir in the taco seasoning. Stir to blend.

2. Drain the meat and transfer it to a large bowl. Add the beans, cheese, enchilada sauce, onion, and green chiles. Stir well to combine.

3. Lay out a tortilla and spread a scant ½ cup filling in a line down one side of the tortilla. Roll the tortilla around the filling, rolling toward the middle of the tortilla. Fold in the sides and continue rolling.

4. Fill and roll the rest of the burritos in the same manner.

Freezing instructions:

Place the rolled burritos in the freezer bags. Chill in the refrigerator before freezing.

To thaw and serve:

Thaw as many burritos as desired in the refrigerator.

To reheat in the microwave: Cook thawed burritos, flipping once, 1 to 2 minutes per burrito, or until hot. You can also reheat them directly from the freezer, without thawing; just add an additional minute or two of cooking time.

To reheat on the griddle: Cook thawed burritos on a hot griddle until the filling is hot and the tortilla is crisp.

To reheat in the oven: Preheat the oven to 350°F. For crispy, oven-baked burritos, bake thawed burritos for 15 to 20 minutes. For softer burritos, wrap each in foil prior to baking. If the burritos are frozen, increase the cooking time 5 to 10 minutes.

Taco Seasoning Mixes and Basic Taco Meat Kit

Prepackaged spice mixes are often costly and can contain dubious ingredients. Fortunately, buying individual spices in bulk can be quite economical, and creating your own spice mixes is a great way to add flavor to any number of dishes without compromising your tastes or your budget. The flavors of spices deteriorate over long storage at room temperature. However, the flavor and intensity of spices are retained for a much longer time when the seasonings are frozen, making custom spice blends a perfect addition to your freezer cooking repertoire. They're a great way to personalize your meals.

In my house, taco seasoning is particularly popular, so I've provided two of my favorite blends, which I use with both ground beef and ground turkey. (They're also great mixed into cooked pinto beans.) Having a stash of pre-seasoned taco meat in your freezer opens up a world of mealtime possibilities. To prepare it, simply stir in 1 to 2 tablespoons of seasoning mix for each pound of meat browning in a skillet. Once no pink remains, drain off the drippings, package, label, chill, and freeze.

Create a simple "taco kit" by packaging 1 pound of precooked meat, 2 cups of shredded cheese, and one 12-count package of soft taco-size flour tortillas. Individually wrap each component and then store them in one larger bag. On taco night, just thaw a bag and add fresh toppings like lettuce, tomatoes, salsa, and sour cream.

Basic Taco Seasoning Mix

This taco seasoning is a standard spice blend that can be mixed into ground beef, shredded chicken, soups, or chilis to give them a little punch. It is also delicious mixed into sour cream as a dip and stirred into marinades and dressings. **○** *Makes about ⅔ cup*

Packaging: Plastic container with lid or pint-size zip-top freezer bag

¼ **cup chili powder**
2 **tablespoons dried oregano**
2 **tablespoons onion flakes**
1 **tablespoon salt**
1 **tablespoon garlic powder**
1 **teaspoon freshly ground black pepper**

Combine all of the ingredients in a small bowl. Place the mixture in an airtight plastic container or freezer bag and store in the freezer. *(continued)*

Chipotle Taco Seasoning Mix

Chipotle chiles, which are smoke-dried jalapeño peppers, add a little heat and a smoky flavor to foods. Once difficult to find but now widely available, they are sold canned in adobo sauce or dried in whole or ground form This seasoning mix can be used in taco meats, chilis, and soups to give a distinctive chipotle flavor. ○ *Makes about ½ cup*

Packaging: Plastic container with lid or pint-size zip-top freezer bag

2 tablespoons chipotle chile powder
2 tablespoons onion flakes
1 tablespoon garlic powder
1 tablespoon salt
1 tablespoon dried oregano
2 teaspoons ground cumin

Combine all of the ingredients in a small bowl. Place the mixture in an airtight plastic container or freezer bag and store in the freezer.

Jamie's Spice Mix

MY SISTER JAMIE has great taste in food. I love learning from her. This spice mix is based on her special blend, one that she gave as a party favor at her wedding when she married into a large Italian family. Add a few shakes to salad dressing, meat marinades, or French fries. It also goes well on pizza. ○ *Makes about ⅔ cup*

Packaging: Pint-size zip-top freezer bag or plastic container with lid

2 tablespoons onion powder
2 tablespoons garlic powder
1½ tablespoons paprika

3 tablespoons chopped fresh basil or 1 tablespoon dried basil

1 tablespoon dried oregano

1 tablespoon fine sea salt

2 teaspoons freshly ground black pepper

1 teaspoon celery seeds

½ teaspoon grated lemon zest

½ teaspoon cayenne pepper

In a small bowl, combine all of the ingredients. Place the mixture in an airtight plastic container or freezer bag and store in the freezer.

Sweet and Spicy Joes

SLOPPY JOES CAN BE TOO SWEET for some palates. This variation retains some of the sweet but adds a spicy kick for variety. If you do prefer a sweeter version, simply add more brown sugar. ○ *Serves 4 to 8*

Packaging: Plastic containers with lids

2 pounds ground beef

1 to 2 cups tomato sauce, depending on how saucy you like it

2½ tablespoons Jamie's Spice Mix (page 90)

1 tablespoon brown sugar

When ready to serve, you will need:

Hamburger buns

Shredded cheddar cheese

Sliced dill pickles

1. In a large skillet, cook the meat over medium-high heat, stirring frequently, until no pink remains.

2. Stir in the tomato sauce, spice mix, and brown sugar. Bring to a bubble and then simmer for 20 minutes.

Freezing instructions:

Divide the meat mixture into meal-size portions in plastic containers. Chill in the refrigerator before freezing.

To thaw and serve:

Thaw in the refrigerator. Reheat the mixture in a saucepan. Spoon the hot mixture onto hamburger buns and top with cheese and pickles. Serve immediately.

Lawnmower Taco

THIS IS A SIMPLE CASSEROLE that my kids love. We call it "lawnmower taco" because it looks, well, like a taco that got stuck in a lawnmower. It comes together easily and is perfect for potlucks or any night when you crave a little comfort food. ○ *Serves 6 to 8*

Packaging: 9 × 13-inch baking dish with lid

1 pound ground beef
1 to 2 tablespoons Basic Taco Seasoning Mix (page 89)
¼ cup unbleached all-purpose flour
2 cups chicken broth
9 ounces tortilla chips, crushed (3 to 4 cups)
2 cup shredded Monterey Jack or cheddar cheese

When ready to serve, you will need:

Shredded lettuce
Salsa
Sour cream
Canned sliced black olives

1. In a large skillet, cook the meat over medium-high heat, stirring frequently, until no pink remains. Sprinkle the taco seasoning and the flour over the cooked meat. Stir well.

2. Stir in the broth and bring the mixture to a simmer. Simmer, stirring occasionally, until the sauce thickens, about 15 minutes.

3. Meanwhile, grease the baking dish. Spread half of the crushed chips across the bottom of the dish. Spoon half of the meat mixture over the chips.

4. Sprinkle half of the cheese over the meat layer. Repeat the layers of chips, meat, and cheese.

Freezing instructions:

Cover the dish and chill in the refrigerator before freezing.

To thaw and serve:

Thaw the casserole in the refrigerator. Preheat the oven to 325°F. Bake the casserole for 20 to 30 minutes, or until bubbly. Serve with the lettuce, salsa, sour cream, and olives.

Soy-Balsamic Burgers

BURGERS ARE A GO-TO SUPPER during the warmer months; there's something so inviting about meat that has been cooked over an open flame. But hamburgers make a great quick meal any time of the year. Having a stash of patties in the freezer makes your prep time even quicker. These burgers are seasoned with balsamic vinegar and soy sauce, adding delicious flavor to the meat.

o *Serves 8*

Packaging: Gallon-size zip-top freezer bag, waxed paper, plastic wrap

2 pounds ground beef
1 tablespoon balsamic vinegar
1 tablespoon soy sauce
1 tablespoon chopped fresh parsley or 1 teaspoon dried parsley flakes
½ teaspoon dried thyme
¼ teaspoon freshly ground black pepper

When ready to serve, you will need:

Hamburger buns
Lettuce leaves or shredded lettuce
Sliced tomatoes
Other toppings, as desired

1. In a large bowl, mix all of the ingredients just until everything is evenly distributed. Don't overmix, as that will make your burgers tough.

2. Divide the mixture into 8 equal portions. Form each portion into a flat hamburger patty.

Freezing instructions:

Place the patties on a baking sheet and freeze until firm. Remove the frozen patties from the sheet and place them in a freezer bag. Seal the bag carefully, removing as much air as possible. Return the burgers to the freezer. Alternatively, you can freeze the burgers in meal-size bundles, separating the patties with waxed paper. Wrap each bundle in plastic wrap and place in a freezer bag.

To thaw and serve:

If you have frozen your hamburger patties individually, simply remove the desired number of patties from the bag. There is no need to thaw them before cooking. If you used the bundle method of packaging, thaw the bundle on a dish in the refrigerator. (You may be able to cook these unthawed as well, if the frozen patties separate easily.) Place the hamburger patties on a hot grill or in a skillet. When the tops of the burgers appear wet, flip them over. Continue cooking until the burgers reach the desired doneness. Serve on buns with lettuce, tomatoes, and other toppings as desired.

Prepping Hamburgers for the Freezer

You might wonder why you should bother prepping hamburgers for the freezer when you can make them up in a matter of minutes right before cooking time. The answers are manifold:

- You can take advantage of grocery sales stocking up on ground beef at a low price rather than paying a premium when the urge for burgers hits.

- Taking a few minutes now gives you the opportunity to "dude" up your burgers with different mix-ins and spices when you have more leisure to do so. This also makes it easier to offer a variety of burgers at one meal.

- Formed and frozen patties can go directly from the freezer to a hot grill, making dinner come together more quickly than a trip to the local burger stand.

Two Basic Prepping Methods

1. Individual freezing

The advantage of individually freezing the burgers is that you can cook as many or as few as you like, while leaving the rest in the freezer. No need to thaw an entire package!

Packaging: Gallon-size zip-top freezer bag

In a large bowl, mix all of the ingredients just until the seasonings are evenly distributed. Don't overmix, as that will make your burgers tough. Divide the mixture into ¼-pound portions, forming each portion into a flat hamburger patty.

Freezing instructions:

Place the patties on a baking sheet and freeze until firm. Remove the frozen patties from the sheet and place them in a labeled zip-top freezer bag. Seal the bag carefully, removing as much air as possible. Return the patties to the freezer.

To serve:

Remove the desired number of patties from the bag. There is no need to thaw them before cooking.

2. Bundling

The selling point of a bundle of hamburger patties is the time you save in the prep stage. You can mix, form, and freeze a number of patties in a matter of minutes. However, you

(continued)

have to pre-plan a bit. If you bundle 12 burgers, then you will probably need to thaw and cook all 12 burgers at once, as they will be more difficult to separate when they are frozen solid, even when separated by waxed paper, as I suggest here.

Packaging: Waxed paper, plastic wrap, zip-top freezer bag

In a large bowl, mix all of the ingredients just until the seasonings are evenly distributed. Don't overmix, as that will make your burgers tough. Divide the mixture into ¼-pound portions, forming each portion into a flat hamburger patty.

Freezing instructions:

Stack the burgers in meal-size bundles, separating the patties with waxed paper. Wrap each bundle in plastic wrap and place in a freezer bag. Store the patties in the freezer.

To thaw and serve:

Thaw the bundle on a dish in the refrigerator and cook as desired.

Outside-In Cheeseburgers

JOIN TWO GREAT TASTES in one by mixing your cheese into this outside-in cheeseburger. The added dill is reminiscent of dill pickles, making this truly an all-in-one burger. ○ *Serves 8*

Packaging: Gallon-size zip-top freezer bag, waxed paper, plastic wrap

2 pounds ground beef
½ cup finely chopped onion
½ cup shredded cheddar cheese
1½ teaspoons fresh chopped dill or ½ teaspoon dried dill
½ teaspoon salt
¼ teaspoon freshly ground black pepper

When ready to serve, you will need:

Hamburger buns
Lettuce leaves or shredded lettuce
Sliced tomatoes
Other toppings, as desired

1. In a large bowl, mix all of the ingredients just until everything is evenly distributed. Don't overmix, as that will make your burgers tough.

2. Divide the mixture into 8 equal portions. Form each portion into a flat hamburger patty.

Freezing instructions:

Place the patties on a baking sheet and freeze until firm. Remove the frozen patties from the sheet and place them in a freezer bag. Seal the bag carefully, removing as much air as possible. Return the burgers to the freezer. Alternatively, you can freeze the burgers in meal-size bundles, separating the patties with waxed paper. Wrap each bundle in plastic wrap and place in a freezer bag.

To thaw and serve:

If you have frozen your hamburger patties individually, simply remove the desired number of patties from the bag. There is no need to thaw them before cooking. If you used the bundle method of packaging, thaw the bundle on a dish in the refrigerator. (You may be able to cook these unthawed as well, if the frozen patties separate easily.) Place the hamburger patties on a hot grill or in a skillet. When the tops of the burgers appear wet, flip them over. Continue cooking until the burgers reach the desired doneness. Serve on buns with lettuce, tomatoes, and other toppings as desired.

Herbed Meatballs

MEATBALLS ARE ONE OF THE HANDIEST meal components to keep in the freezer. They can be added to soup, served atop a bowl of spaghetti, dressed in gravy over mashed potatoes, basted with barbecue sauce on the grill, or spooned into a crusty roll with red sauce for a fabulous hot sandwich.

You can even serve them as meatball sliders on small dinner rolls. This recipe is easy—and just waiting to be finished with your favorite sauce. ● *Serves 12 to 16*

Packaging: Quart- or gallon-size zip-top freezer bags

4 pounds ground beef
3 cups fresh bread crumbs
6 large eggs, beaten
1 cup chopped onion
⅓ cup chopped fresh parsley or 2 tablespoons dried parsley flakes
3 tablespoons chopped fresh basil or 1 tablespoon dried basil
3 cloves garlic, chopped
1 teaspoon kosher salt

1. Line two rimmed baking sheets with heavy-duty foil. Spray the foil lightly with nonstick cooking spray. Preheat the oven to 350°F.

2. In a large bowl, mix all of the ingredients just until everything is evenly distributed. Don't overmix, as that will make your meatballs tough.

3. Form the mixture into golf ball–size balls and place the meatballs on the prepared sheets. Bake the meatballs for 15 minutes, or until they are cooked through.

Freezing instructions:

Divide the meatballs into meal-size portions in freezer bags. Chill the bags in the refrigerator before freezing.

To thaw and serve:

Thaw the meatballs in the refrigerator. Reheat them in your choice of sauce on the stovetop.

VARIATIONS

Barbecue Sauce for Meatballs

Add a little smoky flavor to meatballs by warming them on a hot grill and basting them with this super-spicy sauce. (For less heat, reduce the cayenne pepper.) Serve over mashed potatoes or hot cooked noodles. ● *Makes about 2 cups*

Packaging: 1-cup plastic containers with lids

2 tablespoons olive oil
1 cup finely chopped onion
4 cloves garlic, minced
2 cups tomato sauce
½ cup apple cider vinegar
¼ cup dark brown sugar
1 tablespoon chipotle chile powder
1 teaspoon cayenne pepper, or to taste
⅛ teaspoon crushed red pepper flakes
⅛ teaspoon ground ginger
⅛ teaspoon ground cloves
⅛ teaspoon dry mustard
⅛ teaspoon ground cinnamon

1. In a large saucepan, heat the oil over medium heat. Add the onion and garlic and cook for 8 minutes, or until the onion is tender and starting to caramelize.

2. Add all of the remaining ingredients and stir until well combined. Bring to a low boil, stirring constantly. Reduce the heat, cover, and simmer for 30 minutes, stirring occasionally.

3. Blend the sauce with an immersion blender or in a food processor until smooth.

Freezing instructions:

Divide the sauce into 1-cup plastic containers. Chill the sauce in the refrigerator before freezing.

To thaw and serve:

Thaw the sauce in the refrigerator. Reheat in the microwave or in a pan on the stovetop. Serve as a sauce for meatballs, hot or at room temperature.

Herbed Meatloaf

The basic meatball mixture can also be formed into four meatloaves. Lay out four large sheets of aluminum foil. Divide the meat mixture into four portions, placing one portion on each sheet of foil. Form each of the four portions into a loaf. Wrap each loaf well with the aluminum foil and place them into labeled zip-top freezer bags. Freeze.

To thaw and serve:

Thaw the meatloaf completely in the refrigerator. Preheat the oven to 350°F. Unwrap the meatloaf, place it on a baking sheet, and bake for 45 to 60 minutes or until cooked through.

Swedish Meatballs with Dill

THIS MEATBALL DISH is enjoyed by diners of all ages, particularly when served with mashed potatoes or hot cooked noodles and lingonberry or cranberry sauce. The rich beef gravy will have them licking the plates clean.

○ Serves 12 to 16

Packaging: Quart- or gallon-size zip-top freezer bags, plastic containers with lids

3 pounds ground beef
1 pound ground pork
3 cups fresh bread crumbs
6 large eggs, beaten
1 cup finely chopped onion
3 cloves garlic, minced
⅓ cup chopped fresh parsley or 2 tablespoons dried parsley flakes
¼ cup chopped fresh dill or 1 tablespoon plus 2 teaspoons dried dill
2 teaspoons kosher salt
¼ teaspoon ground allspice
8 cups Beefy Mushroom Gravy (page 81)

1. Line two rimmed baking sheets with heavy-duty foil. Spray the foil lightly with nonstick cooking spray. Preheat the oven to 350°F.

2. In a large bowl, mix the ground meats, bread crumbs, eggs, onion, garlic, parsley, 3 tablespoons of the fresh dill or 1 tablespoon of the dried, salt, and allspice just until everything is evenly distributed. Don't overmix, as that will make your meatballs tough.

3. Form the mixture into golf ball–size balls and place the meatballs on the prepared sheets. Bake the meatballs for 15 minutes, or until they are cooked through.

4. Pour the gravy into a large bowl. Add the remaining 1 tablespoon fresh dill or 2 teaspoons dried and stir to combine.

Freezing instructions:

Divide the meatballs into meal-size portions in freezer bags. Divide the gravy into plastic containers. Chill the meatballs and gravy in the refrigerator before freezing.

To thaw and serve:

Thaw the meatballs and gravy in the refrigerator. Reheat the gravy in a large saucepan on the stovetop, whisking to recombine. Add the meatballs and simmer until heated through. Serve immediately.

Boules de Picolat (Catalan Meatballs)

AS A COLLEGE EXCHANGE STUDENT in France, I was "adopted" by a French family of Catalan descent. They served this traditional Catalan dish to me on my 21st birthday. There is great debate among Catalan families over whether to serve this with boiled potatoes or rice. My host family preferred potatoes. The dish is best made with porcini mushrooms, also known as cèpes, but I've replaced them with the more easily located and economical button mushrooms. ○ *Serves 12 to 16*

Packaging: Quart- or gallon-size zip-top freezer bags

3 pounds ground beef
1 pound ground pork
2 cups chopped onion

3 tablespoons chopped fresh parsley or 1 tablespoon dried parsley flakes

3 cloves garlic, chopped

1 teaspoon salt

½ teaspoon freshly ground black pepper

2 tablespoons olive oil

½ cup coarsely chopped fresh mushrooms

Two 28-ounce cans crushed tomatoes in puree

One 14.5-ounce can diced tomatoes with juices

When ready to serve, you will need:

1 cup green Spanish olives with pimientos

Boiled potatoes or steamed rice

1. Line two rimmed baking sheets with heavy-duty foil. Spray the foil lightly with nonstick cooking spray. Preheat the oven to 350°F.

2. In a large bowl, mix the ground meats, 1 cup of the onion, parsley, garlic, salt, and pepper just until everything is evenly distributed. Don't overmix, as that will make your meatballs tough.

3. Form the mixture into golf ball–size balls and place the meatballs on the prepared sheets. Bake the meatballs for 15 minutes, or until they are cooked through.

4. In a large stockpot, heat the oil over medium-high heat until shimmering. Add the mushrooms and the remaining 1 cup chopped onion to the pot. Cook, stirring, until the onion becomes translucent and the mushrooms start to brown slightly, about 5 minutes. Stir in the crushed tomatoes and diced tomatoes.

5. Add the cooked meatballs to the pot and stir well. Simmer the mixture for 20 minutes.

Freezing instructions:

Divide the meatballs and sauce into meal-size portions in freezer bags. Chill the meatballs and sauce in the refrigerator before storing in the freezer.

To thaw and serve:

Thaw in the refrigerator. Reheat the meatballs and sauce in a saucepan. Stir in the olives and cook until heated through. Serve immediately, along with the potatoes.

Crowd-Pleasing Poultry and Seafood

Ways with Cooked Chicken

Simply cooked chicken is a major building block for many meals. It finds its way into enchiladas, soups, tacos, sandwiches, and salads as a basic, adaptable protein. On busy nights, it's tempting to run for takeout or pick up a rotisserie chicken. But if I've planned ahead, I can instead go to the freezer and grab a bag of precooked shredded chicken. Meals come together in minutes and can be varied in so many ways that we never get bored. Here are three different ways to prepare basic chicken.

Basic Herb-Baked Chicken

YOU CAN MAXIMIZE YOUR SAVINGS by using bone-in chicken breasts. They often go on sale for around $1 per pound, making them a very economical protein. I prefer bone-in chicken breasts because the meat tends to be more flavorful and doesn't dry out the way boneless, skinless chicken breasts sometimes do. ○ *Makes about 6 cups chopped cooked chicken*

Packaging: Quart-size zip-top freezer bags or quart-size plastic containers with lids

6 bone-in chicken breasts
1 teaspoon fine sea salt
1 teaspoon garlic powder
½ teaspoon freshly ground black pepper
1 teaspoon *herbes de Provence*, chili powder, or mixed Italian herbs (optional)

When you sit down to dinner, slip two pans of chicken breasts in the oven to bake while you enjoy your meal. The chicken will be finished cooking by the time you are done eating; it can cool while you clean up dinner. Prep it for the freezer quickly and you're set for several future meals.

1. Preheat the oven to 375°F.

2. Place three chicken breasts in each of two 9 × 13-inch baking dishes. Sprinkle the chicken with salt, garlic powder, pepper, and seasoning, if using.

3. Bake the chicken for 45 minutes to 1 hour, or until the juices run clear when the chicken is pierced with a knife.

4. Remove the chicken from the pan and set aside until cool enough to handle.

5. Remove the chicken meat from the bones. If desired, reserve the bones and skin as well as the pan drippings for making Homemade Chicken Stock (page 108).

6. Chop or shred the chicken, as desired.

Freezing instructions:

If using the chicken in a recipe, proceed with the recipe. Otherwise, place the cooked chicken in freezer bags or containers. Chill the chicken in the refrigerator before freezing.

To thaw and serve:

Thaw the chicken in the refrigerator. Use as desired in recipes.

Versatile Chicken from the Slow Cooker

O N FREEZER-COOKING DAY, it's best to maximize the use of every pot and appliance so that all your "servants" can be working at one time. The slow cooker is no exception. If it isn't already full of soup, chili, or pasta sauce, put the slow cooker to work on chicken. The amount of chicken you can cook at one time will depend on the size of your cooker. Slow cookers work best when filled two-thirds full. ○ *Makes 4 to 6 cups chopped cooked chicken*

Packaging: Quart-size zip-top freezer bags or quart-size plastic containers with lids

4 to 6 bone-in chicken breasts or 1 roasting chicken, giblets removed

1 teaspoon fine sea salt

1 teaspoon garlic powder

½ teaspoon freshly ground black pepper

1 teaspoon *herbes de Provence*, chili powder, or mixed Italian herbs (optional)

1. Sprinkle the chicken breasts or roasting chicken with salt, garlic powder, pepper, and seasoning, if using.

2. Place the chicken in the crock of a 5-quart slow cooker. Cook on LOW for 6 to 8 hours or HIGH for 3 to 4 hours.

3. When the chicken is cooked, remove the chicken from the cooker and set aside until cool enough to handle.

4. Remove the chicken meat from the bones. If desired, reserve the bones and skin as well as the pan drippings for making Homemade Chicken Stock (page 108).

5. Chop or shred the chicken, as desired.

Freezing instructions:

If using the chicken in a recipe, proceed with the recipe. Otherwise, place the cooked chicken in freezer bags or containers. Chill the chicken in the refrigerator before freezing.

Time-Saving Tip

You can start cooking the chicken in the slow cooker right before you go to bed. Set on low heat, it will be done when you awake in the morning.

To thaw and serve:

Thaw the chicken in the refrigerator. Use as desired in recipes.

Simply Poached Chicken

THE TWO TRICKS to tender poached chicken are to avoid boiling it and to allow it to cool in the pan. This method lends itself well to a freezer-cooking session. Get the pan of chicken started, simmer for the allotted time, and then turn it off. While it cools, you can work on other cooking tasks.

○ *Makes about 4 cups chopped cooked chicken*

Packaging: Quart-size zip-top freezer bags or quart-size plastic containers with lids

2 pounds boneless, skinless chicken breasts or tenders
2 bay leaves
4 black peppercorns
1 clove garlic, peeled

1. In a large pot, combine the chicken, bay leaves, peppercorns, garlic, and water. Heat the water just to a boil.

2. Turn down the heat and simmer for 15 to 20 minutes, or until the chicken reaches an internal temperature of 165°F.

3. Turn off the heat and allow the chicken to cool in the liquid.

4. Chop or shred the cooked chicken, as desired.

Freezing instructions:

If using the chicken in a recipe, proceed with the recipe. Otherwise, place the cooked chicken in freezer bags or containers. Chill the chicken in the refrigerator before freezing.

To thaw and serve:

Thaw the chicken in the refrigerator. Use as desired in recipes.

Homemade Chicken Stock

HOMEMADE CHICKEN STOCK is amazingly easy to prepare. It is a tasty component of soups, stews, sauces, and rice dishes, and it's healthier and more economical than its canned or boxed counterparts. Use the carcass from a whole bird or the bones and skin from either the Basic Herb-Baked Chicken (page 104) or the Versatile Chicken from the Slow Cooker (page 105).

○ *Makes about 2 quarts*

Packaging: Quart-size plastic containers with lids

Chicken bones, skin, and drippings from Basic Herb-Baked Chicken (page 104) or
    Versatile Chicken from the Slow Cooker (page 105) *or* the carcass of
    a whole roasted chicken
8 cups water
1 carrot, peeled and chopped
1 medium-size onion, peeled and quartered
2 ribs celery, trimmed and cut into 2-inch pieces
6 black peppercorns
2 whole cloves
1 teaspoon dried thyme
1 teaspoon kosher salt
1 bay leaf

1. Place all of the ingredients in the crock of a 5-quart slow cooker and cook on HIGH for 4 hours or on LOW for 8 hours or overnight. Alternatively, place all of the ingredients in a large stockpot and bring to a gentle boil. Reduce the heat, cover, and simmer for about 3 hours.

2. Strain the stock and discard the solids.

3. Use the stock in your recipe as needed or pour it into containers and allow it to cool.

Freezing instructions:

Chill the chicken stock in the refrigerator. Before freezing, remove the fat that rises to the top when the broth is chilled.

To thaw and serve:

Thaw stock in the refrigerator and reheat in a pan on the stovetop, if necessary, before using in recipes.

Marinated Chicken Pieces

One of the easiest things I pull together for freezer cooking is chicken packed in marinades. Quick to prepare, it's also a speedy meal on the other side of thawing. Cook the marinated chicken on the grill while you make a few side dishes.

Preparing marinated chicken for six dinners takes me about an hour, demonstrating the efficiency of freezer cooking. If I were prepping for one of these meals on any given night, I could easily spend a half hour just trimming the chicken, pulling out the ingredients, and mixing sauces. What could be a cumulative three hours is reduced to one by making bulk batches and preparing several items with like ingredients.

Here's the basic method for easy and quick marinated chicken.

1. Prepare the marinade. Many marinades contain similar ingredients, so making several marinades at once will save time. Assemble, use, and clean up the ingredients once instead of multiple times. Mix the marinades right inside the labeled gallon-size zip-top freezer bags that you will use to store the chicken. If you place each bag in a medium bowl, you can prevent spillage, as the bowl will support the bags while you work. Don't forget to label the bags first. You don't want to try to write on a full bag.

2. Trim the chicken as necessary for the cut you've chosen. Trimming meat is not always a pleasant job, but performing the task in bulk makes it more efficient. Some supermarket meat departments will do the trimming and slicing for you, for little or no charge. Just call and ask. This can save you valuable time in the kitchen. I prefer to marinate boneless, skinless chicken breasts that I halve horizontally into cutlets or slice into strips for stir-fries or fajitas.

3. Add the chicken pieces to the marinades. Squeeze out as much air as possible and massage the bag to distribute the marinade evenly. Lay the sealed bag flat to freeze. Placing the bags on a baking sheet in the freezer will prevent them from slipping through the slats of open freezer shelving. A day or two before serving, pull a bag from the freezer and place it on a tray or dish to thaw completely in the refrigerator.

Easy Chicken (or Turkey) Gravy

BOTTLED AND POWDERED GRAVIES may be convenient, but lots of less-than-desirable ingredients lurk in those packets and cans. Since it's quite easy to make your own gravy, there's no reason to rely on commercial versions. This gravy is a delicious accompaniment to roast chicken dinners and works well in Best-Ever Chicken Pot Pie (page 121). ● *Makes about 2 cups*

Packaging: Pint-size plastic container or canning jar with lid

¼ cup (½ stick) unsalted butter (or fat from chicken or turkey drippings)
¼ cup unbleached all-purpose flour
2 cups chicken broth (or defatted drippings plus enough broth to make 2 cups)
1 teaspoon dried thyme
¼ teaspoon salt
¼ teaspoon freshly ground black pepper

1. In a large stockpot over medium heat, melt the butter. Add the flour and whisk to combine.

2. Heat until the mixture starts to bubble. Whisk in the broth and bring to a boil, stirring constantly.

3. Reduce the heat and simmer until the gravy is thickened, about 5 to 10 minutes. Add the thyme, salt, and pepper. Adjust seasoning to taste.

Freezing instructions:

If using the gravy in a recipe, cool it completely and proceed with the recipe. Otherwise, transfer the gravy to a plastic container or canning jar. Chill the gravy in the refrigerator before freezing.

To thaw and serve:

Allow the gravy to thaw completely in the refrigerator. Reheat in a saucepan over low heat, whisking to recombine.

NOTE: To make a big batch of this gravy, simply multiply all the ingredients by four. The cooking method remains the same, though you may have to add a few minutes to the cooking time.

Spicy Southwest Chicken

THIS MARINADE IS ALMOST LIKE A SALSA. It's full of fresh flavors that miraculously withstand the cold of the freezer and come shining through later. Any leftover grilled chicken can be chopped and served in tacos or atop salads. ○ *Serves 4 to 6*

Packaging: Gallon-size zip-top freezer bag

1 medium-size tomato, quartered
½ medium-size onion, cut into chunks
¼ cup vegetable oil
¼ cup soy sauce
¼ cup fresh cilantro leaves
¼ to ½ jalapeño pepper, chopped, to taste
2 cloves garlic
1 tablespoon freshly squeezed lime juice
4 to 6 boneless, skinless chicken breasts

1. Place the freezer bag in a medium bowl, folding the top over the edges.

2. In a blender or in a food processor fitted with a metal blade, combine the tomato, onion, oil, soy sauce, cilantro, jalapeño, garlic, and lime juice. Blend until smooth.

3. Pour the marinade into the prepared bag. Add the chicken pieces. Seal the bag and massage it gently to combine and distribute the ingredients.

4. Marinate for 2 to 8 hours in the refrigerator if cooking the same day, or freeze immediately.

Freezing instructions:

Freeze the bag flat in the freezer.

To thaw and serve:

A day or two before serving, remove the bag from the freezer and place it on a tray or dish to thaw in the refrigerator. Grill the thawed chicken breasts over a hot fire, turning once, until cooked through.

Naturally Gluten-Free Recipes

If you have a sensitivity or allergy to gluten, enjoying good food can be difficult. Often, suitable recipes are time-intensive or require special ingredients. And running out for takeout on a busy night is not always an option. Thankfully, there is a wide world of foods that are naturally gluten free. Having a stash of such meals in the freezer can be a boon to the busy, gluten-free household. Some families make a habit of stocking their gluten-sensitive college students' freezers with food they can safely eat when away at school. Please read ingredient labels carefully to make sure that you are using gluten-free products in your cooking.

- Versatile Shredded Beef Filling, page 66
- Salsa Verde Beef, page 68
- Oven-Baked Beef Taquitos, page 69
- Red and Green Beef Enchiladas, page 74
- Chipotle-Rubbed Tri-Tip, page 75
- Seasoned Steak with Gorgonzola-Herb Butter, page 78
- Quick and Easy Pepper Steak, page 80
- Vegetable Bolognese, page 83
- Seasoned Taco Meat, page 89
- Soy-Balsamic Burgers (lettuce wrapped), page 93
- Outside-In Cheeseburgers (lettuce wrapped), page 96
- Cooked chicken: Herb-baked, from the slow cooker, or poached, pages 104 to 107
- Spicy Southwest Chicken, page 111
- Spicy Dijon Chicken, page 114
- Tandoori Chicken, page 115
- Garlicky Italian Chicken Breasts, page 117
- Herb-Butter Chicken Tenders, page 118
- Teriyaki Chicken Skewers, page 119
- Creamy Chicken Enchiladas, page 123
- Chicken and Wild Rice Bake, page 129
- Sesame Chicken with Snow Peas and Mushrooms, page 131
- Green Chile Chicken Taquitos, page 133
- Mahi Mahi with Almond-Lime Butter, page 142
- Salmon Packets with Sun-Dried Tomato Pesto and Onions, page 143

Spicy Dijon Chicken

WHO WOULD HAVE THOUGHT that five ingredients could get together and throw a veritable party in your mouth? This Dijon chicken, loosely adapted from one in an old Williams-Sonoma grilling cookbook, pulls that off. Though I highly doubt my French *maman* would have ever added cayenne to her chicken, the Dijon and the pepper combine to give this dish a great kick. You can adjust the heat by increasing or reducing the amount of cayenne; be aware that it will taste spicier once it's cooked. ○ *Serves 4 to 6*

Packaging: Gallon-size zip-top freezer bag

⅓ **cup Dijon mustard**
¼ **cup olive oil**
2 **tablespoons red wine vinegar**
1 **teaspoon cayenne pepper**
4 **to 6 boneless, skinless chicken breasts**

1. Place the freezer bag in a medium bowl, folding the top over the edges.

2. In a small bowl, combine the Dijon mustard, oil, vinegar, and cayenne. Whisk to blend.

3. Pour the marinade into the prepared bag. Add the chicken pieces. Seal the bag and massage gently to combine and distribute the ingredients.

4. Marinate for 2 to 8 hours in the refrigerator if cooking the same day, or freeze immediately.

Freezing instructions:

Freeze the bag flat in the freezer.

To thaw and serve:

A day or two before serving, remove the bag from the freezer and place it on a tray or dish to thaw in the refrigerator. Grill the thawed chicken breasts over a hot fire, turning once, until cooked through.

Tandoori Chicken

TEACHING MY CHILDREN AT HOME, I'VE LEARNED about different cultures and tested out recipes of faraway lands. I wasn't sure my kids would go for tandoori chicken, but I was pleasantly surprised when they loved it. The spices gain strength in the freezer, so I've reduced the amount of seasoning that I would normally use. ○ *Serves 4 to 6*

Packaging: Gallon-size zip-top freezer bag

¾ cup low-fat plain yogurt or buttermilk
2 tablespoons freshly squeezed lemon juice
1 tablespoon olive oil
1 teaspoon paprika
1 teaspoon minced fresh ginger
1 teaspoon curry powder
1 clove garlic, finely chopped
½ teaspoon salt
½ teaspoon chili powder
4 to 6 boneless, skinless chicken breasts

1. Place the freezer bag in a medium bowl, folding the top over the edges. Combine the yogurt, lemon juice, olive oil, paprika, ginger, curry powder, garlic, salt, and chili powder in the bag. Swirl the bowl gently or use a whisk to combine.

2. Add the chicken pieces. Seal the bag and massage gently to combine and distribute the ingredients.

3. Marinate for 2 to 8 hours in the refrigerator if cooking the same day, or freeze immediately.

Freezing instructions:

Freeze the bag flat in the freezer.

To thaw and serve:

A day or two before serving, remove the bag from the freezer and place it on a tray or dish to thaw in the refrigerator. Grill the thawed chicken breasts over a hot fire, turning once, until cooked through.

Easy Caesar Salad with Garlicky Italian Grilled Chicken

In some ways, this is a "mock" Caesar salad. Gone are the raw egg and anchovies. But the dressing still packs quite a punch, and it comes together quickly, making it an ideal accent to a freezer meal. ○ *Serves 4 to 6*

Juice of 1 lemon (about ¼ cup)
1 clove garlic, minced
½ cup olive oil
Salt and freshly ground black pepper
2 to 3 Garlicky Italian Chicken Breasts (page 117)
1 head romaine lettuce, torn into bite-size pieces and refrigerated until ready to serve
¾ cup freshly grated Parmesan cheese
1 cup Homemade Croutons (page 320)

1. In a small glass jar or bowl, combine the lemon juice and garlic. Blend well. Add the olive oil and shake or whisk well to combine. Season the dressing to taste with salt and pepper.

2. Slice the chicken breasts across the grain.

3. In a large salad bowl, toss the lettuce with the dressing. Sprinkle on the cheese and croutons and toss again. Divide the lettuce mixture among serving plates, and top each with a sliced chicken breast. Serve immediately.

Garlicky Italian Chicken Breasts

GRILL UP THIS GARLICKY CHICKEN one night to serve as a main dish, reserving a couple of pieces to chop and toss on Easy Caesar Salad (page 116) the next night. Get two meals from one, with a minimum amount of work. ○ *Serves 4 to 6*

Packaging: Gallon-size zip-top freezer bag

¼ **cup red wine vinegar**
¼ **cup white wine or sherry**
¼ **cup olive oil**
2 **cloves garlic, crushed**
1 **tablespoon chopped fresh basil or 1 teaspoon dried basil**
½ **teaspoon dried oregano**
¼ **teaspoon freshly ground black pepper**
Pinch of sugar
4 **to 6 boneless, skinless chicken breasts**

1. Place the freezer bag in a medium bowl, folding the top over the edges. Combine the vinegar, white wine, oil, garlic, basil, oregano, and sugar in the bag. Swirl the bowl gently to combine the ingredients.

2. Add the chicken pieces. Seal the bag and massage gently to combine and distribute the ingredients.

3. Marinate for 2 to 8 hours in the refrigerator if cooking the same day, or freeze immediately.

Freezing instructions:

Freeze the bag flat in the freezer.

To thaw and serve:

A day or two before serving, remove the bag from the freezer and place it on a tray or dish to thaw in the refrigerator. Grill the thawed chicken breasts over a hot fire, turning once, until cooked through.

Herb Butter Chicken Tenders

T'S AMAZING HOW TENDER a butter marinade can make chicken. Broil or grill the chicken and serve with a quinoa pilaf and green salad for a satisfying summer supper. For a dairy-free version, you can use olive oil in place of the butter.

o *Serves 4 to 6*

Packaging: Gallon-size zip-top freezer bag

¼ cup (½ stick) unsalted butter, melted and cooled
2 tablespoons sherry
½ teaspoon dried thyme
½ teaspoon rubbed sage
¼ teaspoon each dried rosemary, tarragon, and oregano
10 to 12 boneless, skinless chicken breast tenders
Salt and freshly ground black pepper

1. Place the freezer bag in a medium bowl, folding the top over the edges. Combine the butter, sherry, and dried herbs in the bag. Swirl the bowl gently to combine the ingredients.

2. Add the chicken tenders. Seal the bag and massage gently to combine and distribute the ingredients.

3. Marinate for 2 to 8 hours in the refrigerator if cooking the same day, or freeze immediately.

Freezing instructions:

Freeze the bag flat in the freezer.

To thaw and serve:

A day or two before serving, remove the bag from the freezer and place on a tray or dish to thaw in the refrigerator. Grill the thawed chicken breasts over a hot fire, turning once, until cooked through. Season to taste with salt and pepper.

Teriyaki Chicken Skewers

EATING COOKED MEAT OFF A STICK is so much fun. There's something primeval and adventuresome about it. These chicken skewers are easy to pull together once the chicken is prepped and marinated. Grab a bag from the freezer and pack it for the next camping trip or beach cookout. o *Serves 4 to 6*

Packaging: Gallon-size zip-top freezer bag

¼ cup soy sauce
¼ cup dry sherry
3 tablespoons vegetable oil
1 tablespoon sesame oil
2 cloves garlic, minced
1 teaspoon brown sugar
1 teaspoon minced ginger
2 pounds chicken tenders, sliced in half lengthwise

1. Place the freezer bag in a medium bowl, folding the top over the edges. Combine the soy sauce, sherry, oils, garlic, brown sugar, and ginger in the bag. Swirl the bowl gently or use a whisk to combine the ingredients.

2. Add the chicken pieces. Seal the bag and massage gently to combine and distribute the ingredients.

3. Marinate for 2 to 8 hours in the refrigerator if cooking the same day, or freeze immediately.

Freezing instructions:

Freeze the bag flat in the freezer.

To thaw and serve:

Thaw the bag of chicken on a tray in the refrigerator. Thread the chicken pieces on skewers and grill them over a hot fire until cooked through.

Chicken Enchilada Bake with Green Chiles and Jalapeños

EARLY IN OUR MARRIAGE, my husband made it clear that he did not care for canned cream-of-anything soup. Imagine my chagrin, as the majority of the recipes I grew up on started with canned soups. Over time, I've learned tastier and healthier ways to make our meals—without the help of canned soups. This enchilada bake would traditionally contain cream of chicken or cream of celery soup. A homemade version, however, takes only a few minutes longer to prepare on the stovetop. This casserole gets an extra kick from green chiles. ○ *Serves 6 to 8*

Packaging: Two 8-inch baking dishes with lids or one 9 × 13-inch baking dish with lid

3 cups shredded cheddar or Monterey Jack cheese
2 cups Homemade Cream of Celery Soup for Cooking (page 223)
1 cup sour cream
One 4-ounce can chopped green chiles
½ cup chopped onion
1 fresh jalapeño pepper, seeded and finely chopped (optional)
2 teaspoons chili powder
12 corn tortillas, cut into bite-size pieces
3 cups chopped cooked chicken

1. Grease the baking dish(es).

2. In a large bowl, combine 2 cups of the cheese, the celery soup, sour cream, green chiles, onion, jalapeño (if using), and chili powder. Mix well.

3. Stir in the tortillas and the chicken. Spoon the mixture into the prepared baking dish(es).

4. Sprinkle the casserole(s) with the remaining 1 cup cheese.

Freezing instructions:

Cover the dish(es) and chill in the refrigerator before freezing.

To thaw and serve:

Thaw completely in the refrigerator. Preheat the oven to 350°F. Bake for 1 hour, or until hot and bubbly.

Best-Ever Chicken Pot Pie

THIS COZY, ONE-DISH SUPPER is frequently requested at our home. It's also a great recipe to make use of the leftovers of a big roast turkey or chicken supper. Simply put aside a few potatoes before you mash them and reserve any leftover meat, gravy, and vegetables. Fold them all together in a buttery pie crust and stash it in the freezer for dinner later in the month. Feel free to vary the vegetables according to your tastes. ○ *Serves 4 to 6*

Packaging: 9-inch deep-dish pie plate, heavy-duty aluminum foil

2 cups chopped cooked chicken breast
½ cup frozen peas
½ cup diced carrots, cooked
½ cup diced potatoes, cooked
2 cups Easy Chicken (or Turkey) Gravy (page 110)
¼ teaspoon dried sage
¼ teaspoon dried tarragon
2 recipes Versatile Buttery Pie Crust (page 356) or other pie crust

When ready to serve, you will need:

Milk for brushing crust

1. In a large bowl, combine the chicken, peas, carrots, potatoes, gravy, sage, and tarragon; chill the filling until cool to the touch, about 20 minutes.

2. Line the pie plate with one of the two crusts. Pour in the chilled filling. Position the second crust to cover the filling and crimp the edges to seal.

Freezing instructions:

Wrap the pie tightly with foil and freeze, making sure that the pie lies flat in the freezer.

To serve:

Unwrap but do not thaw the pie before baking. Vent the top crust by slashing an ✕ in the frozen crust. Brush with milk. Bake the frozen pie at 450°F for 15 minutes, then reduce the temperature to 375°F and bake until the crust is browned and the filling bubbles, 45 minutes to 1 hour.

Garlicky Chicken Noodle Bake

THIS NOODLE CASSEROLE, full of chicken and cheese with a crisp bread-crumb topping, makes for a hearty supper. Serve with a side salad or steamed vegetables for a complete meal. Be careful not to overcook the noodles. They will soften further during freezing, so cook them just al dente. ○ *Serve 6 to 8*

Packaging: One 9 × 13-inch baking dish with lid or two 8-inch round baking dishes with lids

16 ounces wide egg noodles
2½ cups Easy Chicken (or Turkey) Gravy (page 110)
1 cup freshly grated Parmesan cheese
2 cloves garlic, minced
1 tablespoon chopped fresh parsley or 1 teaspoon dried parsley flakes
1 tablespoon chopped fresh basil or 1 teaspoon dried basil
4 cups chopped cooked chicken
1 cup fresh bread crumbs
¼ cup (½ stick) salted butter, melted

1. Grease the baking dish(es).

2. In a large pot of salted water, cook the egg noodles until al dente, according to the package directions. Drain and cool the noodles.

3. In a large bowl, combine the gravy, Parmesan cheese, garlic, parsley, and basil.

4. Stir in the cooled noodles and chicken. Spoon this mixture into the prepared dish(es).

5. In a small bowl, combine the bread crumbs and melted butter. Sprinkle this crumb mixture over the top of the noodles.

Freezing instructions:

Cover the pans and chill in the refrigerator before freezing.

To thaw and serve:

Thaw in the refrigerator. Preheat the oven to 350°F. Bake for 30 minutes, or until heated through.

Creamy Chicken Enchiladas

THESE CREAMY ENCHILADAS are full of flavor and texture, with a little punch from the chipotle, pepper Jack cheese, and salsa verde, a tangy creaminess from the cream cheese, corn tortillas to give the dish body, and chicken to give it some heart. You'll love how easily these come together.

○ *Serves 4 to 6*

Packaging: Snack-size zip-top freezer bag, 9 × 13-inch baking dish with lid

Vegetable oil, for frying tortillas
12 corn tortillas
4 cups chopped cooked chicken
2 cups shredded pepper Jack cheese
8 ounces cream cheese, softened
½ cup chopped onion
1 teaspoon Chipotle Taco Seasoning Mix (page 90)
Salt and freshly ground black pepper

When ready to serve, you will need:

2 cups salsa verde

1. Fill a skillet with vegetable oil to a depth of 1 inch. Heat over medium heat until the oil shimmers. Fry the tortillas in the hot oil for 30 to 45 seconds each, turning once with tongs. Drain the tortillas on paper towels. Allow the tortillas to cool enough to be easily handled.

2. In a bowl, combine the chicken, 1 cup of the Jack cheese, the cream cheese, onion, and taco seasoning mix. Season the mixture to taste with salt and pepper.

3. Place the remaining 1 cup of Jack cheese in the freezer bag and set aside.

4. Grease the baking dish.

5. Assemble the enchiladas by placing 2 tablespoons filling on each tortilla. Roll and place the enchiladas, seam side down, in the prepared baking dish.

Freezing instructions:

Place the bag of cheese atop the enchiladas, wrap the dish for the freezer, and chill in the refrigerator before freezing.

To thaw and serve:

Thaw completely in the refrigerator. Remove the bag of Jack cheese from the dish. Preheat the oven to 350°F. Pour the salsa over the enchiladas and sprinkle the reserved cheese over the enchiladas. Bake the enchiladas for 20 minutes, or until the dish is heated through and the cheese is melted.

Chicken Divan with Cheddar Crust

F YOU GREW UP in the 1970s and '80s, some version of broccoli-and-chicken casserole will probably be familiar to you. Many, like the one my mom used to make, contain canned soup, curry powder, and mayonnaise. Some are served over rice or noodles; some are served alone. Here, Chicken Divan gets a little makeover with a simple homemade sauce and extra broccoli and chicken. The comfort is still there, but with improved flavor and more wholesome ingredients. I like this version over steamed brown rice. ○ *Serves 6 to 8*

Packaging: One 9 × 13-inch baking dish with lid or two 8-inch square baking dishes with lids

1½ pounds broccoli, cut into florets
4 cups chopped cooked chicken
2 cups Homemade Cream of Celery Soup for Cooking (page 223)
½ cup sour cream
2 tablespoons freshly grated Parmesan cheese
1 tablespoon freshly squeezed lemon juice
1 tablespoon sherry
1 teaspoon Dijon mustard
½ cup bread crumbs
2 tablespoons unsalted butter, melted
1 cup shredded sharp cheddar cheese

1. Grease the baking dish(es).

2. Steam the broccoli just until tender. Arrange the florets in the prepared dish(es).

3. Layer the cooked chicken over the broccoli.

4. In a large bowl, combine the cream of celery soup, sour cream, Parmesan cheese, lemon juice, sherry, and Dijon mustard. Whisk the mixture until smooth, then pour over the chicken layer.

5. In a small bowl, combine the bread crumbs and melted butter. Top the dish with the cheddar cheese and buttered bread crumbs.

Freezing instructions:

Cover and chill in the refrigerator before freezing.

To thaw and serve:

Thaw completely in the refrigerator. Preheat the oven to 350°F. Bake for 30 to 45 minutes, until heated through.

At first glance, stuffed chicken breasts seem like a lot of work, what with the trimming, flattening, filling, rolling, and baking involved. However, stuffed chicken breasts look so elegant on a plate, it's a shame to relegate them to special occasions. Thanks to freezer cooking and assembly-line preparation, you can enjoy this dish any night. Try one of the next two recipes, then branch out with other fillings of your choice.

Stuffed Chicken Parmesan

LIKE AN OUTSIDE-IN CHICKEN PARMESAN, this chicken is filled with mozzarella cheese, breaded, and baked. Serve it with pasta and a simple red sauce, like Easy Slow Cooker Red Sauce (page 205), and give it all a thorough dusting of Parmesan cheese. ○ *Serves 4 to 8*

Packaging: 1 or 2 baking dishes with lids, depending on how many breasts you will serve at each meal

1½ cups bread crumbs
1 tablespoon chopped fresh basil or 1 teaspoon dried basil
1 teaspoon garlic powder
½ teaspoon dried oregano
4 boneless, skinless chicken breasts, trimmed and cut in half horizontally
4 ounces mozzarella cheese, cut into eight ½-ounce sticks

When ready to serve, you will need:

2 cups Easy Slow Cooker Red Sauce (page 205)

1. Grease the baking dish(es) and set aside.

2. In a small bowl, combine the bread crumbs, basil, garlic powder, and oregano. Set the mixture aside.

3. Place the chicken pieces on a clean, flat surface and cover them with a sheet of plastic wrap. Using a kitchen mallet, pound the chicken pieces to flatten slightly.

4. Place a stick of cheese on each piece of chicken. Roll the chicken around the cheese, tucking in the sides as you roll.

5. Roll each stuffed breast in the bread crumb mixture and place it in the prepared baking dish(es).

Freezing instructions:

Once all the chicken breasts have been filled, rolled, and placed in the prepared dish(es), cover the dishes and chill in the refrigerator before freezing.

To thaw and serve:

Thaw the chicken breasts in the refrigerator. Preheat the oven to 350°F. Bake for 40 minutes to 1 hour, until the chicken is cooked through and the juices run clear.

Garlic Butter Chicken with Lemon Sauce

MY HUSBAND'S FAVORITE DINNER is a lemon chicken that is quite time-intensive. It's a "once-a-year" kind of meal, but I've streamlined it here in this stuffed chicken breast recipe. Some of the garlic butter oozes out of the chicken into the pan. The garlic butter and the juices of the chicken are quickly mixed with lemon juice and a little more butter to create a delectable sauce. Enjoy this meal with rice pilaf. ○ *Serves 4 to 8*

Packaging: 1 or 2 baking dishes with lids, depending on how many breasts you will serve at each meal

1½ cups bread crumbs
1 tablespoon finely chopped fresh parsley or 1 teaspoon dried parsley flakes
1 teaspoon dried thyme
½ cup (1 stick) salted butter, softened
1 teaspoon minced garlic
4 boneless, skinless chicken breasts, trimmed and cut in half horizontally

When ready to serve, you will need:

Juice of 1 lemon
2 tablespoons salted butter, melted

1. Grease the baking dish(es) and set aside.

2. In a small bowl, combine the bread crumbs, 1½ tablespoons of the fresh parsley or 1 teaspoon parsley flakes, and thyme. Set the mixture aside.

3. In another small bowl, cream together the ½ cup butter, garlic, and remaining 1½ teaspoons fresh parsley or ¼ teaspoon parsley flakes. Chill the butter mixture just until it will hold its shape when formed. Form the garlic butter into 8 logs. Chill until ready to use.

4. Place the chicken pieces on a clean, flat surface and cover with a sheet of plastic wrap. Using a kitchen mallet, pound the chicken pieces to flatten slightly.

5. Place a garlic butter log on each piece of chicken. Roll the chicken around the butter, tucking in the sides as you roll.

6. Roll each stuffed breast in the prepared bread crumb mixture and place it in the prepared baking dish(es).

Freezing instructions:

Once all the chicken breasts have been filled, rolled, and placed in the prepared dish(es), cover the pans and chill in the refrigerator before freezing.

To thaw and serve:

Thaw the chicken breasts in the refrigerator. Preheat the oven to 350°F. Bake for 40 minutes to 1 hour, until the chicken is cooked through and the juices run clear. Remove the cooked chicken breasts to a platter and tent with foil. Add the lemon juice and the melted butter to the juices in the pan. Stir well to combine. Serve this sauce with the chicken.

Chicken and Wild Rice Bake

CHICKEN, VEGETABLES, AND HERBS, as well as wild and brown rice, combine in a delicious dish that is both hearty and elegant. This dish is prepped as a kit to assemble on the day of baking. In this way, valuable time is saved by getting a lot of prep work out of the way. Quickly freezing the vegetables eliminates the need to thaw them before stirring them into the rice mixture.

○ Serves 4 to 6

Packaging: 2-gallon, 1-gallon, quart-, and sandwich-size zip-top freezer bags

½ cup chopped onion

½ cup chopped fresh mushrooms (optional)

1 rib celery, chopped (optional)

3 bone-in chicken breasts or mixed chicken pieces (about 2 pounds)

1 recipe Herbed Vinaigrette (page 130) or ½ cup other favorite vinaigrette

2 cups uncooked brown rice

2 tablespoons wild rice

½ teaspoon dried thyme

¼ teaspoon freshly ground black pepper

When ready to serve, you will need:

4 cups chicken broth or water, or a combination

1. Label the 2-gallon freezer bag "Chicken and Wild Rice Bake" and include baking instructions.

2. Spread the onion, mushrooms (if using), and celery (if using) in a single layer on a parchment-lined baking sheet. Freeze for about 20 minutes.

3. Combine the chicken breasts and vinaigrette in the gallon-size freezer bag. Seal and massage the bag to coat the chicken.

4. Combine the rice and seasonings in the quart-size freezer bag.

5. Remove the vegetables from the freezer, place them in the sandwich bag, and seal.

6. Place all three bags in the labeled 2-gallon bag. Freeze.

To thaw and serve:

Remove the bag containing the marinade and chicken from the larger bag. Place the bag of chicken in a dish and thaw completely in the refrigerator. The remaining ingredients can stay in the freezer.

When ready to cook, preheat the oven to 375°F. Spray a 9 × 13-inch baking dish with nonstick cooking spray. Combine the rice mixture and the vegetables in the pan. Stir in the broth. Remove the thawed chicken pieces from the marinade and place them atop the rice. Discard the marinade. Cover the pan with foil and bake for 1 hour. Uncover the pan and bake for an additional 45 minutes to 1 hour, until the rice absorbs most of the liquid and the chicken is cooked through and the juices run clear. Remove the chicken from the pan and cut each breast in half. Serve immediately.

Herbed Vinaigrette

◦ *Makes about ½ cup*

Juice of ½ lemon
1 tablespoon red wine vinegar
1 teaspoon Dijon mustard
1 clove garlic, minced
¼ teaspoon dried thyme
¼ teaspoon dried tarragon
⅛ teaspoon freshly ground black pepper
¼ cup extra-virgin olive oil

In a small bowl, combine the lemon juice, vinegar, mustard, garlic, herbs, and pepper. Stir well. Add the olive oil in a thin stream, whisking to combine.

Sesame Chicken with Snow Peas and Mushrooms

SESAME CHICKEN IS A TAKEOUT FAVORITE. This chicken dish comes together easily and is fantastic to have on hand for a quick "takeout" fix without leaving the house. Serve it over rice. ○ *Serve 4 to 6*

Packaging: Freezer containers with lids or gallon-size zip-top freezer bags

1½ pounds boneless, skinless chicken breasts, sliced into 1 × ¼-inch-thick strips
2 cloves garlic, minced
1 teaspoon minced fresh ginger
⅛ teaspoon crushed red pepper flakes
3 teaspoons sesame seeds
½ cup chicken broth
2 tablespoons soy sauce
1 tablespoon dry sherry
1 tablespoon cornstarch
1 teaspoon sesame oil
¼ teaspoon sugar
¼ cup vegetable oil
8 ounces sliced fresh mushrooms
6 ounces snow peas

1. In a medium bowl, combine the chicken strips, garlic, ginger, and crushed red pepper flakes. Set aside.

2. In a large dry skillet over medium heat, toast the sesame seeds until lightly browned. Remove them from the pan and set aside. Do not wash the pan.

3. In a small bowl, prepare the cooking sauce by combining the chicken broth, soy sauce, dry sherry, cornstarch, sesame oil, and sugar. Stir until well blended.

4. In the skillet, heat 2 tablespoons of the vegetable oil over high heat. Add the chicken and cook for about 3 minutes. Remove the chicken to a platter with a slotted spoon.

5. Lower the heat to medium-high and add the remaining 2 tablespoons of oil to the skillet. Add the mushrooms and cook, stirring, until tender and starting to brown, about 3 minutes. Add the snow peas and cook 1 minute more, stirring.

6. Add the chicken, sesame seeds, and cooking sauce to the pan. Cook over medium heat, stirring, until the sauce has thickened.

Freezing instructions:

Divide the chicken mixture into meal-size portions in plastic containers or freezer bags. Chill in the refrigerator before freezing.

To thaw and serve:

Thaw completely in the refrigerator. Heat the chicken, vegetables, and sauce in a saucepan until hot and bubbly.

Chipotle Chicken and Onion Wraps

F ROZEN BURRITOS are great on-the-go food. But this particular version takes "to go" to a whole new level. Filled with a creamy chipotle chicken mixture, these burritos will disappear quickly. ○ *Serves 6 to 12*

Packaging: Gallon-size zip-top freezer bags

1 tablespoon salted butter
½ cup finely chopped onion
6 cups diced cooked chicken
8 ounces Neufchâtel cheese, softened
2 tablespoons chopped chipotle chile peppers in adobo sauce
1 tablespoon chopped fresh parsley or 1 teaspoon dried parsley flakes
12 burrito-size flour tortillas

1. In a small sauté pan, melt the butter over medium heat. Add the onion and cook, stirring, until the onion is translucent. Cover the pan and reduce the heat to low. Allow the onion to cook for about 5 minutes more. Remove the lid and stir the onion, continuing to cook until it is very tender and starting to brown.

2. Combine the chicken, Neufchâtel cheese, cooked onions, chipotle chile and sauce, and parsley in a large bowl. Stir well. (You can combine these ingredients in the bowl of a stand mixer, mixing on low speed just until combined.)

3. Assemble the wraps by laying each tortilla on a flat surface. Spread a scant ½ cup of the chicken filling down the center of each tortilla.

4. Roll the tortillas up, folding in the sides as you go. Place the wraps in the freezer bag(s).

Freezing instructions:

Seal the wraps in the bag(s), removing as much air as possible. Store in the freezer.

To thaw and serve:

The wraps can be heated directly from the freezer or thawed. Microwave a frozen wrap on a plate for 2 to 3 minutes, turning once. Or thaw the burritos in the refrigerator and then crisp them on a hot griddle until the filling is hot.

Green Chile Chicken Taquitos

MANY, MANY MOONS AGO, my sisters and I found a recipe that vaguely resembled chicken taquitos. We made them all through our teen years, despite the excess of not-very-spicy canned picante sauce the recipe called for. While I still love a trip down memory lane, I've switched my allegiance to these taquitos, with their spicier and slightly more sophisticated filling. ○ *Serves 4 to 6*

Packaging: Plastic containers with lids or gallon-size zip-top freezer bags

Vegetable oil, for frying tortillas
24 corn tortillas
2 cups shredded cooked chicken
One 4-ounce can diced green chiles
2 scallions, finely chopped
1 teaspoon chipotle chile powder
1 to 2 tablespoons chicken broth, as needed
Salt and freshly ground black pepper

When ready to serve, you will need:

Sour cream
Super-Simple Guacamole (page 71)
Easy Homemade Salsa (page 71)

1. Fill a skillet with vegetable oil to a depth of 1 inch. Heat over medium heat until the oil shimmers. Fry the tortillas in the hot oil for 30 to 45 seconds each, turning once with tongs. Drain the tortillas on paper towels. Allow the tortillas to cool enough to be easily handled.

2. In a bowl, combine the shredded chicken, green chiles, scallions, and chile powder. Moisten, if necessary, with the chicken broth. Season the mixture to taste with salt and pepper.

3. To assemble the taquitos, roll 1 to 2 tablespoons of filling tightly into each tortilla. Secure the taquitos with toothpicks and set them on a tray lined with plastic wrap or waxed paper.

Freezing instructions:

Place the tray in the freezer for about 20 minutes, or until the taquitos are partially frozen but not so firm that you can't remove the toothpicks. If the toothpicks get frozen stuck, that's fine; you can store them with the toothpicks, though you may not be able to pack them as compactly. Once frozen, pack the taquitos into freezer bags or containers and store them in the freezer.

To serve:

Place the frozen taquitos, seam side down, on a baking tray and bake at 475°F for 15 to 25 minutes, turning once. Check for crispness after 15 minutes. Serve with the sour cream, guacamole, and salsa.

Chicken-Bacon Subs

SUCCULENT CHICKEN, CRISP BACON, melted cheese, and rich garlic butter present a feast for the senses in this sandwich. Certainly, sandwiches aren't difficult to prepare. But knowing that a large gourmet sub is waiting at home, ready to be popped in the oven, is likely to deter us from stopping for fast food. Get a large, soft, Italian-style loaf for this sub, not a crusty baguette-style bread.

○ Serves 4

Packaging: Heavy-duty aluminum foil

1 large loaf Italian-style bread, 14 to 16 inches in length
½ cup Garlic Butter (page 136)
2 cups shredded cooked chicken
¼ cup chopped bacon, cooked until crisp
5 ounces sliced mozzarella or Monterey Jack cheese

1. Slice the bread in half horizontally and place the halves on a large sheet of heavy-duty aluminum foil. Spread the garlic butter on the bottom half of the bread.

2. Arrange the shredded chicken on top of the garlic butter. Sprinkle the chicken with the chopped bacon. Layer the cheese over the top.

3. Place the top half of the bread over the cheese.

Freezing instructions:

Wrap the sub tightly in foil and freeze.

To thaw and serve:

Thaw the sub completely in the refrigerator. Preheat the oven to 350°F. Bake the sub for 25 to 30 minutes, until the cheese is melted and the filling is hot. Remove the foil and slice into four portions.

Garlic Butter

○ *Makes ½ cup*

½ cup unsalted butter, softened
2 cloves garlic, chopped
1½ teaspoons chopped fresh parsley or ½ teaspoon dried parsley flakes

In a small bowl, combine all of the ingredients. Blend well.

Make-Ahead Roast Turkey

BELIEVE IT OR NOT, a roast turkey can be successfully frozen and served later—without tasting like last Christmas's leftovers. And though you may not want to make your big meal a "freezer meal," it's nice to know that you can if need be. Not only can you save yourself a great deal of work on serving day, you can also take advantage of sale prices. Cook and freeze the birds you get on special for a roast turkey dinner or turkey sandwich any night of the year.

○ *Serves 10 to 12 (for a 20-pound turkey)*

Packaging: Heavy-duty aluminum foil, gallon-size zip-top freezer bags

1 tablespoon unbleached all-purpose flour
1 large turkey (up to 20 pounds), thawed, rinsed, and giblets removed
1 medium-size onion, quartered
¾ cup (1½ sticks) unsalted butter, softened
2 teaspoons minced garlic
Salt and freshly ground black pepper

1. Preheat the oven to 350°F. Place the flour in a large turkey oven bag and shake, according to the manufacturer's directions. Place the turkey in the prepared bag and place the onions in the cavity.

2. In a small bowl, combine ½ cup of the butter and the garlic. Spread the garlic butter all over the turkey. Season the bird generously with salt and pepper. Close the bag and bake according to the oven bag directions.

3. Carve the cooked turkey. Reserve the drippings for making soup or Easy Chicken (or Turkey) Gravy, page 110.

Freezing instructions:

Arrange the turkey slices and pieces in meal-size portions on sheets of foil. Dot the turkey portions generously with the remaining ¼ cup butter. Wrap the turkey securely and place the bundles in freezer bags.

To thaw and serve:

Thaw the roast turkey bundles in the refrigerator. Unwrap the turkey and place it in a roasting pan; moisten with turkey drippings or broth. Cover the pan loosely with foil. Preheat the oven to 325°F. Reheat the turkey until it reaches an internal temperature of 165°F, 15 to 30 minutes depending on how much turkey you are reheating.

Got Turkey?

Cooked turkey can often be used in place of cooked chicken in recipes. While turkey has a richer flavor, it is just as freezer-friendly as its barnyard counterpart. Try turkey in one of these recipes as a great way to use up holiday leftovers.

- Chicken Enchilada Bake with Green Chiles and Jalapeños, page 120
- Best-Ever Chicken Pot Pie, page 121
- Garlicky Chicken Noodle Bake, page 122
- Creamy Chicken Enchiladas, page 123
- Chicken Divan with Cheddar Crust, page 124
- Chipotle Chicken and Onion Wraps, page 132
- Green Chile Chicken Taquitos, page 133
- Chicken-Bacon Subs, page 135

Spicy Taco Lasagna

THIS TURKEY LASAGNA is an interesting twist on a classic, featuring spicy cheese and salsa as well as cream cheese in the filling. Hats off to cookbook author Ann Hodgman for the cream cheese sauce; it's the best. There's no need to cook the noodles, as they will soften during freezing and while the lasagna cooks in the oven. Serve this with sour cream, cilantro, and sliced avocado. ○ *Serves 6 to 8*

Packaging: 9 × 13-inch baking dish with lid

1 pound ground turkey
2 cups shredded pepper Jack cheese
2 cups shredded cheddar cheese
3 cups Easy Slow Cooker Red Sauce (page 205) or other favorite red sauce
1 cup Easy Homemade Salsa (page 71) or other favorite salsa
1 cup chicken broth
8 ounces cream cheese
6 to 8 regular (not no-boil) lasagna noodles

When ready to serve, you will need:

Sour cream
Sliced avocado
Chopped fresh cilantro

1. In a large skillet over medium-high heat, brown the ground turkey, breaking it up as it cooks, until it is no longer pink. Drain if necessary.

2. In a bowl, combine the shredded cheeses. In another bowl, combine the browned turkey, red sauce, and salsa.

3. In a medium saucepan, bring the chicken broth to a simmer. Add the cream cheese and whisk until smooth. Set aside.

4. Spray the baking dish with nonstick cooking spray. Spread half the turkey mixture in the bottom of the dish. Sprinkle with 1 cup of the cheese.

5. Arrange 3 or 4 of the uncooked lasagna noodles over the cheese layer, breaking them as necessary to fit. Pour the cream cheese mixture over the noodles. Sprinkle with 1 cup of the cheese.

6. Arrange the remaining lasagna noodles over the cream cheese layer. Spread the remaining turkey mixture over the noodles. Sprinkle on the remaining cheese.

Freezing instructions:

Cover the cooled dish and chill in the refrigerator before freezing.

To thaw and serve:

Thaw the lasagna completely in the refrigerator. Preheat the oven to 350°F and bake for 45 minutes to 1 hour, until brown and bubbly. Allow the lasagna to rest for 10 minutes before cutting. Top each serving with sour cream, sliced avocado, and chopped cilantro.

Turkey Burgers with Scallions

TURKEY BURGERS, when well seasoned, are an excellent alternative to traditional hamburgers. These burgers are tender and juicy. Ground turkey is rather sticky, making it difficult to form. Using wet hands to shape the patties will help. ○ *Serves 4*

Packaging: Zip-top freezer bags, waxed paper, plastic wrap

1¼ pounds ground turkey
½ cup fresh bread crumbs
¼ cup finely chopped scallions
1 tablespoon sherry
1 teaspoon salt
½ teaspoon freshly ground black pepper

When ready to serve, you will need:

Hamburger buns
Lettuce leaves or shredded lettuce
Sliced tomatoes
Other toppings, as desired

1. In a large bowl, mix all of the ingredients just until everything is evenly distributed. Don't overmix, as that will make your burgers tough.

2. Divide the mixture into 4 equal portions. Form each portion into a flat patty.

Freezing instructions:

Place the patties on a baking sheet and freeze until firm. Remove the frozen patties from the sheet and place them in a freezer bag. Seal the bag carefully, removing as much air as possible. Return the burgers to the freezer. Alternatively, you can freeze the burgers in meal-size bundles, separating the patties with waxed paper. Wrap each bundle in plastic wrap and place in a freezer bag.

To thaw and serve:

If you have frozen your hamburger patties individually, simply remove the desired number of patties from the bag. There is no need to thaw them before cooking. If you used the bundle method of packaging, thaw the bundle on a dish in the refrigerator. (You may be able to cook these unthawed as well, if the frozen patties separate easily.) Place the hamburger patties on a hot grill or in a skillet. When the tops of the burgers appear wet, flip them over. Continue cooking until the burgers reach the desired doneness. Serve on buns with lettuce, tomatoes, and other toppings as desired.

Tarragon Turkey Burgers with Blue Cheese and Chipotle Mayo

CHIPOTLE MAYONNAISE and flavorful blue cheese crown these herbed burgers. No one will miss the all-beef patty. o *Serves 4*

Packaging: Zip-top freezer bags, waxed paper, plastic wrap

1¼ pounds ground turkey
¼ cup chopped scallions
1½ teaspoons chopped fresh tarragon leaves or ½ teaspoon dried tarragon
½ teaspoon kosher salt
¼ teaspoon freshly ground black pepper

When ready to serve, you will need:

½ cup crumbled blue cheese
½ cup mayonnaise
1 chipotle chile in adobo sauce, finely chopped
Hamburger buns
Lettuce leaves or shredded lettuce
Sliced tomatoes
Sliced red onion
Other toppings, as desired

1. In a large bowl, mix all of the ingredients just until everything is evenly distributed. Don't overmix, as that will make your burgers tough.

2. Divide the mixture into 4 equal portions. Form each portion into a flat patty.

Freezing instructions:

Place the patties on a baking sheet and freeze until firm. Remove the frozen patties from the sheet and place them in a freezer bag. Seal the bag carefully, removing as much air as possible. Return the burgers to the freezer. Alternatively, you can freeze the burgers in meal-size bundles, separating the patties with waxed paper. Wrap each bundle in plastic wrap and place in a freezer bag.

To thaw and serve:

If you have frozen your hamburger patties individually, simply remove the desired number of patties from the bag. There is no need to thaw them before cooking. If you used the bundle method of packaging, thaw the bundle on a dish in the refrigerator. (You may be able to cook these unthawed as well, if the frozen patties separate easily.) Place the hamburger patties on a hot grill or in a skillet. When the tops of the burgers appear wet, flip them over. Continue cooking until the burgers reach the desired doneness.

Top the patties with the blue cheese and allow it to melt slightly before removing the burgers from the heat. In a small bowl, combine the mayonnaise with the chopped chipotle chile and its sauce. Serve the burgers on buns with the mayonnaise, lettuce, tomato, red onion, and other toppings as desired.

Mahi Mahi with Almond-Lime Butter

WHENEVER I SERVE THIS SIMPLE FISH with almond-lime butter, folks just can't get enough of it. With the flavors and textures of lime zest, toasted almonds, and dill, this butter sauce blends delectably into the fish. ○ *Serves 4*

Packaging: Plastic wrap, gallon-size zip-top freezer bag

4 mahi mahi fillets, 5 to 8 ounces each, wrapped securely in freezer paper
½ cup (1 stick) salted butter, softened
¼ cup toasted sliced almonds
1½ teaspoons chopped fresh dill or ½ teaspoon dried dill
Grated zest of 1 lime
½ teaspoon kosher salt
Freshly ground black pepper

1. Place the fish in the freezer bag. Place the bag in the freezer.

2. In a small bowl, combine the softened butter, almonds, dill, lime zest, and salt. Blend well.

3. Lay out a small sheet of plastic wrap. Spoon the compound butter onto the center of the plastic wrap. Using the plastic wrap as a guide, form the butter into a narrow log. Wrap the butter securely in the plastic wrap and place the butter log in the freezer bag with the fish. Seal and return the bag to the freezer.

To thaw and serve:

Thaw the bag in the refrigerator. Season the thawed fillets with salt and pepper and cook them, turning once, on a hot, oiled grill until the fish starts to flake, 10 to 15 minutes. Meanwhile, allow the butter to soften. Top each fillet with a few slices of the compound butter. The butter will melt quickly atop the hot fish, forming a sauce. Serve immediately.

Salmon Packets with Sun-Dried Tomato Pesto and Onions

SALMON IS A HEALTHFUL FISH that is readily available. It is delicious when topped with sun-dried tomato pesto and tender onions. Cooking fish in foil packets keeps it moist. Store a kit of toppings and fish in the freezer and assemble it right before cooking on the grill. ○ *Serves 4*

Packaging: Gallon-size zip-top freezer bag, 2 sandwich bags

4 salmon fillets, 5 to 8 ounces each, wrapped securely in freezer paper
¼ cup Sun-Dried Tomato Pesto (page 206)
1 medium-size red onion, thickly sliced

1. Place the fish fillets in the freezer bag. Place in the freezer.

2. Place the tomato pesto in a sandwich bag and seal.

3. Place the onion slices in the other sandwich bag and seal. Place these bags in the larger bag in the freezer.

To thaw and serve:

Thaw the bag in the refrigerator. Lay out four sheets of aluminum foil. Place 1 fillet on each piece of foil. Spread 1 tablespoon of pesto over each fillet. Top the pesto with several slices of red onion. Fold the foil over the fish to create a sealed packet. Cook the packets on a hot grill until the fish begins to flake, 10 to 15 minutes. Serve immediately.

Hoisin-Glazed Salmon Fillets

THIS TANGY FISH IS DELICIOUS served with rice and grilled vegetables. It's a grilled fish dinner that comes together in just a short time. The marinade thaws quickly at room temperature, and the salmon does not need to marinate for long. ○ *Serves 4*

Packaging: Plastic wrap, gallon-size zip-top freezer bag, small plastic container with lid

4 salmon fillets, 5 to 8 ounces each, wrapped securely in freezer paper
¼ cup rice vinegar
¼ cup soy sauce
1 tablespoon chopped fresh ginger
1 tablespoon hoisin sauce

1. Place the fish fillets in the freezer bag. Place in the freezer.

2. In the plastic container, combine the rice vinegar, soy sauce, ginger, and hoisin sauce. Mix well and seal the container. Place this container in the larger bag in the freezer.

To thaw and serve:

Thaw the bag in the refrigerator. Stir the marinade to recombine. Lay the thawed fillets in a shallow dish, then drizzle them with the thawed marinade. Allow the fish to marinate for 20 minutes. Cook the fish on a hot grill until it starts to flake, 10 to 15 minutes.

Crumb-Topped Cod Fillets

FRIED FISH IS A DELICIOUS and decadent treat, but it can be a nuisance to prepare. This crumb-topped fish dish offers the crunch and flavor without much work. Having a seasoned bread crumb mixture in the freezer makes quick work of this meal. It's just as easy as frozen fish sticks, but much better. Any white fish can be used. ○ *Serves 4*

Packaging: Gallon-size zip-top freezer bag, snack-size bag

4 cod fillets or other white fish, 5 to 8 ounces each, wrapped securely in freezer paper
½ cup panko bread crumbs
1 tablespoon fresh chopped dill or 1 teaspoon dried dill
1 teaspoon garlic powder
Grated zest of 1 lemon
½ teaspoon sesame seeds
½ teaspoon paprika
½ teaspoon salt

When ready to serve, you will need:

1 tablespoon olive oil
Lemon wedges

1. Place the fish fillets in the freezer bag. Place in the freezer.

2. In a small bowl, combine the bread crumbs, dill, garlic powder, lemon zest, sesame seeds, paprika, and salt. Place the crumb mixture in the snack-size bag and place this bag in the larger bag in the freezer.

To thaw and serve:

Thaw the bag in the refrigerator. Preheat the oven to 400°F and line a rimmed baking sheet with parchment paper. Place the fish fillets on the prepared baking sheet. Brush the thawed fillets with the olive oil and sprinkle with the seasoned bread crumbs. Bake the fish in the oven until it flakes easily, 10 to 12 minutes depending on the thickness of the fillets. Serve immediately, with lemon wedges on the side.

Tarragon-and-Lemon-Rubbed Fish

HAVING YOUR OWN CUSTOM-MADE spice blends on hand makes a cookout quick and easy. Store them in the freezer to preserve their freshness. This classic combination of tarragon and lemon goes well with all kinds of fish, from delicate fillets to thick, rich steaks. ○ *Serves 4*

Packaging: Gallon-size zip-top freezer bag, snack-size bag

4 fish fillets or steaks, such as salmon, 5 to 8 ounces each, wrapped securely in freezer paper
1 tablespoon chopped fresh parsley or 1 teaspoon dried parsley flakes
1 teaspoon grated lemon zest
1 teaspoon garlic powder
1 teaspoon dried tarragon
1 teaspoon kosher salt
¼ teaspoon freshly ground black pepper
¼ teaspoon paprika

When ready to serve, you will need:

1 tablespoon olive oil

1. Place the fish fillets in the freezer bag. Place in the freezer.

2. In a small bowl, combine the parsley, lemon zest, garlic powder, tarragon, salt, pepper, and paprika. Place the spice mixture in the snack-size bag and place this bag in the larger bag in the freezer.

To thaw and serve:

Thaw the bag in the refrigerator. Brush the thawed fillets with the olive oil and rub the seasoning all over the fish. Cook on a hot grill or in a stovetop grill pan, turning once, until the fish starts to flake, 10 to 15 minutes.

Grilled Tilapia or Shrimp Tacos

FISH OR SHRIMP TACOS are a delicious twist on Mexican food. Popular in Baja California, they are often served with fresh cabbage and a delectable white sauce. Fried fish is popular as a taco filling, but grilling the seafood is easier and healthier. Package this meal as a kit to be assembled and cooked right before serving. ○ *Serves 4*

Packaging: Gallon-size zip-top freezer bag, snack-size bag

1 pound tilapia fillets or medium-size shrimp (31 to 40 count), peeled and
    deveined, wrapped securely in freezer paper
1 tablespoon paprika
1 teaspoon sesame seeds
½ teaspoon ground ginger
½ teaspoon freshly ground black pepper
1½ teaspoons chopped fresh dill or ½ teaspoon dried dill
½ teaspoon salt
¼ teaspoon cayenne pepper

When ready to serve, you will need:

1 tablespoon olive oil
Corn tortillas, warmed
Shredded green or red cabbage
Chopped fresh cilantro
Yogurt-Dill Dressing (page 77)
Easy Homemade Salsa (page 71)
Lime wedges

1. Place the fish fillets or shrimp in the freezer bag. Place in the freezer.

2. In a small bowl, combine the paprika, sesame seeds, ginger, pepper, dill, salt, and cayenne. Place the spice mixture in the snack-size bag and place this bag in the larger bag in the freezer.

To thaw and serve:

Thaw the bag in the refrigerator. Brush the thawed fillets or shrimp with the olive oil and sprinkle with the seasoning. Cook the seafood on a hot grill or in a stovetop grill pan, turning once, until the fish starts to flake or the shrimp are pink, 7 to 10 minutes. Assemble the tacos by placing a small portion of seafood on each tortilla. Top the fish with shredded cabbage and chopped cilantro. Drizzle the tacos with the yogurt-dill dressing and serve with salsa and lime wedges.

Things to Serve When You Forgot to Thaw

Water, water, every where, nor any drop to drink. So cried the Ancient Mariner. And you may empathize with his plight if you ever find yourself with a freezer full of food and nothing to eat for dinner! This can easily happen if you forget to pull items from the freezer in time to thaw adequately. But never fear—there is a way out of these doldrums.

The following items either thaw quickly or can be cooked or reheated directly from the freezer, without thawing.

- Oven-Baked Beef Taquitos, page 69
- Mexican Beef Tortas, page 71
- Not Your Convenience Store's Frozen Burritos, page 87
- Seasoned Taco Meat, page 89
- Sweet and Spicy Joes, page 91
- Herbed Meatballs, page 97, with Easy Slow Cooker Red Sauce, page 205, or Barbecue Sauce for Meatballs, page 98
- Swedish Meatballs with Dill, page 100
- Best-Ever Chicken Pot Pie, page 121
- Chipotle Chicken and Onion Wraps, page 132
- Green Chile Chicken Taquitos, page 133
- Any of the red sauces, pages 201 to 205
- Any of the soups, pages 208 to 232
- French Bread Pizza Dippers, page 246
- Deep-Dish Focaccia Pizza Your Way, page 247
- Spinach and Cheese Calzones, page 249

Spicy Shrimp and Tomatoes

SUCCULENT SHRIMP and juicy tomatoes are a great combination in this dish. When you're ready to serve, the seafood cooks quickly in the tangy sauce, making for a speedy freezer meal. Serve this spicy mixture over hot cooked rice or with cornbread. ○ *Serves 6 to 10*

Packaging: 2 quart-size plastic containers with lids

2 tablespoons olive oil

1 cup chopped red or green bell pepper, or a combination

1 cup chopped onion

1 cup chopped celery

1 tablespoon chopped garlic

One 14.5-ounce can diced tomatoes, with their juices

One 15-ounce can tomato sauce

1 cup water

One 6-ounce can tomato paste

1 teaspoon smoked paprika

1 teaspoon dried thyme

1 teaspoon salt

1 teaspoon dried oregano

1 bay leaf

½ teaspoon freshly ground black pepper

½ teaspoon chipotle chile powder

⅛ teaspoon crushed red pepper flakes

When ready to serve, you will need:

2 pounds shrimp (41 to 50 count), peeled and deveined

1. In a large stockpot, heat the oil over medium heat until shimmering. Add the peppers, onion, celery, and garlic, and cook until the vegetables are tender and the onions are translucent, about 10 minutes.

2. Stir in the tomatoes, tomato sauce, water, tomato paste, and seasonings. Bring the mixture to a low boil. Simmer for 20 minutes.

3. Ladle the sauce into the quart-size plastic containers. Allow the sauce to cool to room temperature.

Freezing instructions:

Cover and chill the sauce in the refrigerator before storing in the freezer.

To thaw and serve:

Thaw the sauce and the shrimp (if necessary) in the refrigerator. Heat the sauce in a large saucepan over medium heat. Add the shrimp to the sauce and cook for 3 to 5 minutes, until the shrimp are pink. Adjust the seasonings to taste.

Sure-Fire Pork and Sausage

Versatile Slow-Cooked Carnitas

CARNITAS ("LITTLE MEATS" IN SPANISH) is a seasoned, shredded pork filling used for tacos, tostadas, and tamales. Traditionally, the pork shoulder is boiled and then roasted. Here, it is prepared in a slow cooker for a simpler yet equally delicious result. The moist and juicy carnitas freezes and reheats quite well, making it a perfect addition to your freezer cooking arsenal. Instead of a shoulder roast, you can use country-style pork strips, which often go on sale.

○ Serves 10 to 12

Packaging: Quart-size zip-top freezer bags or plastic containers with lids

One 3- to 4-pound pork shoulder roast
Salt and freshly ground black pepper
1 medium-size onion, chopped
½ teaspoon dried oregano
¼ cup water

1. Place the pork roast in a 4-quart slow cooker. Season the meat generously with salt and pepper. Add the chopped onion and sprinkle the oregano over all. Add the water to the pot.

2. Cook on LOW for 8 hours or on HIGH for about 4 hours. The meat should be very tender and shred easily.

3. Remove the meat from the pot. Strain the juices and reserve them to add to chili, stew, or soup.

4. Shred and cut the meat into bite-size pieces.

Freezing instructions:

Divide the carnitas into meal-size portions in freezer bags or containers. Chill the meat in the refrigerator before freezing.

To thaw and serve:

Thaw the meat in the refrigerator. Preheat the oven to 350°F. Place the meat in a baking dish and reheat for 15 minutes, until hot. Adjust the seasonings to taste.

Southwest Seasoned Pork Chops

THESE PORK CHOPS gain a depth of flavor from the simple marinade and the grill. Pair these chops with fried potatoes, corn, and black beans for a hearty meal. Mix up a batch of Basic Taco Seasoning Mix (page 89) first, as that spice blend plays a starring role in the marinade. o *Serves 4*

Packaging: Gallon-size zip-top freezer bag

¼ cup red wine vinegar
¼ cup vegetable oil
1 tablespoon Basic Taco Seasoning Mix (page 89)
4 boneless pork chops, about ½ inch thick

1. Place the freezer bag in a medium bowl, folding the top over the edges. Pour in the vinegar and oil, and add the taco seasoning. Massage the bag to combine the marinade ingredients.

2. Add the pork chops to the bag. Seal the bag, squeezing out as much air as possible. Massage the bag to distribute the marinade evenly.

Freezing instructions:

Freeze the bag flat in the freezer.

To thaw and serve:

Thaw the chops on a tray or dish in the refrigerator. Grill or broil the thawed pork chops, turning once, until cooked through, 10 to 15 minutes. Serve hot.

Pork Chile Verde with Hominy and Carrots

THIS PORK DISH always gets rave reviews. It's simple but filling, with a touch of the Southwest. Serve it with rice, salsa, sour cream, and chopped cilantro.

A time-saving technique during a freezer cooking session is to have one or even two slow cookers going while you prepare other food items. Not only does it make good use of your time in the kitchen, it also takes advantage of the technology available to you. You can even start a stew or sauce in the slow cooker several hours before you begin your intensive cooking session. In this way, you'll have a great head start on the cooking process. o *Serves 8 to 10*

Packaging: Plastic containers with lids

1½ pounds boneless shoulder blade pork strips (also called country-style ribs)
Salt and freshly ground black pepper
1 tablespoon olive oil
1 cup coarsely chopped onion
One 4-ounce can chopped green chiles
½ teaspoon ground cumin
2 cups salsa verde
One 15.5-ounce can hominy, rinsed and drained
2 cups baby carrots

1. Season the pork generously with salt and pepper.

2. In a large skillet over medium heat, heat the oil. Brown the pork strips, turning until browned on all sides. Transfer the pork strips to a 5-quart slow cooker or a large heavy pot.

3. Add the onion, chiles, and cumin to the drippings in the skillet. Sauté the onions until they are translucent and starting to brown, about 5 minutes. Add the onion mixture to the pork in the slow cooker or pot.

4. Stir in the salsa verde and the hominy.

5. If using the slow cooker, cover and cook on LOW for 4 to 6 hours. If using a pot, bring the mixture to a low simmer, and simmer for about 2 hours.

6. If using the slow cooker, stir in the carrots an hour before the end of cooking time. If using a pot, stir in the carrots 20 minutes before the end of cooking time.

Freezing instructions:

Divide the pork, vegetables, and sauce into meal-size portions in plastic containers. Chill in the refrigerator before storing in the freezer.

To thaw and serve:

Thaw the pork in the refrigerator. Reheat in a saucepan and serve.

Cranberry Pork Chops

THIS MEAL IS IDEAL for a cold, blustery day. Cranberries, onions, and spices join forces to flavor the pork chops as they simmer in the slow cooker. Prep couldn't be easier, as the meat and seasonings are ready to go in one zip-top freezer bag. Just empty the bag into the cooker, turn it on, and go about your day.

○ *Serves 4*

Packaging: Gallon-size zip-top freezer bag

2 tablespoons salted butter
½ cup chopped onion
¼ cup chopped celery
1 clove garlic, chopped
1 cup fresh cranberries
4 boneless pork chops, about ½ inch thick
¼ teaspoon freshly ground black pepper
½ teaspoon dried thyme
2 tablespoons brown sugar

When ready to serve, you will need:

¼ cup chicken broth or vegetable broth

1. In a large skillet, melt the butter over medium heat. Add the onion, celery, and garlic, and cook, stirring, until the vegetables are tender. Set the mixture aside to cool completely.

2. Place the cooled, sautéed vegetables, cranberries, pork chops, pepper, thyme, and brown sugar in the freezer bag.

3. Seal the bag, squeezing out as much air as possible. Massage the bag to distribute the ingredients evenly.

Freezing instructions:

Freeze the bag flat in the freezer.

To thaw and serve:

Thaw the pork chops on a tray or dish in the refrigerator. On the morning of the day you plan to serve this dish, empty the contents of the bag into a 4-quart slow cooker and add ¼ cup broth. Cook on LOW for 6 to 8 hours, or until the pork chops are cooked through.

Tips for Cooking When You Have Kids Around

The first time I tackled a big freezer cooking day, I was seven months pregnant, with the swollen ankles to prove it. My friend Jessika and I spent two days cooking in my 50-square-foot kitchen. We were both married without kids, and we produced about 40 meals to feed ourselves and our husbands.

The next time we tackled the job, I had a newborn. Needless to say, things were a bit different. Thankfully, I had my mother on baby duty. We cooked while she rocked the baby; I took occasional pit stops to nurse.

Since then my little family has almost tripled in size. With six kids ranging in age from toddler to teen, ours is a busy household, as you can imagine. But we've all gotta eat! While there are still nights when I cook a meal from scratch to serve my brood, I love to be able to pull a full meal or just a few meal components from the freezer to make my time in the kitchen easier and quicker.

How do you cook up a storm with little people about? Over the years, I've developed a number of approaches to cooking with kids and, sometimes, in spite of them. These same strategies also come in handy when I'm preparing big holiday meals.

- Get a babysitter. My mom, also known as Nanna, often comes to spend the day or weekend with us for the express purpose of watching the kids so that I can fill the freezer. If your "nanna" is not available, enlist the aid of a teenage "mother's helper." I'm willing to pay for babysitting if I know it will buy me time.

- Make judicious use of videos, audio resources, and computer games. Call this "free babysitting," if you will. It may not be the same as a human babysitter, but I'm okay

Pork and Chile Tamales

TAMALES ARE A CHRISTMAS TRADITION in Mexico and southern California. Though I was born and raised in southern California, I did not grow up enjoying homemade tamales. I wish I had! Years ago, my husband suggested that we learn how to make them ourselves. Now, we often keep a few batches of tamales stashed in the freezer. They freeze beautifully and are a delicious snack, lunch, or dinner. ○ *Serves 12 to 15*

Packaging: Quart- or gallon-size zip-top freezer bags

with using electronic devices to keep my kids entertained and out of mischief while I work toward better dinners and family nights. I also break up the electronic activities with Play-Doh sessions, snacks and lunches, and other independent play. If your children are school aged, cooking while they're at school may be the best way to fill your freezer.

- Have snacks ready before you start cooking. It's hard to interrupt a big cooking session to prep another meal, so have kid-friendly foods at the ready. You could even pack a little sack lunch for each child. That will give them something to look forward to.

- Cook during naptime and after the kids are in bed. There have been many nights when I've burned the midnight oil in the kitchen. I know the kids are safe, and I can work more quickly without interruptions. It's also a great time for my husband and me to catch up with each other. A freezer cooking date night? I'm all over that!

- Get your spouse or partner to plan a day out with the kiddos. Explain the benefits of a big freezer cooking day and ask that he or she take the kids out for the day. This will buy you the peace and quiet to get a lot accomplished in a short amount of time.

- Include them! I'm a firm believer in teaching kids to cook at a young age. My little ones love to be in on the action. And for my bigger kids, this is about learning valuable life skills. Picky eaters might also be more excited to try new foods if they've had a hand in the preparation.

1 package dried corn husks

1⅓ cups unsalted butter, softened

4 cups masa harina

2 teaspoons salt

2 to 3 cups chicken broth

2 cups Versatile Slow-Cooked Carnitas (page 152)

½ to 1 cup red chile sauce or enchilada sauce

When ready to serve, you will need:

Additional red chile sauce or enchilada sauce
Sour cream
Easy Homemade Salsa (page 71)

1. Soak the corn husks in warm water until pliable, up to several hours. Remove any silks or debris from the husks and rinse the husks thoroughly. Keep the husks damp until ready to use.

2. In a large bowl, whip the butter until light and fluffy. Blend in the masa harina, salt, and 2 cups of chicken broth. Blend well. Add more chicken broth until the dough holds together well. It should have the consistency of soft cookie dough. Cover the prepared masa with a damp cloth and keep it cool until ready to use.

3. In a medium bowl, combine the carnitas and enough of the red chile sauce to moisten it. Taste for seasoning and adjust as desired.

4. For each tamale, lay a presoaked husk flat on a work surface with the tip away from you. Spread 2 tablespoons masa on the husk, in a 5 × 4-inch rectangle. Spoon 2 tablespoons carnitas filling in a line down the center of the masa rectangle.

5. Fold the right side of the corn husk over the center of the filling, then fold the left side over the filling, wrapping any uncovered husk around the tamale. Fold the ends over.

6. Lay each tamale in a steamer basket, folded side down to hold it shut. Once all the tamales are folded and arranged in the steamer, place the steamer basket in a large pot over a few inches of boiling water. Make sure that the steam can move freely around the tamales; don't pack them in too tightly.

7. Cover the pot and turn the heat to medium so that the water will boil gently. Steam the tamales for 45 minutes to 1 hour.

8. To test for doneness, remove one tamale from the top of the stack and one from the middle. Open them; they are done if the masa dough is firm, does not stick to the husk, and does not have a raw, doughy taste.

Freezing instructions:

Cool the tamales completely and package them in freezer bags. Chill in the refrigerator before freezing.

To serve:

Steam the frozen tamales for 20 to 30 minutes or until heated through. Or microwave frozen tamales on a plate, covered with a damp paper towel, for 1 to 2 minutes per tamale. Serve the tamales with red chile sauce, sour cream, and salsa.

Soy-Ginger Pork Tenderloin

THIS ASIAN-FLAVORED PORK TENDERLOIN marinates as it thaws in the refrigerator, making for simple last-minute preparation. Once thawed, this easy but elegant meal can go from refrigerator to table in about 30 minutes. Serve with rice and vegetables on the side. o *Serves 4*

Packaging: Gallon-size zip-top freezer bag

¼ cup rice vinegar
¼ cup vegetable oil
3 tablespoons soy sauce
1 teaspoon minced fresh ginger
½ teaspoon crushed garlic
¼ teaspoon freshly ground black pepper
¼ teaspoon crushed red pepper flakes
One 1-pound pork tenderloin

1. Place the freezer bag in a medium bowl, folding the top over the edges. Pour in the vinegar, oil, and soy sauce, and add the ginger, garlic, black pepper, and red pepper flakes. Massage the bag to combine the marinade ingredients.

2. Add the tenderloin to the bag. Seal the bag, squeezing out as much air as possible. Massage the bag to distribute the marinade evenly.

Freezing instructions:

Freeze the bag flat in the freezer.

To thaw and serve:

Thaw the tenderloin on a tray in the refrigerator. Preheat the oven to 375°F. Remove the tenderloin from the bag and place it in a baking dish. Cook the tenderloin until an instant-read thermometer registers 145°F for medium or 160°F for well done, 30 to 40 minutes. Alternatively, the tenderloin can be cooked on a grill for about 30 minutes, turning once. Allow the tenderloin to rest for about 10 minutes after cooking. Slice and serve.

Pulled Pork Sandwiches with Asian Slaw and Tangy Barbecue Sauce

A DINNER THAT MIGHT TAKE HOURS to prepare requires only minutes to assemble when you have succulent pulled pork ready in the freezer. Pair the tender meat with a tangy barbecue sauce and an Asian-inspired coleslaw for a great dinner. ◦ *Serves 8 to 12*

Packaging: Quart- or gallon-size zip-top freezer bags

1½ teaspoons garlic powder
1 teaspoon onion powder
1 teaspoon chili powder
1 teaspoon salt
½ teaspoon freshly ground black pepper
½ teaspoon ground cumin
½ teaspoon ground ginger
One 2½-pound boneless pork shoulder

When ready to serve, you will need:

Kaiser rolls or hamburger buns
Asian Slaw (recipe follows)
Tangy Asian Barbecue Sauce (recipe follows)

1. In a small bowl, combine the garlic powder, onion powder, chili powder, salt, pepper, cumin, and ginger.

2. Rub the spice mixture all over the pork shoulder.

3. Place the seasoned pork shoulder in a 5-quart slow cooker. Turn the slow cooker to HIGH for 30 minutes. Then reduce it to LOW and continue to cook for 6 to 8 hours, or until the meat is pull-apart tender.

4. Remove the meat from the pot. Strain the juices and save them to add to chili, stew, or soup.

5. Cut and shred the meat into bite-size pieces.

Freezing instructions:

Cool the meat completely and divide into meal-size portions in freezer bags. Squeeze out the excess air and chill in the refrigerator before freezing.

To thaw and serve:

Thaw the meat in the refrigerator, then place it in a baking dish. Adjust the seasonings to taste. Preheat the oven to 350°F. Reheat the meat for 15 minutes, or until heated through. Serve immediately on buns, topped with slaw and sauce.

Asian Slaw

○ *Makes about 4 cups*

Packaging: Quart-size zip-top freezer bag

½ cup rice vinegar
2 tablespoons soy sauce
1 tablespoon sesame oil
1 tablespoon minced fresh ginger
1 tablespoon olive oil
1 pound coleslaw mix
½ cup chopped scallions

When ready to serve, you will need:

¼ cup chopped fresh cilantro
2 tablespoons sesame seeds, toasted
One 8-ounce can water chestnuts, drained and chopped

1. In a large bowl, combine the rice vinegar, soy sauce, sesame oil, ginger, and olive oil. Whisk to blend.

2. Stir in the coleslaw mix and scallions. Toss to coat.

Freezing instructions:

Spoon the slaw into the freezer bag and seal. Freeze.

To thaw and serve:

Thaw the slaw in the refrigerator on a tray to catch any drips. Just before serving, stir in the chopped cilantro, sesame seeds, and water chestnuts.

Tangy Asian Barbecue Sauce

This sauce comes together quickly on the stovetop. It's a delicious accompaniment to pulled pork, grilled meats, and meatballs. o *Makes about 2½ cups*

Packaging: Plastic containers with lids

2 tablespoons olive oil
½ cup chopped onion
One 15-ounce can tomato sauce
½ cup hoisin sauce
¼ cup soy sauce
1 tablespoon chopped fresh ginger
1 tablespoon sesame oil
¼ teaspoon red pepper flakes

1. In a large saucepan, heat the oil over medium heat. Add the onion and cook for 8 minutes, or until the onions are tender and starting to caramelize.

2. Add the remaining ingredients and stir until well combined. Bring to a low boil, stirring constantly. Reduce the heat and simmer, covered, for 30 minutes, stirring occasionally.

Freezing instructions:

Divide the sauce into meal-size portions in plastic containers. Chill in the refrigerator before freezing.

To thaw and serve:

Thaw the sauce in the refrigerator. Reheat in a saucepan. Serve immediately.

Grilled Caribbean Pork Tenderloin

EXOTIC SPICE RUBS can pack a pricey punch if you buy them premixed. But you can make your own, saving you money and time. This pork rub was a pleasant surprise to my family. They were initially skeptical of the Caribbean spices, but the proof was on the empty plate! Serve this taste of the Caribbean with a side of rice and Fresh Mango Salsa (page 164). ◦ *Serves 4*

Packaging: Gallon-size zip-top freezer bag, snack-size zip-top freezer bag

One 1- to 1½-pound boneless pork tenderloin, in its original wrapper
1 teaspoon garlic powder
1 teaspoon dried thyme
1 teaspoon grated lime zest
½ teaspoon ground allspice
½ teaspoon ground nutmeg
½ teaspoon kosher salt
¼ teaspoon cayenne pepper
¼ teaspoon ground cinnamon
¼ teaspoon freshly ground black pepper

When ready to serve, you will need:

2 tablespoons olive oil
Fresh Mango Salsa (page 164)

1. Place the tenderloin in the large freezer bag.

2. In the snack-size bag, combine all of the remaining ingredients. Seal the bag, removing as much air as possible.

3. Place the spice rub bag into the larger bag. Seal the larger bag, squeezing out as much air as possible.

Freezing instructions:

Store the bag in the freezer.

To thaw and serve:

Thaw the bag in the refrigerator on a tray to catch any drips. Remove the tenderloin from its wrappings and brush all over with some of the olive oil. Shake the spice mix to recombine the spices. Rub the spice mixture all over the tenderloin. Allow the meat to sit for 15 minutes. Brush a grill grate with the remaining oil. Cook the tenderloin on a hot grill until it reaches an internal temperature of 145°F for medium and 160°F for well done, 20 to 30 minutes. Allow the meat to rest for 10 minutes before slicing. Serve with Fresh Mango Salsa.

Fresh Mango Salsa

o *Makes about 2 cups*

1 mango, peeled, pitted, and chopped
¼ cup chopped fresh cilantro
Juice of 1 lime
1 jalapeño pepper, finely chopped
2 tablespoons chopped red onion

In a small bowl, combine all of the ingredients. Stir gently. Serve immediately.

Herb-Crusted Pork Roast

DIJON MUSTARD and apple cider vinegar flavor this hearty main dish. The roast is pre-seasoned and then frozen uncooked. On the morning of serving day, place the thawed roast in the slow cooker and await the enticing aromas that will fill your home. ○ *Serves 4*

Packaging: Gallon-size zip-top freezer bag

1 tablespoon Dijon mustard
½ teaspoon dried thyme
1½ teaspoons cider vinegar
½ teaspoon rubbed sage
½ teaspoon dried rosemary
⅛ teaspoon freshly ground black pepper
One 2-pound pork loin roast

1. In a small bowl, combine the mustard, thyme, cider vinegar, sage, rosemary, and black pepper. Stir until a smooth paste forms.

2. Rub the paste all over the pork roast. Place the roast inside the freezer bag. Seal the bag, squeezing out as much air as possible.

Freezing instructions:

Store the roast in the freezer.

To thaw and serve:

Thaw the bag on a tray in the refrigerator. Place the roast in a 4-quart slow cooker. Cook the roast on LOW for 6 to 8 hours or until cooked through. Alternatively, the pork can be roasted the oven. Preheat the oven to 375°F, cover the roast with foil, and cook for 45 minutes to 1 hour. Remove the foil for the last 15 minutes to brown the roast. The pork should reach an internal temperature of 145°F for medium and 160°F for well done. Remove the roast from the slow cooker (or oven) and allow it to rest for 10 minutes before slicing and serving.

Gingery Pork and Mushroom Lettuce Wraps

YOU MIGHT NOT EXPECT a meal involving a lettuce wrap to be freezer-friendly. But it can be if you prepare the cooked component first and store it in the freezer. Add the lettuce leaves and other fresh elements right before serving. The ginger-seasoned pork and mushrooms come together quickly and easily for a light summertime supper or elegant appetizer. ○ *Serves 4*

Packaging: Quart-size zip-top freezer bag or plastic container with lid

1 pound ground pork
8 ounces fresh mushrooms, finely chopped
2 teaspoons minced fresh ginger
2 cloves garlic, minced
⅛ teaspoon red pepper flakes
1 tablespoon sherry
1 tablespoon soy sauce
1 tablespoon water
1 tablespoon cornstarch

When ready to serve, you will need:

Lettuce leaves
Chopped fresh cilantro
Chopped scallions
Shredded carrots
Asian Dipping Sauce (recipe follows), soy sauce, sriracha sauce, or chili sauce

1. In a large skillet, cook the pork and mushrooms over medium-high heat until the pork is cooked through and the mushrooms start to brown slightly, about 10 minutes.

2. Stir in the ginger, garlic, and red pepper.

3. In a small bowl, combine the sherry, soy sauce, water, and cornstarch. Add the sauce to the skillet and cook, stirring, until the sauce thickens.

Freezing instructions:

Cool the pork mixture to room temperature. Spoon the mixture into a freezer bag or plastic container. Chill the mixture in the refrigerator before freezing.

To thaw and serve:

Thaw the pork mixture in the refrigerator. Reheat the mixture in a large skillet or in the microwave. Spoon several spoonfuls of the pork mixture into each lettuce leaf. Top with cilantro, scallion, and carrot. Serve with the sauce of your choice.

Asian Dipping Sauce

This recipe from my friend Jessika also makes a great dipping sauce for pot stickers or spring rolls. ○ *Makes about 1 cup*

⅓ cup soy sauce
¼ cup rice vinegar
3 cloves garlic, minced
2 tablespoons sesame oil
2 tablespoons sugar
1 tablespoon minced fresh ginger
¼ teaspoon freshly ground black pepper
¼ teaspoon crushed red pepper flakes

Combine all of the ingredients in a glass bowl and microwave until warmed through. Alternatively, heat the sauce over low heat in a small saucepan.

Shells Stuffed with Pork, Mushrooms, and Onions

THESE SHELLS HAVE A MAGICAL QUALITY. Even the pickiest of eaters will devour them in seconds. I know, because I've watched it happen numerous times. The delicately seasoned pork is mild without being bland. Use a great sauce like Easy Slow Cooker Red Sauce (page 205) for an exceptional meal. And do not overcook the noodles; they will soften further during freezing and baking. For smaller portions, simply divide the shells into smaller baking dishes. ○ *Serves 4 to 6*

Packaging: 9 × 13-inch baking dish with lid

12 ounces jumbo pasta shells
1¼ pounds ground pork
½ cup diced onion
1 cup finely chopped fresh mushrooms
¼ teaspoon dried oregano
¼ teaspoon dried thyme
Salt and freshly ground black pepper
3 cups shredded mozzarella cheese
¼ cup freshly grated Parmesan cheese
3 cups Easy Slow Cooker Red Sauce (page 205) or other favorite red sauce

1. In a large pot of boiling, salted water, cook the shells according to the package directions just until al dente. Drain and set aside to cool.

2. In a large skillet over medium heat, cook the pork, onion, and mushrooms for about 10 minutes or until the meat is no longer pink. Stir in the oregano and thyme. Season the mixture to taste with salt and pepper. Transfer to a large bowl to cool.

3. Add 2 cups of the mozzarella cheese and the Parmesan cheese to the cooled pork mixture and stir to combine.

4. Grease the baking dish. Fill the cooled shells with the pork mixture and arrange them in the prepared baking dish. Top the filled shells with the pasta sauce. Sprinkle the shells with the remaining 1 cup mozzarella cheese.

Freezing instructions:

Cover and chill the casserole in the refrigerator before freezing.

To thaw and serve:

Thaw the shells in the refrigerator. Preheat the oven to 375°F. Bake for 15 to 20 minutes, until hot and bubbly. Serve immediately.

Make-Ahead Baked Bacon

BACON FOR THE FREEZER? Really? Yes, really. Having precooked bacon on hand enables you to make a quick BLT or breakfast sandwich. It also helps you prepare in advance for weekend brunches or a houseful of guests. And everything is better with bacon! Grab a few slices whenever you want to add a little smoky crunch to a dish.

The easiest way to cook bacon is in the oven, not in a pan on the stove. The mess and time are both greatly reduced. Just watch it carefully to prevent burning.

o Serves 4

Packaging: Gallon-size zip-top freezer bag

1 pound sliced bacon

1. Preheat the oven to 375°F. Line a rimmed baking sheet with aluminum foil.

2. Separate the slices of bacon and lay them on the sheet. Avoid overlapping the slices if possible.

3. Bake for 15 to 20 minutes, turning the slices over about midway through the cooking time. As oven temperatures and thickness of bacon can vary, check often to prevent burning. Once the bacon is cooked to your desired doneness, remove the pan from the oven.

4. Drain the bacon on paper towels.

Freezing instructions:

Place the strips of bacon on a foil-lined tray in the freezer and freeze. Once the bacon is frozen, place the slices in the freezer bag. Seal the bag, squeezing out as much air as possible.

To thaw and serve:

Remove the desired number of bacon slices from the freezer bag and reheat in a pan on the stovetop or between paper towels in the microwave until hot. Serve immediately.

Ham and Swiss Potato Gratin

THIS CHEESY, MEATY GRATIN is perfect for a cold winter's night. It's filling and rich and just begging for a nice glass of wine, a crisp salad, and a roaring fire to eat it by.

This casserole uses a homemade cream of celery soup that brings flavor and richness without the dubious ingredients of the canned version. ● *Serves 4*

Packaging: 9 × 13-inch baking dish with lid

2 cups Homemade Cream of Celery Soup for Cooking (page 223)
1 tablespoon Dijon mustard
½ cup heavy cream
One 32-ounce bag frozen shredded potatoes (do not thaw)
2 cups shredded Swiss cheese
8 ounces diced ham
1 cup bread crumbs
2½ tablespoons unsalted butter, melted

1. Grease the baking dish.

2. In a large bowl, combine the celery soup, Dijon mustard, and cream. Stir in the potatoes, cheese, and ham. Spoon the mixture into the prepared baking dish.

3. In a small bowl, combine the bread crumbs and butter. Sprinkle the buttered bread crumbs over the potato mixture.

Freezing instructions:

Cover and freeze.

To thaw and serve:

Thaw the dish in the refrigerator. Preheat the oven to 350°F. Bake for about 1 hour, or until bubbly. Serve immediately.

Zesty Italian Melts

MY HUSBAND'S FAVORITE SANDWICH features Italian meats and herbed mayonnaise on a roll, which we often eat cold and freshly made. I've transformed it here into a freezer-friendly sub that's baked or grilled before serving, resulting in hot, melty, meaty goodness. Serve this one with a salad or a cup of vegetable soup. ○ *Serves 8*

Packaging: Heavy-duty aluminum foil, 3 to 4 gallon-size zip-top freezer bags

½ cup (1 stick) unsalted butter, softened
2 teaspoons chopped fresh basil or ½ teaspoon dried basil
1 teaspoon minced garlic
¼ teaspoon dried oregano
8 Italian rolls, sliced lengthwise, with one long edge attached
8 slices ham
24 slices salami
8 slices mozzarella cheese

1. In a small bowl, combine the softened butter, basil, garlic, and oregano. Blend well. Spread a thin layer of the garlic butter on each roll.

2. Layer one slice of ham, three slices of salami, and one slice of cheese on each roll. Close the rolls and wrap each tightly with aluminum foil.

Freezing instructions:

Place all the wrapped rolls in the freezer bags. Store the sandwiches in the freezer.

To thaw and serve:

Thaw the desired number of sandwiches in the refrigerator. Preheat the oven to 325°F. Bake the wrapped sandwiches for 15 to 25 minutes, or until the bread is crusty and the cheese is melted. Alternatively, you can cook the thawed sandwiches in a panini press until hot.

Queso Fundido

THIS MEAL HAS BEEN A MAINSTAY in our family for more than a decade. Delicious and easy to prepare, it's got a little kick, thanks to the cheese and the hot sausage. It's ideal for taking to a potluck or to share with a friend. Serve a green salad, beans, and rice as side dishes. For milder flavor, use mild Italian sausage and Monterey Jack cheese. o *Serves 4*

Packaging: 8-inch pie plate or other 1-quart baking dish with lid or foil

1 pound hot Italian sausage, casings removed
1 cup chopped onion
2 cups shredded pepper Jack cheese

When ready to serve, you will need:

12 corn tortillas or soft taco-size flour tortillas
Sour cream
Easy Homemade Salsa (page 71)

1. In a large skillet, brown the sausage and onion over medium-high heat, breaking up any big chunks of meat with the back of a spoon, for about 10 minutes, or until the meat is just cooked and no longer pink. Drain off any grease.

2. Grease the pie plate. Spoon the mixture into the pie plate and set aside to cool.

3. Cover the cooled sausage with the shredded cheese.

Freezing instructions:

Wrap the pie plate in foil and place it inside a zip-top freezer bag. Chill the dish in the refrigerator before freezing.

To thaw and serve:

Thaw the pie plate in the refrigerator. Preheat the oven to 350°F. Bake, uncovered, for 15 to 20 minutes, or until the cheese is melted and bubbling. Serve with the tortillas, sour cream, and salsa.

Herbed Pork Sausage Patties

WANT A CHANGE OF PACE from your regular burger? Looking for a spicy accompaniment to your eggs in the morning? How about a simple homemade sausage? You can't go wrong with this version, which mixes up quickly and freezes beautifully. Store the patties, cooked or uncooked, in the freezer for quick breakfast or lunch fare. ○ *Serves 6*

Packaging: Waxed paper, plastic wrap, gallon-size zip-top freezer bag

1 pound lean ground pork
2 tablespoons salted butter, softened
2 cloves garlic, chopped
1 teaspoon salt
½ teaspoon onion powder
¼ teaspoon freshly ground black pepper
¼ teaspoon rubbed sage
⅛ teaspoon dried thyme
⅛ teaspoon paprika
⅛ teaspoon cayenne pepper
⅛ teaspoon dry mustard

1. In the bowl of a stand mixer, mix all of the ingredients until the mixture is well blended and starts to bind together.

2. With wet hands, divide the pork mixture into six equal portions. Pat each portion into a flat patty.

Freezing instructions:

If freezing uncooked, stack the patties with a square of waxed paper between each one. Wrap the stack in plastic wrap and place in a freezer bag.

If freezing precooked, preheat the oven to 400°F and cook the patties on a foil-lined rimmed baking sheet, flipping once, for 10 to 15 minutes, or until cooked through. Drain the cooked patties on paper towels. Cool completely. Freeze the patties on a tray, and then transfer to a freezer bag. Seal the bag, squeezing out as much air as possible. Return the patties to the freezer.

To thaw and serve:

For uncooked patties, thaw in the refrigerator. Preheat the oven to 400°F. Bake the unwrapped patties on a foil-lined rimmed baking sheet, flipping once, for 10 to 15 minutes, or until cooked through.

For cooked patties, thaw in the refrigerator. Preheat the oven to 400°F. Reheat the patties 5 to 10 minutes, or until heated through. You can also reheat them without thawing; add about 5 minutes to the oven time.

Red Sauce with Sausage

THIS MEATY RED SAUCE is simple and delicious. It freezes well and complements pasta dishes beautifully. One of the secrets to its rich flavor is cooking the sausages in the sauce. Feel free to use sweet sausage, spicy sausage, or a mixture. If you are pressed for time, omit the sausages, stir in some beef broth, and reduce the cooking time to 2 hours total. ○ *Serves 10 to 12*

Packaging: Glass jars or plastic containers with lids, quart-size zip-top freezer bags for the sausages

2 tablespoons olive oil

1 cup chopped onion

2 cloves garlic, chopped

Four 28-ounce cans tomato puree

3 cups water

1 tablespoon salt

3 tablespoons chopped fresh Italian parsley or 1 tablespoon dried parsley flakes

3 tablespoons chopped fresh basil or 1 tablespoon dried basil

1½ teaspoons dried oregano

¼ teaspoon red pepper flakes

2 pounds Italian sausage links

When ready to serve, you will need:

Cooked pasta

1. In a large pot, heat the olive oil over medium heat and cook the onion and garlic until softened. Add the tomato puree and water. Stir to mix thoroughly, then add the salt, parsley, basil, oregano, and red pepper flakes.

2. Cover and simmer for 2 hours, stirring occasionally. Add the sausages and cook, covered, for another 2 hours.

Freezing instructions:

Divide the sausages into meal-size portions in freezer bags. Squeeze out as much air as possible and seal the bags. Pour the sauce into containers. Chill the sausages and the sauce in the refrigerator before storing in the freezer.

To thaw and serve:

Thaw a container of sauce and a bag of sausages in the refrigerator. Reheat them together in a saucepan and serve over pasta.

Penne with Italian Sausage and Tricolor Peppers

WHEN WE WERE BROKE college students living in France, my friend Sarah and I often prepared a simple pasta dish with tomatoes and vegetables. We didn't have the extra coin to add meat. This dish is reminiscent of what we ate in those days, only with mild Italian sausage added to give it a little more oomph. This sauce freezes beautifully. It's delicious over pasta, served with sliced baguette for soaking up the juices. ○ *Serves 6 to 8*

Packaging: Plastic containers with lids

1 tablespoon olive oil

· 12 ounces bulk mild Italian sausage

2 cloves garlic, minced

½ cup each diced green, red, and yellow bell pepper

½ cup julienned sun-dried tomatoes

One 15-ounce can tomato sauce

One 6-ounce can tomato paste

1 tablespoon chopped fresh basil or 1 teaspoon dried basil

1 tablespoon chopped fresh parsley or 1 teaspoon dried parsley flakes

¼ teaspoon freshly ground black pepper

¼ teaspoon red pepper flakes

2 cups water

When ready to serve, you will need:

Cooked penne

1. In a large saucepan, heat the oil over medium heat. Add the sausage and garlic. Cook, stirring, until the sausage just starts to brown, about 10 minutes.

2. Add the bell peppers. Cook, stirring, until the peppers have softened, about 5 minutes more.

3. Stir in the sun-dried tomatoes, tomato sauce, tomato paste, basil, parsley, black pepper, red pepper flakes, and water.

4. Bring the sauce to a low boil. Reduce the heat and simmer for 20 minutes.

Freezing instructions:

Divide the sauce into meal-size portions in plastic containers. Chill in the refrigerator before freezing.

To thaw and serve:

Thaw the sauce in the refrigerator. Reheat in a saucepan and serve over pasta.

Wild Boar Italian Sausage with Spicy Tomato Sauce

FREEZER MEALS DON'T NEED TO BE BORING. In this case, reheating the sausage on the grill gives it a smoky flavor you wouldn't get from the stovetop.

If you can't find wild boar sausage, Italian pork sausages will work just as well. The red pepper gives the sauce a nice kick, but you can reduce it to tone down the spiciness, if you prefer. Serve the sausages and sauce with pasta or polenta and lots of grated Parmesan for sprinkling. ○ *Serves 4 to 6*

Packaging: Plastic containers with lids, quart-size zip-top freezer bags

1 tablespoon olive oil
½ cup finely chopped carrot
½ cup chopped onion
One 15-ounce can tomato sauce
One 14.5-ounce can diced tomatoes with juices
2 tablespoons chopped fresh basil or 2 teaspoons dried basil
¼ teaspoon red pepper flakes
1 teaspoon kosher salt
⅛ teaspoon freshly ground black pepper
4 wild boar Italian sausage links

When ready to serve, you will need:

Cooked pasta or polenta
Freshly grated Parmesan cheese

1. In a large pot, heat the olive oil over medium heat until shimmering. Add the carrot and onion. Sauté the vegetables until very tender, about 10 minutes.

2. Add the tomato sauce, diced tomatoes, basil, red pepper flakes, salt, and black pepper. Stir to combine. Bring to a low boil.

3. Submerge the sausage links in the sauce. Cover the pot slightly. Simmer for 1 hour.

Freezing instructions:

Divide the sausages into meal-size portions in freezer bags. Squeeze out as much air as possible and seal the bags. Pour the sauce into containers. Chill the sauce and the sausages in the refrigerator before storing in the freezer.

To thaw and serve:

Thaw a container of sauce and a bag of sausages in the refrigerator. Reheat the sauce in a saucepan. Brown the sausages on a hot grill. Slice the sausages on the diagonal. Serve the hot sausages and sauce over cooked pasta or polenta. Top with Parmesan.

Meatless Marvels

Seasoned Versatile Pinto Beans

OUR FAMILY BATTLED ITS WAY out of debt years ago. Today we live debt-free, in part because we enjoyed a "rice and beans" diet for a time. This recipe, so easy and satisfying, is still a mainstay in our menu rotation. It's an ideal freezer staple to have on hand. Although canned beans are certainly convenient, they can be high in sodium, and it's more economical to cook your own. It is quite simple to cook dried beans and freeze them in 2-cup portions. Reheating them is just as easy as opening a can. ○ *Makes 6 cups cooked beans*

Packaging: Pint-size containers with lids or pint-size zip-top freezer bags

1 pound dried pinto beans, rinsed and picked over
1 cup chopped onion
2 teaspoons chopped garlic
1 tablespoon salt
¼ teaspoon freshly ground black pepper

Place the beans in a pot and add enough water to cover by at least 2 inches. Allow the beans to soak for at least 6 hours, or as long as overnight. Drain and rinse the beans.

To cook in a slow cooker:

Place the beans in a 5-quart slow cooker. Add the chopped onion, garlic, and enough water to cover the beans by about 1 inch. Cook on LOW for 6 to 8 hours. Drain the beans partially, leaving a small amount of water in the pot. Season with salt and pepper. Mash the beans slightly.

To cook on the stovetop:

Place the soaked and rinsed beans, the chopped onion, garlic, and water to cover in a large stockpot. Bring to a boil. Reduce the heat to a simmer and partially cover. Cook for about 2 hours, stirring frequently, adding more water if necessary. Once the beans are tender, drain them, mash them slightly, and season with salt and pepper.

Freezing instructions:

If using in a recipe, proceed with the recipe. Otherwise, divide the beans into 2-cup portions (about the amount of beans in a typical can) in containers or freezer bags. Chill in the refrigerator before freezing.

To thaw and serve:

Thaw the beans in the refrigerator or reheat them directly from the freezer. Reheat them in a pan on the stovetop or in a microwave-safe dish in the microwave.

If Your Freezer Has Experienced a Power Failure

Once you pack your freezer with the fruits of your labor, the last thing you want is to lose it all to a power failure. It happened to me once when the ground fault interrupter, or GFI, in the garage tripped the breaker and broke power to the freezer. I called my husband, crying. All he could get out of my mumbling was the word "died." Needless to say, he had a minor panic attack until I was able to clarify that it was an appliance and not a child or parent.

Since then, we've installed a small, inexpensive freezer alarm. It lets out a loud wail any time the freezer gets too warm. It's fairly sensitive, able to detect the slightest changes in temperature when I load it with food, so I rest easy, trusting that it will let me know—loud and clear—when it starts to get hot under the collar.

To help provide a buffer in case of a power failure, fill any empty spots in the freezer with water bottles or milk jugs filled with water. They will act as insulation, helping the freezer run more efficiently. (A full freezer runs better than an empty one.) In case of a power failure, the frozen water bottles should keep the contents of the freezer cold until the power comes back on. Add water bottles to your freezer gradually, as the appliance has to work harder if a lot of unfrozen items are added at one time.

If the power does go out or the door is left open, all is not lost. The food may be safe to use if there are still ice crystals present. If the power is out, keep the freezer closed and do not open it. According to the USDA, a full freezer that is kept shut can keep food safe for up to two days. You can refreeze food that is partly frozen, still has ice crystals, and/or is no warmer than 40°F. Discard any food that has been warmer than 40°F for longer than 2 hours, as well as anything that has been touched by raw meat juices.

Bean and Cheese Nacho Bake

THIS VERSATILE BEAN AND CHEESE CASSEROLE can be served as a main dish, accompanied by salad and rice, or as an appetizer with chips. Using homemade salsa will give it a fresher taste. ○ *Serves 6 to 8*

Packaging: 9 × 13-inch baking dish with lid

3 cups canned refried beans
⅓ cup finely chopped onion
1 teaspoon chopped garlic
1 cup Easy Homemade Salsa (page 71) or other favorite salsa
⅔ cup canned sliced black olives, drained
1 cup tomato sauce
2 cups shredded pepper Jack cheese
1 cup ricotta cheese
⅔ cup sour cream
½ teaspoon ground cumin
6½ ounces crushed tortilla chips (about 3 cups)

1. Grease the baking dish.

2. In a large bowl, combine the beans, onion, garlic, salsa, black olives, and tomato sauce.

3. In another bowl, combine 1 cup of the Jack cheese, the ricotta, sour cream, and cumin.

4. Place half of the chips in the bottom of the baking dish, spreading to cover. Spread half of the bean mixture over the chips. Spread all of the cheese mixture over the bean layer. Repeat the layers, using the remaining chips, bean mixture, and remaining 1 cup Jack cheese.

Freezing instructions:

Cover and chill in the refrigerator before freezing.

To thaw and serve:

Thaw the casserole in the refrigerator. Preheat the oven to 350°F. Bake for 40 minutes, or until the casserole is hot and the cheese is bubbly.

Quick and Easy Cheese Enchiladas

IMAGINE DELICIOUS Mexican fare for supper—without having to wait hours for a table. This meal is it! Partnered with rice and beans and a green salad, cheese enchiladas make an ideal meatless meal.

This recipe yields two large pans of a dozen enchiladas each. But you can package them in whatever size baking dishes best suit the number of people you're serving. ○ *Serves 8 to 12*

Packaging: Two 9 × 13-inch baking dishes with lids

Vegetable oil, for frying
24 corn tortillas
4 cups shredded cheddar and/or Monterey Jack cheese
One 28-ounce can red enchilada sauce
One 2.25-ounce can sliced black olives
¼ cup sliced scallions

1. Fill a skillet with vegetable oil to a depth of 1 inch. Heat over medium heat until the oil shimmers. Fry the tortillas in the hot oil until the texture is a bit leathery but not crisp, 20 to 30 seconds, turning once. Drain the tortillas on paper towels and set aside until cool enough to handle.

2. Grease the baking dishes.

3. Set aside 1 cup of cheese. For each enchilada, place a small handful of cheese down the center of each tortilla, roll up, and place, seam side down, in a greased baking dish. Continue until all the tortillas are rolled and the baking dishes are filled. You should be able to fit 12 enchiladas in each dish.

4. Pour the enchilada sauce over the tops of the rolled tortillas. Sprinkle the reserved 1 cup cheese as well as the olives and scallions over the top.

Freezing instructions:

Cover the enchiladas and chill in the refrigerator before freezing.

To thaw and serve:

Thaw the enchiladas in the refrigerator. Preheat the oven to 350°F. Bake the enchiladas until they are heated through and the cheese is melted, about 15 minutes. You can also bake this directly from the freezer; allow an extra 15 to 30 minutes of baking time.

Cozy Cheese and Potato Casserole

AT FIRST GLANCE, you might confuse this delectable concoction of potatoes and cheese with the "church potatoes" or hash brown casseroles of yore. However, unlike its predecessors, this potato bake features a homemade cream of celery soup that puts the canned version to shame. It's important to use frozen potatoes in this dish; uncooked fresh potatoes will blacken in the freezer. Commercially frozen hash brown potatoes work exceptionally well here. Don't let them thaw as you mix up this casserole. Stir it up quickly, spoon it into the pan, and pop it into the freezer. ○ *Serves 6 to 8*

Packaging: 9 × 13-inch baking dish with lid

2 cups Homemade Cream of Celery Soup for Cooking (page 223), chilled
1½ cups shredded cheddar cheese
1 cup sour cream
1 teaspoon kosher salt
¼ teaspoon freshly ground black pepper
One 32-ounce bag frozen shredded potatoes
1 teaspoon paprika

1. Grease the baking dish.

2. In a large bowl, combine the celery soup, cheese, sour cream, salt, and pepper. Stir in the frozen shredded potatoes, combining well.

3. Spoon the potato mixture into the prepared dish. Sprinkle the paprika over the top.

Freezing instructions:

Cover and freeze.

To thaw and serve:

Thaw the casserole in the refrigerator. Preheat the oven to 375°F. Bake the casserole for about 1 hour, or until it is heated through and the cheese is melted.

Six-Layer Nachos

THIS NACHO PLATE IS ALWAYS A HIT. Whether served as an appetizer or a "snacky" dinner, it's a crowd-pleaser. For the meat-eaters, you can add a layer of seasoned taco meat (page 89), but it's not necessary; it's packed full of flavor as it is. Make several pans at once so that you always have a quick appetizer, snack, or dinner on hand. ○ *Serves 4 as a main dish, 6 to 8 as an appetizer*

Packaging: 8-inch pie plate, foil, gallon-size zip-top freezer bag

1 cup canned refried beans
½ cup enchilada sauce
1 cup shredded cheddar cheese
2 tablespoons chopped green chiles
2 tablespoons sliced black olives
2 tablespoons chopped onion

When ready to serve, you will need:

Tortilla chips
Sour cream
Easy Homemade Salsa (page 71)
Sliced avocado or Super-Simple Guacamole (page 71)
Other toppings as desired, such as chopped tomatoes or shredded lettuce

1. Grease the pie plate.

2. Spread the refried beans across the bottom of the plate. Drizzle the enchilada sauce over the beans. Sprinkle the cheese over the sauce. Sprinkle the green chiles, black olives, and chopped onion over the cheese layer.

Freezing instructions:

Cover the pan with foil and slip the pan inside the freezer bag, taking care not to tip the pan. Freeze.

To thaw and serve:

Thaw the nachos in the refrigerator. Preheat the oven to 350°F. Bake the nachos for 15 to 20 minutes, until hot and bubbly. Serve with the tortilla chips and toppings.

Green Chile Rice Casserole

RICE, CHEESE, AND CHILES combine in a comfort-food dish that will disappear quickly. Brown rice boasts a denser texture and a nuttier flavor than white rice. It also holds up better in the freezer, making it the perfect base for this rich and creamy casserole. You will want to cook the rice ahead of time so that it can cool before you assemble the casserole. Sour cream adds great flavor, but Greek yogurt has it beat with less fat and extra protein. o *Serves 4 to 6*

Packaging: 8-inch square baking dish or 3-quart baking dish with lid

3 cups cooked brown rice, at room temperature
16 ounces plain Greek-style yogurt or sour cream
2 cups shredded cheddar cheese
One 4-ounce can chopped green chiles
1 tablespoon finely chopped jalapeño peppers
¼ teaspoon ground cumin
⅛ teaspoon freshly ground black pepper

Grease the baking dish. Combine all of the ingredients in a large bowl. Spoon the mixture into the prepared pan.

Freezing instructions:

Cover and chill in the refrigerator before freezing.

To thaw and serve:

Thaw the dish in the refrigerator. Preheat the oven to 350°F. Bake the casserole for 25 to 40 minutes, or until heated through.

Pepper Jack and Chile Burritos

FROZEN BURRITOS MAKE QUICK SNACKS or main dishes. After an overnight thaw in the refrigerator, these will crisp perfectly on a hot griddle, for a healthier alternative to chimichangas. Top with enchilada sauce, shredded lettuce, tomatoes, and sour cream. For even quicker eats, simply microwave the frozen burritos for a minute or two. To prevent the burritos from cracking when you roll them, use fresh tortillas that are at room temperature. ○ *Serves 6 to 12*

Packaging: Gallon-size zip-top freezer bags, aluminum foil or plastic wrap (optional)

4 cups canned refried beans or Seasoned Versatile Pinto Beans (page 180)
2 cups shredded pepper Jack cheese
One 4-ounce can chopped green chiles
12 burrito-size flour tortillas

1. In a large bowl, combine the beans, cheese, and green chiles.

2. Fill the burritos by spooning a scant ½ cup of the filling down the center of each tortilla. Roll it up, tucking in the sides as you go. As each burrito is rolled, place it in a freezer bag. If you like, you can wrap each burrito in aluminum foil or plastic wrap before placing it in the freezer bag.

Freezing instructions:

Seal the burritos in the bags, squeezing out as much air as possible. Store the bags of burritos in the freezer.

To thaw and serve:

Thaw as many burritos as desired in the refrigerator.

To reheat in the microwave: Cook thawed burritos, flipping once, 1 to 2 minutes per burrito, or until hot. You can also reheat them directly from the freezer, without thawing; just add an additional minute or two of cooking time.

To reheat on the griddle: Cook thawed burritos on a hot griddle until the filling is hot and the tortilla is crisp.

To reheat in the oven: Preheat the oven to 350°F. For crispy burritos, bake thawed burritos for 15 to 20 minutes. For softer burritos, wrap each in foil prior to baking. If the burritos are frozen, increase the cooking time 5 to 10 minutes.

Easy Stovetop Ratatouille

A TRADITIONAL FRENCH VEGETABLE STEW, ratatouille is summer captured in a bowl. There is great debate over the proper preparation of ratatouille; this simple version is mixed in one pot and simmered on the stovetop. This vegan dish is good served hot or even at room temperature. Provide lots of sliced baguette for soaking up the juices. Avoid overcooking the vegetables, so that they are not soggy when reheated. o *Serves 6 to 8*

Packaging: Plastic containers with lids

¼ cup olive oil
1 cup chopped onion
1 tablespoon chopped garlic
1 red bell pepper, chopped
1 green bell pepper, chopped
1 medium zucchini, sliced into ¼-inch-thick half-moons

1 small yellow squash, sliced

1 eggplant, peeled and cubed

4 ounces fresh mushrooms, sliced

Two 14.5-ounce cans petite diced tomatoes with juices

1½ teaspoons *herbes de Provence*

1 teaspoon kosher salt

1. In a large heavy pot, heat the oil over medium heat until shimmering. Add the onion and garlic, and cook until the onions are translucent.

2. Add the peppers, zucchini, yellow squash, eggplant, and mushrooms, and sauté for about 5 minutes, stirring occasionally.

3. Add the tomatoes, *herbes de Provence*, and salt. Stir to combine. Cook for about 30 minutes, or until the vegetables are just tender.

Freezing instructions:

Divide the ratatouille into meal-size portions in plastic containers and chill in the refrigerator before freezing.

To thaw and serve:

Thaw the ratatouille in the refrigerator. Reheat in a saucepan. Serve hot, warm, or at room temperature.

Italian-Spiced Cheesewiches

MY MOM MADE something similar to these cheesewiches when I was a kid. We loved them; they were like cheese pizza undercover. The updated version is even better! I've freshened up the seasonings and replaced canned soup with tomato sauce and fresh garlic. These toasty, flavorful cheese sandwiches are the perfect complement to a cup of soup or a bowl of salad for a hearty lunch or supper. ○ *Serves 6 to 12*

Packaging: Heavy-duty aluminum foil, gallon-size zip-top freezer bags

4 cups shredded sharp cheddar cheese

2 cups tomato sauce

½ cup canned chopped black olives, drained

¼ cup olive oil

2 teaspoons chopped garlic

1½ teaspoons chopped fresh basil or ½ teaspoon dried basil

½ teaspoon dried oregano

½ teaspoon dried thyme

¼ teaspoon freshly ground black pepper

12 kaiser rolls

1. In a large bowl, combine the cheese, tomato sauce, olives, olive oil, garlic, basil, oregano, thyme, and black pepper.

2. Slice each roll in half, leaving the top and bottom attached on one side. Scoop out the insides of the rolls, leaving a 1-inch shell. Crumble the inner bread portions and add to the cheese mixture. Stir the mixture to combine all the ingredients well.

3. Fill the rolls with the cheese mixture. Close each roll and wrap in foil.

Freezing instructions:

Place all the foil-wrapped rolls in one or two freezer bags and freeze.

To thaw and serve:

Thaw the desired number of rolls in the refrigerator. Preheat the oven to 350°F. Bake thawed, foil-wrapped rolls for 15 to 25 minutes, until the bread is crusty and the cheese is melted.

Red Lentil Dal

SEASONED LENTILS, OR DAL, are staples in much of India. While this preparation is not as spicy as some, it has a warmth that will please the palate. Cooked lentils freeze and reheat well, making this an ideal dish for bulk cooking. Thanks to my Indian pen pal and fellow blogger Prerna Malik from The

Mom Writes, for her tips on Indian cuisine. Serve the dal with rice and roti (Indian flat bread). ○ *Serves 4 to 6*

Packaging: Plastic containers with lids

2 cups red lentils, rinsed and picked over
2 tablespoons olive oil
1 cup chopped onion
1 teaspoon chopped fresh ginger
1 teaspoon ground cumin
1 teaspoon chopped garlic
1 teaspoon red curry powder
1 teaspoon salt
½ teaspoon ground turmeric
One 14.5-ounce can petite diced tomatoes with juices
4 cups water

1. Soak the lentils for 20 minutes.

2. Meanwhile, in a large stockpot, heat the oil over medium heat until shimmering. Add the onion and cook until translucent. Stir in the ginger, cumin, garlic, curry powder, salt, and turmeric. Cook for about 1 minute, stirring.

3. Add the tomatoes, stirring and scraping up any browned bits.

4. Drain the lentils and add them to the pot, along with the 4 cups water. Simmer for about 20 minutes, or until the lentils are tender.

Freezing instructions:

Divide the dal into meal-size portions in plastic containers. Chill in the refrigerator before freezing.

To thaw and serve:

Thaw the dal in the refrigerator. Reheat in a saucepan until heated through.

Tahini Vegetable Patties

THESE VEGGIE PATTIES combine the flavors of falafel and fresh vegetables, making for a delicious and filling dish. Serve them with Greek yogurt, chopped fresh cilantro, and crumbled feta cheese, or stuff them into pita breads, if you like. Make smaller patties to serve as appetizers. ● *Serves 4*

Packaging: Waxed paper, quart-size zip-top freezer bag

1 tablespoon olive oil
½ cup shredded zucchini
½ cup chopped red bell pepper
½ cup chopped onion
1 tablespoon finely chopped jalapeño pepper
1 teaspoon chopped garlic
One 15-ounce can garbanzo beans, drained
1¾ cups fresh bread crumbs
2 large eggs, beaten
2 tablespoons tahini
1 teaspoon kosher salt

When ready to serve, you will need:

Olive oil, for frying
Plain Greek-style yogurt
Chopped fresh cilantro
Crumbled feta cheese

1. In a large skillet over medium-high heat, heat the olive oil. Sauté the zucchini, bell pepper, onion, jalapeño, and garlic. Cook the mixture until the vegetables are tender, about 7 minutes. Remove from the heat and set aside to cool.

2. In the bowl of a food processor, pulse the garbanzo beans until coarsely chopped. Alternatively, you can mash them with a potato masher.

3. In a large bowl, combine the sautéed vegetables, garbanzo beans, bread crumbs, eggs, tahini, and salt. Stir gently to combine. Form the mixture into 4 patties.

Freezing instructions:

Stack the patties with a square of waxed paper between each one. Place in a freezer bag and freeze.

To thaw and serve:

Thaw the patties in the refrigerator. Heat 1 to 2 tablespoons olive oil in a skillet and fry the patties in the hot oil until hot and browned. Serve with the yogurt, cilantro, and feta for toppings.

Potatoes Stuffed with Caramelized Onions and Dubliner Cheese

TWICE-BAKED POTATOES reach new heights of deliciousness with the addition of caramelized onions and sharp Dubliner cheese. Since these potatoes freeze and reheat so well, it's worth making a big batch so you can enjoy an elegant potato dish any night of the week. Serve these stuffed potatoes with a side salad. You can substitute sharp cheddar cheese for the Dubliner if you'd rather.

o *Serves 8*

Packaging: Plastic wrap, gallon-size zip top freezer bags

8 large baking potatoes
2 tablespoons olive oil
1 cup chopped onion
1 teaspoon chopped garlic
1 cup sour cream
1 cup shredded Dubliner or sharp cheddar cheese
¼ cup (½ stick) unsalted butter, softened
1 tablespoon chopped fresh parsley or 1 teaspoon dried parsley flakes
½ teaspoon kosher salt
½ teaspoon freshly ground black pepper

1. Pierce each potato several times with a fork. Bake the potatoes in the oven at 350°F for 1 hour or until tender, or microwave them until cooked through. Set the potatoes aside until cool enough to handle.

2. In a medium skillet, heat the olive oil over medium heat until shimmering. Add the onions and garlic, and cook until the onions are translucent. Turn the heat to low, cover, and cook 5 minutes more. Remove the lid and stir. Continue to cook until the onions start to brown lightly around the edges. Remove the pan from the heat and set the mixture aside to cool.

3. Cut ¼ inch off the top of each baked potato and discard or reserve for another use. Scoop out the insides of each potato, leaving a ¼-inch-thick shell. Place the scooped-out potato in a large bowl and mash with a potato masher.

4. Stir the onion mixture, sour cream, ¾ cup of the Dubliner cheese, the butter, parsley, salt, and pepper into the mashed potatoes. Stir well to combine.

5. Fill the potato shells with the mixture. Sprinkle the remaining ¼ cup of Dubliner cheese over the tops of the potatoes.

Freezing instructions:

Allow the potatoes to cool to room temperature. Wrap each potato in plastic wrap and place the potatoes in freezer bags. Chill in the refrigerator before freezing.

To thaw and serve:

Thaw the potatoes in the refrigerator. Preheat the oven to 375°F. Unwrap the potatoes and place them on a baking sheet. Reheat the potatoes for 15 to 20 minutes, until heated through. Serve immediately.

Broccoli Gratin with Tarragon and Buttered Bread Crumbs

THIS CREAMY BROCCOLI-AND-CHEESE CASSEROLE makes a delicious meatless main dish when accompanied by a salad and bread. Homemade cream of celery soup replaces the canned variety often seen in traditional casseroles. ○ *Serves 4 to 6*

Packaging: 9 × 13-inch baking dish with lid

1½ pounds broccoli florets (about 9 cups)
2 cups Homemade Cream of Celery Soup for Cooking (page 223)
½ teaspoon dried tarragon
1 cup shredded cheddar cheese
1 cup fresh bread crumbs
2 tablespoons salted butter, melted

1. Grease the baking dish. Steam the broccoli florets until crisp-tender, 8 to 10 minutes.

2. In a large bowl, combine the broccoli, cream of celery soup, tarragon, and ½ cup of the cheddar cheese. Stir gently to combine. Spread the mixture in the bottom of the prepared baking dish. Sprinkle the remaining ½ cup cheddar cheese over the top.

3. In a small bowl, combine the bread crumbs and melted butter. Sprinkle this over the cheese layer.

Freezing instructions:

Cover and chill in the refrigerator before freezing.

To thaw and serve:

Thaw the dish in the refrigerator. Preheat the oven to 350°F. Bake the gratin for 30 to 45 minutes, or until hot and bubbly.

Roasted Vegetable Quiche

FULL OF PROTEIN AND FLAVOR, a quiche goes wonderfully with a fresh salad on the side. This savory pie is bursting with roasted vegetables and creamy eggs and cheese. Although you can use a store-bought crust, consider making the Versatile Buttery Pie Crust (page 356) to take this dish over the top.

o *Makes one 9-inch quiche*

Packaging: 9-inch pie plate, heavy-duty aluminum foil

2 cups chopped vegetables, such as zucchini, onion, bell pepper, or broccoli, or a combination
2 tablespoons olive oil
Salt and freshly ground black pepper
1 unbaked 9-inch single pie shell
1 cup shredded cheddar cheese tossed with 2 tablespoons unbleached all-purpose flour
3 large eggs
1½ cups cream or half-and-half

1. Preheat the oven to 400°F. In a large bowl, combine the vegetables and olive oil. Season the vegetables generously with salt and pepper. Transfer the vegetables to a shallow baking dish and roast them in the preheated oven for 15 to 30 minutes, or until tender, stirring occasionally to prevent sticking. Transfer the cooked vegetables to a plate to cool.

2. Once the vegetables have cooled, spread them in the bottom of the unbaked pie shell. Sprinkle the cheddar cheese over the top.

3. In a bowl, beat the eggs. Stir in the cream and ⅛ teaspoon black pepper. Pour the egg mixture over the vegetables and cheese in the pie shell.

Freezing instructions:

Place the pie plate flat in the freezer. Freeze until firm. Wrap the frozen quiche well with foil. Return to the freezer.

To serve:

Preheat the oven to 400°F. Bake the frozen quiche, uncovered (no need to thaw), for 30 to 45 minutes, or until a knife inserted in the center comes out clean.

Individual Greek Egg Casseroles

I N MY HUSBAND'S HOMETOWN, there used to be a delightful family-owned Greek restaurant where we often ate as newlyweds. One of my favorite meals at Pavlako's was the Greek eggs, which featured the delicious combination of spinach and feta. I've re-created Pavlako's Greek eggs in this individual egg casserole, which makes a delicious lunch or dinner when served with a side salad and a roll. Make several individual casseroles at one time by multiplying the recipe, lining up all the dishes and ingredients, and preparing them assembly-line style. ○ *Serves 1*

Packaging: 2-cup baking dish with lid

1 cup soft bread cubes from an Italian loaf
⅓ cup crumbled feta cheese
¼ cup chopped frozen spinach, thawed and squeezed dry
2 large eggs, beaten
½ cup milk
Pinch of freshly ground black pepper

1. Grease the baking dish. Spread the bread cubes across the bottom of the dish. Sprinkle the feta cheese and spinach over the bread cubes.

2. In a small bowl, whisk together the eggs, milk, and black pepper. Pour the egg mixture over the bread and cheese.

Freezing instructions:

Cover and freeze.

To thaw and serve:

Thaw the casserole in the refrigerator. Preheat the oven to 350°F. Bake the casserole for 25 minutes or until the top is puffy and a tester inserted in the center comes out clean. Alternatively, bake directly from the freezer for 40 to 45 minutes.

Baked Manicotti with Sun-Dried Tomatoes and Thyme

NOODLES AND CHEESE are a beautiful combination. They can be prepared casually, as in a pasta salad or mac and cheese, or they can be dressed up, as in this manicotti. Manicotti can seem intimidating to prepare, since the large pasta tubes tear easily. To help them hold their shape, cook the noodles just until al dente or a tad firmer. The noodles will soften upon freezing and with further baking in the oven. I've called for one large pan here, but feel free to package the manicotti in smaller baking dishes or store them in freezer bags without the sauce (freeze the sauce separately). That way, you can bake whatever quantity you want at serving time. ● *Serves 5 to 7*

Packaging: 9 × 13-inch baking dish with lid

1 package manicotti (about 14 manicotti)
2 cups shredded mozzarella cheese
15 ounces ricotta cheese
½ cup finely chopped sun-dried tomatoes
½ teaspoon dried thyme
¼ teaspoon freshly ground black pepper
3 cups Easy Slow Cooker Red Sauce (page 205) or other favorite sauce

1. Grease the baking dish.

2. Cook the manicotti just until al dente, according to the package directions. Drain the noodles.

3. In a large bowl, combine 1 cup of the mozzarella cheese, the ricotta, sun-dried tomatoes, thyme, and black pepper. Stir well to combine.

3. Fill the cooked manicotti by spooning a heaping tablespoon of the mixture into each one. You can also fill the manicotti using a piping bag made out of a quart-size freezer bag. Spoon the cheese filling into the bag and seal. Snip off one corner of the bag and pipe the filling into the cooked manicotti.

4. Arrange the manicotti in the prepared baking dish. Pour the sauce over the manicotti. Sprinkle the remaining 1 cup mozzarella cheese over the sauce.

Freezing instructions:

Cover and chill the pan in the refrigerator before freezing.

To thaw and serve:

Thaw the manicotti in the refrigerator. Preheat the oven to 350°F. Bake the pasta until heated through, about 30 minutes.

Pesto Penne and Cheese

RICH PESTO AND INTENSE sun-dried tomatoes take the humble mac-and-cheese casserole up a few notches. Serve this with a green salad and a glass of great wine. ○ *Serves 6 to 8*

Packaging: 9 × 13-inch inch baking dish with lid

One 16-ounce package penne
1½ cups shredded mozzarella cheese
8 ounces cubed Monterey Jack cheese
1 cup sour cream
¾ cup Jullenned sun-dried tomatoes
½ cup pesto
Salt and freshly ground black pepper

When ready to serve, you will need:

1 tablespoon chopped fresh parsley or 1 teaspoon dried parsley flakes

1. Grease the baking dish. Cook the pasta just until al dente, according to the package directions. Drain.

2. Meanwhile, in a large bowl, combine 1 cup of the mozzarella cheese, the Monterey Jack, sour cream, sun-dried tomatoes, and pesto. Season the mixture to taste with salt and pepper. Stir in the drained noodles.

3. Spoon the mixture into the baking dish. Sprinkle the remaining ½ cup mozzarella cheese over the top.

Freezing instructions:

Cover and chill the pan in the refrigerator before freezing.

To thaw and serve:

Thaw the macaroni and cheese in the refrigerator. Preheat the oven to 350°F. Bake the casserole until heated through, about 30 minutes. Stir to recombine the cheese sauce and noodles before serving. Sprinkle the parsley over the top.

Spinach and Feta Manicotti with Lemon and Oregano

SPINACH AND FETA CHEESE are happy companions in a number of Greek dishes. But they steal the show in this easy baked pasta dish. As with the Baked Manicotti with Sun-Dried Tomatoes and Thyme (page 198), remember to cook the noodles just until al dente or a tad firmer. The noodles will soften upon freezing and with further baking in the oven. And, if you like, package them in smaller baking dishes or store them in freezer bags without the sauce (freeze the sauce separately). That way, you can bake whatever quantity you want at serving time. ○ *Serves 5 to 7*

Packaging: 9 × 13-inch baking dish with lid

1 package manicotti (about 14 manicotti)
One 16-ounce package frozen chopped spinach, thawed and squeezed dry
2 cups shredded mozzarella cheese
2 cups ricotta cheese
1 cup crumbled feta cheese
1 large egg, beaten

Grated zest of 1 lemon

¼ teaspoon dried oregano

3 to 4 cups Tomato Sauce with Oregano and Kalamata Olives (page 201) or
other favorite red sauce

1. Grease the baking dish.

2. Cook the manicotti just until al dente, according to the package directions. Drain the noodles.

3. In a large bowl, combine the spinach, 1 cup of the mozzarella cheese, the ricotta, feta cheese, egg, lemon zest, and oregano. Stir well to combine.

4. Fill the cooked manicotti by spooning a heaping tablespoon of the mixture into each one. You can also fill the manicotti using a piping bag made out of a quart-size freezer bag. Spoon the cheese filling into the bag and seal. Snip off one corner of the bag and pipe the filling into the cooked manicotti.

5. Arrange the manicotti in the prepared baking dish. Pour the sauce over the manicotti. Sprinkle the remaining 1 cup mozzarella cheese over the sauce.

Freezing instructions:

Cover and chill the pan in the refrigerator before freezing.

To thaw and serve:

Thaw the manicotti in the refrigerator. Preheat the oven to 350°F. Bake the pasta until heated through, about 30 minutes.

Tomato Sauce with Oregano and Kalamata Olives

THIS MEDITERRANEAN-STYLE SAUCE is delicious served over pasta, as a dipping sauce for bread, or even on pizza. It also makes a delicious topping for the Spinach and Feta Manicotti with Lemon and Oregano (page 200).

○ Makes about 6 cups

Packaging: Plastic containers with lids

2 tablespoons olive oil
½ cup chopped onion
1 teaspoon chopped garlic
¼ cup white wine
Two 14.5-ounce cans petite diced tomatoes with juices
One 15-ounce can tomato sauce
⅓ cup chopped kalamata olives
2 teaspoons dried oregano
⅛ teaspoon freshly ground black pepper

1. In a large stockpot, heat the olive oil over medium heat until shimmering. Add the onion and garlic, and cook, stirring, until the onion becomes translucent, about 5 minutes.

2. Add the white wine and stir, scraping up any brown bits. Add the diced tomatoes, tomato sauce, olives, oregano, and black pepper. Simmer the mixture for 30 minutes. Taste and adjust the seasonings.

Freezing instructions:

Divide the sauce into meal-size portions in plastic containers. Chill in the refrigerator before freezing.

To thaw and serve:

Thaw the sauce in the refrigerator. Reheat in a saucepan on the stovetop or in a microwave-safe dish in the microwave.

Quick and Spicy Marinara Sauce

MAKING HOMEMADE PASTA SAUCES is one of the easiest and most satisfying of cooking pursuits. Not only can you tailor them to your preference, you also control all the ingredients. No high-fructose corn syrup here! While many jarred sauces are full of sweeteners, sodium, and additives, this one tastes of vegetables and spices. It also comes together in a flash. You can certainly let it simmer for several hours, but you don't have to, since the flavors blend during freezing. This sauce can also be prepared in a 5-quart slow cooker; cook it on HIGH for 4 hours or LOW for 6 to 8 hours. ○ *Makes 14 to 16 cups sauce*

Packaging: Plastic containers with lids

¼ cup olive oil
2 cups chopped onion
1 tablespoon chopped garlic
1 cup finely chopped carrot
½ cup chopped bell pepper (red, green, or a combination)
½ cup chopped celery
Four 28-ounce cans crushed tomatoes
⅓ cup Jamie's Spice Mix (page 90)
2 to 3 cups water

1. In a large stockpot, heat the olive oil over medium heat until shimmering. Add the onion and garlic, and cook, stirring, for about 5 minutes, or until the onions are translucent.

2. Add the carrot, pepper, and celery, and cook, stirring occasionally, 5 minutes more.

3. Stir in the crushed tomatoes, spice mix, and enough water to achieve the desired consistency. Stir well to blend.

4. Simmer the sauce on the stovetop for 1 hour, or until the carrots are tender.

5. For a smoother sauce, blend it in batches in a blender or food processor, or puree it using an immersion blender.

Freezing instructions:

Divide the sauce into meal-size portions in plastic containers. Chill in the refrigerator before freezing.

To thaw and serve:

Thaw the sauce in the refrigerator. Reheat it in a saucepan over low heat, whisking to recombine. Add a small amount of water if necessary to achieve the desired consistency.

Potluck-Friendly Main Dishes

One of the goals of bulk cooking is to free up your time so you can spend it on other things. If you have a freezer full of homemade convenience foods, you can easily attend potlucks and other group meals, feast in hand. You're more likely to arrive with a smile on your face if you haven't spent the previous few hours fussing over food.

The following items travel well in a slow cooker or covered dish. You can now buy insulated carriers to keep both slow cookers and baking dishes warm between home and your destination.

- Red and Green Beef Enchiladas, page 74
- Vegetable-Beef Lasagna, page 85
- Shepherd's Pie with Green Chile Mashed Potatoes, page 86
- Sweet and Spicy Joes, page 91
- Lawnmower Taco, page 92
- Chicken Enchilada Bake with Green Chiles and Jalapeños, page 120
- Best-Ever Chicken Pot Pie, page 121
- Garlicky Chicken Noodle Bake, page 122
- Creamy Chicken Enchiladas, page 123
- Chicken Divan with Cheddar Crust, page 124
- Ham and Swiss Potato Gratin, page 170
- Bean and Cheese Nacho Bake, page 182
- Quick and Easy Cheese Enchiladas, page 183
- Cozy Cheese and Potato Casserole, page 184
- Roasted Vegetable Quiche, page 196
- Pesto Penne and Cheese, page 199
- Spinach and Feta Manicotti with Lemon and Oregano, page 200
- Bacon-Cheddar Egg Bake, page 273
- Eggs Florentine Casserole, page 275
- Savory Ham and Swiss Clafouti, page 277
- Chile and Sausage Oven Frittata, page 278

Easy Slow Cooker Red Sauce

WHEN MY FAMILY NEEDED to economize years ago, I started making my own pasta sauce, and I haven't looked back. About once a month I cook up a big batch, divide it into 2-cup portions, and freeze it. I never buy jarred sauce; we enjoy the homemade version so much more. Serve this sauce over your favorite noodles, or use it in lasagna and other casseroles.

o *Makes 14 to 16 cups*

Packaging: Plastic containers with lids

¼ cup olive oil
2 large onions, diced
1 tablespoon chopped garlic
Four 28-ounce cans crushed tomatoes
1 to 2 cups water
1 tablespoon salt
⅓ cup chopped fresh basil or 2 tablespoons dried basil
3 tablespoons chopped fresh parsley or 1 tablespoon dried parsley flakes
½ teaspoon red pepper flakes

In a large skillet, heat the olive oil over medium heat. Add the onions and garlic and cook until softened. Spoon the onion mixture into a 5-quart or larger slow cooker. Add the crushed tomatoes, water, salt, basil, parsley, and red pepper flakes. Cover and cook on LOW for at least 4 hours. Adjust the seasonings to taste.

Freezing instructions:

Divide the sauce into meal-size portions in plastic containers. Chill in the refrigerator before freezing.

To thaw and serve:

Thaw the sauce in the refrigerator. Reheat in a saucepan over low heat, whisking to recombine.

Sun-Dried Tomato Pesto

SUN-DRIED TOMATOES create a vibrant pesto that works beautifully on pizza, hot pasta, and pasta salads; you can mix it into hamburgers or use it as a topping for chicken breasts. A little goes a long way in adding sunny summer flavor. ○ *Makes 2½ cups*

Packaging: Plastic containers with lids or pint-size zip-top freezer bags

2 cups sun-dried tomatoes
1 cup freshly grated Parmesan cheese
¾ cup walnuts or pine nuts
3 tablespoons chopped fresh basil or 1 tablespoon dried basil
1 tablespoon chopped garlic
1 teaspoon freshly ground black pepper
¼ teaspoon red pepper flakes
¾ cup olive oil

1. In a food processor fitted with a metal blade, combine the sun-dried tomatoes, cheese, nuts, basil, garlic, black pepper, and red pepper flakes. Process until smooth.

2. With the machine running, pour in the olive oil in a slow stream. Process until combined.

Freezing instructions:

Divide into ½-cup portions in plastic containers and chill in the refrigerator before freezing.

To thaw and serve:

Thaw in the refrigerator. Stir to recombine the ingredients before using.

Soup's On

Cheddar Soup with Zucchini, Broccoli, and Carrots

FANCY CAFÉS CHARGE A PRETTY PENNY for their cheese and broccoli soup. Save money and eat at home in style. Keep single-serving containers of this soup on hand for quick lunches and suppers. ○ *Serves 4 to 6*

Packaging: Plastic containers with lids

¼ cup (½ stick) unsalted butter
2 cloves garlic, minced
½ medium-size zucchini, shredded
1 carrot, peeled and shredded
½ medium-size onion, shredded
1 head broccoli, chopped into small florets (about 3 cups)
3 cups reduced-sodium chicken broth
¼ cup unbleached all-purpose flour
2 cups milk
2 cups shredded cheddar cheese
Salt and freshly ground black pepper

1. In a large saucepan, melt 2 tablespoons of the butter. Add the garlic, zucchini, carrot, and onion. Sauté until the vegetables are tender, about 10 minutes.

2. Stir in the broccoli and broth. Simmer until the broccoli is tender, about 10 minutes.

3. Meanwhile, melt the remaining 2 tablespoons butter in a large pot over medium heat. Whisk in the flour and cook for a minute or two. Whisk in the milk until smooth. Simmer until thickened. Whisk in the cheddar cheese gradually, stirring to incorporate.

4. Pour the vegetable mixture into the cheese mixture, stirring to combine. Season to taste with salt and pepper.

Freezing instructions:

Portion the soup into meal-size plastic containers. Cool to room temperature. Cover and chill in the refrigerator before freezing.

To thaw and serve:

Thaw the soup in the refrigerator. Reheat in a saucepan until heated through, stirring to recombine. Serve immediately.

Taco Soup with Hominy

TACO SOUP IS GENERALLY A WINNER with children. However, many recipes call for packaged seasoning mixes, which are laden with sodium. I've tweaked those recipes to suit my family's tastes and budget. This cooks in the slow cooker, and it's so easy my 5-year-old son can put it together. I cook the meat and open the cans, and he can do the rest. How simple is that? **o** *Serves 6 to 8*

Packaging: Plastic containers with lids

1 pound ground beef or turkey
One 28-ounce can crushed tomatoes
Two 15-ounce cans black beans, rinsed and drained
One 15.5-ounce can hominy, drained
One 15-ounce can kidney beans, rinsed and drained
One 15-ounce can pinto beans, rinsed and drained
1 to 2 cups water
1 cup red enchilada sauce
3 tablespoons chopped fresh parsley or 1 tablespoon dried parsley flakes
1 tablespoon dried oregano
1 tablespoon onion powder
1 teaspoon garlic powder
Freshly ground black pepper

When ready to serve, you will need:

Salsa
Shredded cheddar cheese
Sour cream

1. In a large skillet over medium heat, brown the meat until it is no longer pink, breaking it up with the back of a spoon as it cooks. Drain.

2. Combine all of the ingredients in a 5-quart slow cooker. Cook on HIGH for 4 to 6 hours.

Freezing instructions:

Divide the soup into meal-size portions in plastic containers. Chill in the refrigerator before freezing.

To thaw and serve:

Thaw the soup in the refrigerator. Reheat in a saucepan until heated through, stirring to recombine. Serve immediately with the salsa, cheese, and sour cream.

Not Your Mother's Chicken Noodle Soup

CANNED SOUP WAS A STANDARD for many of us growing up. But keeping a freezer full of soup is just as easy as canned—and much healthier and more delicious. This version is loaded with tender bits of vegetables and chicken and boasts a slightly Asian twist with sesame oil, cilantro, and spicy red pepper. The noodles will absorb more water and soften in the freezer, so it is fine to cook them al dente. ● *Serves 6 to 8*

Packaging: Plastic containers with lids

2 tablespoons sesame oil
1 medium-size onion, grated
1 teaspoon chopped garlic
1 teaspoon chopped fresh ginger
2 carrots, shredded
1 small zucchini, shredded
8 cups reduced-sodium or homemade chicken broth
2 cups chopped cooked chicken
⅛ to ¼ teaspoon red pepper flakes

Salt and freshly ground black pepper

8 ounces wide egg noodles

When ready to serve, you will need:

2 tablespoons chopped fresh cilantro
Lime wedges

1. In a large stockpot, heat the sesame oil over medium heat. Add the onion, garlic, and ginger, and sauté until translucent, about 5 minutes. Stir in the carrots and zucchini and cook a few minutes more.

2. Stir in the chicken broth. Bring the soup to a boil and stir in the chicken, red pepper flakes, and salt and pepper to taste. Simmer for 15 minutes. Stir in the egg noodles and continue to simmer the soup until they are al dente.

Freezing instructions:

Divide the soup into meal-size portions in plastic containers. Chill in the refrigerator before freezing.

To thaw and serve:

Thaw the soup in the refrigerator. Reheat in a saucepan until heated through. Sprinkle the fresh cilantro over the top before serving. Serve with the lime wedges.

Cheesy Butternut Squash Soup with Herbs

BELIEVE IT OR NOT, I had never eaten butternut squash until our CSA provided an abundance of them one fall. My parents don't like squash; neither does my husband. So there wasn't much opportunity for us to get acquainted before. But we are fast friends now. The squash plays so nicely with cheddar in this soup. Happiness in a spoon! I like to package it in single servings for quick lunches.

o Serves 6 to 8

Packaging: Plastic containers with lids

5 tablespoons salted butter
One 2-pound butternut squash, peeled, seeded, and cubed, or
    two 12-ounce packages cubed squash
1½ cups chopped onion
1 cup chopped celery
1 cup chopped carrot
1 cup diced potato
5 cups reduced-sodium chicken broth or water
¼ teaspoon rubbed sage
¼ teaspoon dried thyme
⅛ teaspoon dried marjoram
¼ cup unbleached all-purpose flour
2 cups milk
2 cups shredded cheddar cheese
Salt and freshly ground black pepper

1. In a large stockpot, melt 3 tablespoons of the butter over medium heat. Add the butternut squash and onion. Cook for about 5 minutes, stirring occasionally.

2. Add the celery, carrot, and potato. Cook 5 minutes more, stirring occasionally.

3. Add the chicken broth, sage, thyme, and marjoram, and bring to a boil. Reduce the heat and simmer until the vegetables are tender, about 30 minutes.

4. Meanwhile, melt the remaining 2 tablespoons butter in a large pot over medium heat. Whisk in the flour and cook for a minute or two. Whisk in the milk until smooth. Simmer until thickened. Whisk in the cheddar cheese gradually, stirring to incorporate. Remove from the heat.

5. Puree the vegetable mixture with an immersion blender or in a food processor, in batches if necessary. Stir in the cheese mixture. Season with salt and pepper to taste.

Freezing instructions:

Divide the soup into meal-size portions in plastic containers. Chill in the refrigerator before freezing.

To thaw and serve:

Thaw the soup in the refrigerator. Reheat in a saucepan until heated through.

How Freezer Cooking Helps Me

Here's how readers of my blog LifeasMOM.com answered these questions: How does freezer cooking help you? How does it help your family eat better? How do you make it work for your life?

The key is to be flexible. When I have time and my husband has time, I will cook for an entire day while he watches the kids. Other times, I simply double a recipe in the slow cooker or on the stove and freeze half. I make whatever I can in a very limited time, such as cooking up beans when I am doing other things around the house. Then I freeze them and I save money by not having to buy canned beans.

—Melissa Batai, MomsPlans.com

Freezer cooking is rarely something I set out to do but just what happens when cooking nearly every dinner from scratch. Huge batches of soup, for example, are just as easy as small batches, so to avoid wasting the leftovers, freezing becomes a necessity. On the other end of the process, it's a joy to have a quick and easy meal for those nights when I've just not planned well, have no inspiration, or am simply tired. I'm not as tempted to eat out or use convenience foods, which helps our budget and our overall nutrition, and I also freeze a lot of "parts" of meals, like chicken stock and chopped vegetables, so I can cook fresh more quickly and healthfully.

—Katie Kimball, KitchenStewardship.com

Freezer cooking is like an emergency fund for my freezer. Having a stash of meal components at the ready turns my foodie crisis moments into mere inconveniences. It keeps us eating well and for a lot less! **—Amy McGuire, AmysFinerThings.com**

Split Pea Soup with Bacon and Thyme

N THIS HEARTY, FLAVORFUL SPLIT PEA SOUP, the bacon and thyme go particularly well with the creamy goodness of the peas, making for a delightful supper.

o *Serves 8*

Packaging: Plastic containers with lids

4 slices lower-salt bacon, finely chopped
1½ cups chopped onion
1 cup chopped carrot
3 quarts water
1 pound split peas, picked over and rinsed
1 bay leaf
1 tablespoon fine sea salt
½ teaspoon dried marjoram
½ teaspoon dried thyme
¼ teaspoon freshly ground black pepper

1. In a large stockpot, cook the bacon and onion over medium heat until the bacon is crisp and the onion has begun to turn translucent, about 5 to 10 minutes.

2. Add the carrot, reduce the heat to low, and cook for about 2 minutes.

3. Add the water, peas, bay leaf, salt, marjoram, thyme, and pepper. Bring to a boil. Reduce the heat to low, cover, and simmer for 2 hours.

4. Remove the bay leaf. Puree the soup with an immersion blender or in a food processor or blender, in batches if necessary. Adjust the seasonings to taste.

Freezing instructions:

Divide the soup into meal-size portions in plastic containers. Chill in the refrigerator before freezing.

To thaw and serve:

Thaw the soup in the refrigerator. Reheat in a saucepan until heated through.

White Bean Soup with Vegetables

THOUGH I GREW UP in a meat-and-potatoes family, I've been pleasantly surprised to discover how satisfying meatless meals can be. Not only are they less expensive, there's a freshness that always shines through. This filling, flavorful white bean soup contains no meat or dairy, making it a great dish to serve to vegetarian or vegan friends. Omit the jalapeño for a less spicy soup.

○ Serves 6 to 8

Packaging: Plastic containers with lids

¼ cup olive oil
½ cup chopped onion
1½ teaspoons crushed garlic
1 cup chopped red potato
½ cup chopped carrot
½ cup chopped celery
¼ cup chopped red bell pepper
1 tablespoon chopped jalapeño pepper (optional)
1 pound Great Northern white beans, rinsed, picked over, and soaked
    according to package directions, then drained
6 cups water
3 tablespoons chopped fresh parsley or 1 tablespoon dried parsley flakes
1 tablespoon Jamie's Spice Mix (page 90)
1 teaspoon salt
Freshly ground black pepper

1. In a large stockpot, heat the oil over medium heat until shimmering. Sauté the onion and garlic until the onion start to turn translucent, about 5 minutes.

2. Add the potato, carrot, celery, bell pepper, and jalapeño, if using, to the pot, and cook, stirring occasionally, 5 minutes more.

3. Add the beans, water, parsley, spice mix, and salt to the pot. Bring to a low boil and simmer, covered, for 2 to 3 hours, until the beans are tender. Alternatively, the soup can be cooked in a 4- or 5-quart slow cooker on LOW for 6 to 8 hours or on HIGH for 4 hours. Adjust the seasonings to taste.

Freezing instructions:

Divide the soup into meal-size portions in plastic containers. Chill in the refrigerator before freezing.

To thaw and serve:

Thaw the soup in the refrigerator. Reheat in a saucepan until heated through.

Creamy Cauliflower Soup

THIS CREAMY SOUP makes a perfectly simple supper for cold winter nights. Just add bread and a green salad. Full of vegetables and cheese, it can also be served as a starter for a more elegant meal. ○ *Serves 8*

Packaging: Plastic containers with lids

2 tablespoons plus ⅓ cup salted butter
1 cup chopped celery
½ cup chopped carrot
⅓ cup chopped onion
4 cups water
1 head cauliflower, cut into florets (about 5 cups)
1½ teaspoons chopped fresh dill or ½ teaspoon dried dill
1 teaspoon salt
1½ teaspoons Jamie's Spice Mix (page 90)
½ cup unbleached all-purpose flour
4 cups milk
4 ounces cream cheese, cubed
Salt and freshly ground pepper

1. In a large stockpot, melt the 2 tablespoons butter over medium heat. Add the celery, carrot, and onion, and cook, stirring occasionally, until the onion turns translucent, about 5 minutes.

2. Add the water, cauliflower, dill, salt, and spice mix. Bring to a low boil. Reduce the heat and simmer for 30 to 40 minutes, or until the vegetables are tender.

3. Meanwhile, melt the remaining ⅓ cup butter in a large pot over medium heat. Whisk in the flour and cook for a minute or two. Whisk in the milk until smooth. Simmer until thickened. Whisk in the cream cheese, stirring to incorporate.

4. Once the cauliflower and other vegetables are tender, blend the mixture with an immersion blender, leaving some chunks of vegetables.

5. Add the milk mixture to the vegetable mixture, stirring to incorporate. Adjust the seasonings to taste.

Freezing instructions:

Divide the soup into meal-size portions in plastic containers. Chill in the refrigerator before freezing.

To thaw and serve:

Thaw the soup in the refrigerator. Reheat in a saucepan until heated through, stirring to recombine.

Beef and Barley Soup with Dill

BEEF AND BARLEY are a classic combination. They bring iron, protein, and that stick-to-your-ribs comfort that we often look for in soups. The addition of vegetables and dill to this soup makes it shine a little more brightly. Package it in 2-cup portions for easy lunches to take to the office or enjoy at home.

○ *Serves 8*

Packaging: Plastic containers with lids

2 tablespoons olive oil

2 pounds boneless chuck roast, finely cubed

1 cup chopped onion

1 teaspoon chopped garlic

½ cup chopped celery

½ cup chopped mushrooms

½ cup chopped carrot

¾ cup pearl barley, rinsed

½ cup white wine

8 cups reduced-sodium beef broth

1 tablespoon chopped fresh dill or 1 teaspoon dried dill

Salt and freshly ground black pepper

1. In a large stockpot, heat the oil over medium heat until shimmering. Add the beef cubes and cook, stirring, for 5 minutes. Add the onion and garlic, and cook 5 minutes more. Add the celery, mushrooms, and carrot, and cook 5 minutes more.

2. Add the barley and cook, stirring, until the barley is lightly browned, 5 to 10 minutes.

3. Add the white wine and cook a minute or two, scraping up any browned bits. Stir in the beef broth and dill. Season to taste with salt and pepper.

4. Simmer the soup, partially covered, for 1 hour, or until the barley and beef are tender. Adjust the seasonings to taste.

Freezing instructions:

Divide the soup into meal-size portions in plastic containers. Chill in the refrigerator before freezing.

To thaw and serve:

Thaw the soup in the refrigerator. Reheat in a saucepan until heated through, stirring to recombine.

Black Bean Soup with Jalapeño

SOME BLACK BEAN SOUPS are laden with bacon. While bacon is not a bad thing, this soup is different in that the flavor of vegetables and beans shines through. Serve it with crusty bread and cheddar cheese or a dollop of sour cream. The soup can be prepared with dried beans, but for quicker cooking, use canned black beans. ○ *Serves 6 to 8*

Packaging: Plastic containers with lids

1 pound dried black beans, rinsed, picked over, and soaked according to package directions, then drained, or four 15-ounce cans black beans, rinsed and drained

6 cups reduced-sodium chicken broth or vegetable broth

1 tablespoon olive oil

1 cup shredded carrot

1 cup chopped onion

1 cup chopped celery

1 tablespoon finely chopped jalapeño pepper

1 teaspoon chopped garlic

1 cup shredded potato

1 bay leaf

1 to 2 teaspoons kosher salt

1 teaspoon dried oregano

½ teaspoon ground cumin

¼ teaspoon freshly ground black pepper

1 tablespoon freshly squeezed lemon juice or lime juice

1. In a large stockpot, combine the soaked dried beans and broth. Bring to a boil and simmer for 2 hours, or until the beans are tender. If you're using canned beans, simply combine the beans and broth and move on to step 2.

2. In a large heavy skillet, heat the oil over medium heat until shimmering. Sauté the carrot, onion, celery, jalapeño, and garlic until crisp-tender, about 5 minutes.

3. Transfer the sautéed vegetables to the pot along with the shredded potato, bay leaf, salt, oregano, cumin, and pepper. Stir well and simmer for 1 hour.

4. Remove the bay leaf and discard it. Stir in the lemon juice. This is a chunky soup. If you prefer it smoother, puree the soup with an immersion blender or in a food processor or blender, in batches if necessary. Adjust the seasonings to taste.

Freezing instructions:

Divide the soup into meal-size portions in plastic containers. Chill in the refrigerator before freezing.

To thaw and serve:

Thaw the soup in the refrigerator. Reheat in a saucepan until heated through, stirring to recombine.

Fish Chowder with Red Potatoes and Corn

THIS CHOWDER IS FULL OF FLAVOR, with bell pepper, onion, potatoes, dill, and corn. Chunks of cod or salmon take it up a few notches. Prepare the base soup or sauce and freeze it, then add the fish right before serving. It's a perfect blend of flavor and convenience. This chowder can easily make dinner for two nights. Consider dividing the chowder into two plastic containers with lids.

o *Serves 8*

Packaging: Plastic containers with lids

1 tablespoon olive oil
½ cup chopped onion
1 cup chopped bell pepper (red, green, or a combination)
6 cups Homemade Cream of Celery Soup for Cooking (page 223)
1½ cups frozen or canned corn kernels, drained if canned
Grated zest of 1 lemon

2 tablespoons chopped fresh dill or 1 tablespoon dried dill

4 cups (about 2 pounds) cooked and cubed red potatoes (microwave or steam them)

Salt and freshly ground black pepper

When ready to serve, you will need:

10 ounces salmon or cod fillets, cut into 1-inch cubes

1. In a large stockpot, heat the oil over medium heat until shimmering. Add the onion and sauté until the onion starts to become translucent, 3 to 4 minutes. Add the bell pepper and cook until tender, about 5 minutes.

2. Stir in the cream of celery soup, corn, lemon zest, dill, and potatoes. Add water to thin the soup to the desired consistency. Simmer the soup for 20 minutes. Season to taste with salt and pepper.

Freezing instructions:

Divide the chowder into meal-size portions in plastic containers. Chill in the refrigerator before freezing.

To thaw and serve:

Thaw the chowder in the refrigerator. Reheat in a saucepan until heated through, stirring to recombine. Stir the fish chunks into the hot chowder. Continue cooking until the fish is cooked through, 10 to 15 minutes. Adjust the seasonings to taste. Serve immediately.

Tortilla Soup with Shrimp

VEGETABLES, SEASONINGS, AND BROTH combine to make a flavorful soup base that is frozen; shrimp are stirred in during the last few minutes of cooking to make it an extra-special bowl of goodness. For a less spicy soup, reduce or omit the jalapeños. o *Serves 8*

Packaging: Plastic containers with lids

2 tablespoons olive oil

1 cup chopped onion

1 cup sliced carrot

½ cup chopped bell pepper (red, green, or a combination)

1 jalapeño pepper, finely chopped (optional)

One 14.5-ounce can petite diced tomatoes with juices

One 15-ounce can black beans, rinsed and drained

One 15.5-ounce can hominy, rinsed and drained

7 cups reduced-sodium chicken broth

1 teaspoon dried oregano

Salt and freshly ground black pepper

When ready to serve, you will need:

8 ounces medium shrimp, shelled and deveined

Crushed tortilla chips

Chopped fresh cilantro

1. In a large stockpot, heat the oil over medium heat until shimmering. Add the onion and sauté until it starts to turn translucent, about 5 minutes.

2. Add the carrot, bell pepper, and jalapeño, and cook about 5 minutes more.

3. Stir in the tomatoes, black beans, hominy, broth, and oregano. Simmer for 20 minutes. Season with salt and pepper to taste.

Freezing instructions:

Divide the soup into meal-size portions in plastic containers. Chill in the refrigerator before freezing.

To thaw and serve:

Thaw the soup in the refrigerator. Reheat in a saucepan until heated through. Stir the shrimp into the soup. Continue cooking until the shrimp has turned pink, about 10 minutes. Place a small handful of crushed tortilla chips into each bowl. Ladle the hot soup over the chips. Top with chopped cilantro and serve immediately.

Homemade Cream of Celery Soup for Cooking

CANNED CREAM SOUP has been a resource for busy home cooks for more than 50 years. However, a quick glance at the label tells us that there might be better foods to feed our bodies. Cook up a bulk batch of this vegetarian cream of celery soup to use in cooking instead. For a richer flavor, use chicken broth or vegetable broth instead of water. ○ *Makes about 2 cups*

Packaging: Plastic container with lid

¼ cup (½ stick) salted butter
¼ cup unbleached all-purpose flour
1 cup milk
1 cup water
2 tablespoons chopped celery
1 tablespoon freshly grated Parmesan cheese
1 teaspoon salt
¼ teaspoon freshly ground black pepper
¼ teaspoon onion powder
⅛ teaspoon paprika

1. In a large stockpot, melt the butter over medium heat. Stir in the flour and cook until the mixture bubbles. Cook 1 minute more, stirring.

2. Whisk in the milk and water, stirring constantly, until the mixture thickens to a sauce-like consistency.

3. Stir in the celery, Parmesan cheese, salt, black pepper, onion powder, and paprika. Simmer for 5 minutes.

Freezing instructions:

If using the soup in a recipe, cool it completely and proceed with the recipe. Otherwise, transfer the soup to a plastic container. Chill the soup in the refrigerator before freezing.

To thaw and serve:

Thaw the soup in the refrigerator. Use as directed in recipes.

NOTE: To make a big batch of this soup, simply multiply all the ingredients by four. The cooking method remains the same.

Chicken Cacciatore Stew

THIS CHICKEN STEW, made with tender white meat, sweet tomatoes, and woodsy mushrooms, is sure to please everyone at your table. And since you don't have to break a sweat to make it, you'll have a smile on your face as well. Serve it with crusty bread for a hearty meal. ○ *Serves 6 to 8*

Packaging: Plastic containers with lids

¼ cup olive oil
1 cup chopped onion
1 red bell pepper, chopped
1 green bell pepper, chopped
8 ounces fresh mushrooms, cleaned and quartered
One 14.5-ounce can petite diced tomatoes with juices
One 15-ounce can tomato sauce
4 pounds chicken tenders or boneless, skinless chicken breasts, cut into 1-inch chunks
1 teaspoon dried rosemary
Salt and freshly ground black pepper

1. In a large stockpot, heat the oil over medium heat until shimmering. Add the onion, bell peppers, and mushrooms, and cook until the vegetables are very tender, about 7 minutes.

2. Stir in the tomatoes, tomato sauce, chicken, and rosemary. Season generously with salt and pepper.

3. Bring to a simmer. Cover and cook on low heat for about 20 minutes, stirring occasionally, until the chicken is cooked through.

Freezing instructions:

Divide the stew into meal-size portions in plastic containers. Chill in the refrigerator before freezing.

To thaw and serve:

Thaw the stew in the refrigerator. Reheat it in a saucepan until heated through, stirring to recombine.

Our Favorite Irish Stew

T**HIS IS OUR FAMILY'S** traditional St. Patrick's Day fare. The saint of the Emerald Isle had, of course, been a shepherd, and so this simple, authentic meal is one we share in his honor. It is delicious served with slices of Irish soda bread and chunks of Dubliner cheese. ○ *Serves 6 to 8*

Packaging: Plastic containers with lids

¼ cup unbleached all-purpose flour
1 teaspoon salt
½ teaspoon freshly ground black pepper
2 pounds chuck roast, cut into 1-inch cubes
2 tablespoons vegetable oil
1 cup finely chopped onion
½ cup beef broth
1 bay leaf
2 cups baby carrots
4 medium potatoes, peeled and cut into 1-inch chunks

1. Combine the flour, salt, and pepper in a large zip-top bag. Add the beef cubes, seal, and shake to coat all the cubes with the flour.

2. In a large skillet, heat the oil over medium heat until shimmering. Brown the beef cubes on all sides, in batches if necessary. As the meat browns, transfer it to a 5-quart slow cooker.

3. Add the onion to the drippings in the skillet and sauté until tender, 5 to 7 minutes. Add the onions to the slow cooker.

4. Stir in the beef broth and the bay leaf. Cook the stew on LOW for 4 hours.

5. Add the carrots and potatoes and stir gently to combine. Cook on LOW 4 hours more, or until the meat and vegetables are tender. Adjust the seasonings to taste.

Freezing instructions:

Divide the stew into meal-size portions in plastic containers. Chill in the refrigerator before freezing.

To thaw and serve:

Thaw the stew in the refrigerator. Reheat in a saucepan until heated through.

Beef Stew with Eggplant and Carrots

FOR A COZY SUPPER OF COMFORT FOOD, this stew hits the mark; it is absolutely delicious, especially when served over mashed potatoes. The eggplant adds richness and great flavor. ○ *Serves 8*

Packaging: Plastic containers with lids

¼ cup olive oil
3 pounds boneless chuck roast, cut into 1-inch cubes
Salt and freshly ground black pepper
1 medium-size onion, diced
3 cloves garlic, minced
2 bay leaves
3 tablespoons unbleached all-purpose flour
2 teaspoons dried thyme
2 cups reduced-sodium beef broth
2 cups peeled and diced eggplant
2 cups peeled and sliced carrots

When ready to serve, you will need:

Cream Cheese Mashed Potatoes (page 82) or other favorite mashed potatoes

1. In a large skillet, heat 2 tablespoons of the oil over medium heat until shimmering. Brown the beef cubes on all sides, in batches if necessary. Transfer the beef to a 5-quart slow cooker and season with salt and pepper.

2. Add the onion and garlic to the drippings in the skillet. Sauté until translucent, about 5 minutes. Add the bay leaves, flour, and thyme. Stir to combine. Stir in the beef broth, scraping up any browned bits. Transfer the broth and onion mixture to the slow cooker. Cook on LOW for 4 hours.

3. In a large skillet, heat the remaining 2 tablespoons olive oil over medium-high heat until shimmering. Sauté the eggplant, stirring, for about 7 minutes. Stir the eggplant and the carrots into the stew in the slow cooker. Continue to cook 2 hours more. Season to taste with salt and pepper.

Freezing instructions:

Divide the stew into meal-size portions in plastic containers. Chill in the refrigerator before freezing.

To thaw and serve:

Thaw the stew in the refrigerator. Reheat in a saucepan until heated through. Serve over mashed potatoes.

Hearty Beef Stew with Olives

MY FOUR BOYS are self-proclaimed "meat-atarians." Though they do enjoy meatless meals, they absolutely devour this hearty beef stew boasting the bright flavor of lime and spicy chiles from the enchilada sauce. Serve it over rice or boiled potatoes. ○ *Serves 6 to 8*

Packaging: Plastic containers with lids

½ cup unbleached all-purpose flour

1 teaspoon salt

½ teaspoon freshly ground black pepper

2 pounds boneless chuck roast, cubed

2 tablespoons olive oil

½ cup chopped onion

¼ cup freshly squeezed lime juice

¼ cup canned red chile sauce or enchilada sauce

1½ teaspoons dried oregano

One 5-ounce jar green Spanish olives (with or without pimientos), drained

1. Combine the flour, salt, and pepper in a large zip-top bag. Add the beef cubes, seal, and shake to coat all the cubes with the flour.

2. In a large skillet, heat the oil over medium heat until shimmering. Brown the beef cubes, in batches if necessary. Transfer the browned beef to a 4-quart slow cooker.

3. Add the onion to the skillet and cook, stirring, until it starts to become translucent, about 5 minutes. Add the lime juice, stirring to scrape up any browned bits. Add the enchilada sauce and oregano and stir to combine.

4. Transfer this mixture to the slow cooker. Cook the stew on LOW for 6 to 8 hours. In the last 20 minutes of cooking, stir in the green olives. Adjust the seasonings to taste.

Freezing instructions:

Divide the stew into meal-size portions in plastic containers. Chill in the refrigerator before freezing.

To thaw and serve:

Thaw the stew in the refrigerator. Reheat in a saucepan until heated through.

Quick and Easy Texas Chili

A TRADITIONAL BOWL OF RED is simply meat and chiles—no beans. While beans certainly fill the dish with fiber, they aren't acceptable in some parts of the country. And the no-beans variety is extremely tasty and freezer-friendly. Serve this Texas-style chili over chips or with cornbread. It can even fill up burritos or be served over hot cooked noodles. Feel free to make this with ground turkey; simply reduce the cayenne pepper to ¼ teaspoon, to complement the milder flavor of turkey. ○ *Serves 4 to 6*

Packaging: Plastic containers with lids

2½ pounds ground beef or ground turkey
1 medium-size onion, chopped
2 cloves garlic, minced
One 15-ounce can tomato sauce
2 tablespoons chili powder
1 teaspoon salt
1 teaspoon dried oregano
1 teaspoon ground cumin
½ teaspoon cayenne pepper

1. In a large pot, cook the ground beef, onion, and garlic over medium heat, stirring, until the meat is browned and the onion starts to turn translucent, about 10 minutes.

2. Stir in the tomato sauce, chili powder, salt, oregano, cumin, and cayenne pepper. Simmer for 15 minutes, stirring occasionally. Adjust the seasonings to taste.

Freezing instructions:

Divide the chili into meal-size portions in plastic containers. Chill in the refrigerator before freezing.

To thaw and serve:

Thaw the chili in the refrigerator. Reheat in a saucepan until heated through. Serve immediately.

Chihuahua Chili

'VE BEEN MAKING THIS CHILI for more than a decade. It's flavorful and filling, with just enough kick. When I'm going to feed a crowd, this is my go-to, easy-to-serve recipe. Just dish up bowls of red, offer a selection of toppings and a basket of bread and butter, and you're good to go. If you'd like, you can make this in the slow cooker. After you sauté the onions and garlic, simply combine all of the ingredients in a 5-quart slow cooker and cook on LOW for 6 to 8 hours ○ *Serves 8 to 12*

Packaging: Plastic containers with lids

1 pound ground beef
2 cups chopped onion
3 tablespoons chopped garlic
Two 29-ounce cans (or four 15-ounce cans) pinto beans, rinsed and drained
Two 15-ounce cans black beans, rinsed and drained
2 cups tomato sauce
1 cup enchilada sauce
One 12-ounce bottle beer
1 tablespoon ground cumin
1 tablespoon chili powder

When ready to serve, you will need:

Sour cream
Shredded cheddar cheese
Chopped fresh cilantro

1. In a large pot, cook the ground beef, onion, and garlic over medium heat, stirring, until the meat is browned and the onion starts to turn translucent, about 10 minutes.

2. Add the beans, tomato sauce, enchilada sauce, beer, cumin, and chili powder. Stir the mixture well to combine.

3. Bring the chili to a low boil. Reduce the heat to low. Simmer, partially covered, until the chili is slightly thickened and the flavors have mingled, about 1 hour.

Freezing instructions:

Divide the chili into meal-size portions in plastic containers. Chill in the refrigerator before freezing.

To thaw and serve:

Thaw the chili in the refrigerator. Reheat in a saucepan until heated through. Serve immediately with the sour cream, cheese, and cilantro.

Smoky Multi-Bean Vegetarian Chili

GOING MEATLESS can be a great way to cut costs and improve health. This chili, adapted from one Jessika shared with me years ago, is full of fiber from beans and lentils. It also boasts a warm, smoky flavor from the ground chipotle chile powder. You can certainly use regular chili powder, but you'll miss out on the smoked flavor of the chipotles. o *Serves 8 to 10*

Packaging: Plastic containers with lids

2 tablespoons olive oil
1 cup chopped onion
3 cloves garlic, chopped
½ cup chopped red or green bell pepper
One 4-ounce can chopped green chiles
2 teaspoons ground cumin
1 teaspoon chipotle chile powder
1 teaspoon fine sea salt
½ teaspoon dried oregano
2 cups water
Two 15-ounce cans black beans, rinsed and drained
One 15-ounce can red beans, rinsed and drained
1½ cups frozen or canned corn, drained if canned
1 cup lentils, rinsed and picked over
1 cup tomato sauce
Salt and freshly ground black pepper

1. In a large stockpot over medium heat, heat the oil until shimmering. Cook the onions and garlic until the onion starts to become translucent, about 5 minutes.

2. Add the bell pepper, chiles, cumin, chipotle chile powder, salt, and oregano. Stir to combine, reduce the heat to low, and cook for about a minute.

3. Add the water, beans, corn, lentils, and tomato sauce. Bring to a boil. Reduce the heat to low and cover. Simmer for about 1 hour, or until the lentils are tender. Alternatively, you can cook the chili in a 5-quart slow cooker on LOW for 4 to 6 hours. Adjust the seasonings with salt and pepper to taste.

Freezing instructions:

Divide the chili into meal-size portions in plastic containers. Chill in the refrigerator before freezing.

To thaw and serve:

Thaw the chili in the refrigerator. Reheat in a saucepan until heated through.

Perfect Pizzas

Basic Pizza Dough

MANY GROCERY STORES now sell pizza dough in the refrigerated section. But it's not difficult to make your own. By doing so, you can customize the ingredients and save money. To speed things up, I use a bread machine to mix the dough. This gives me a more consistent texture and keeps the kitchen cleaner. But you can very easily mix up this dough in a stand mixer or by hand, if you prefer.

Preparing the dough takes about 2 hours from start to finish. However, I can break up that prep time by mixing and freezing the dough one day and letting it thaw and rise another day. This helps me use my time in the kitchen more efficiently.

For bulk dough making, I usually start one batch in the bread machine and then get my KitchenAid stand mixer going on another. I freeze the dough after it has risen for only 30 minutes, placing each greased dough ball in a plastic sandwich bag and then storing them in a larger freezer bag or paired with other ingredients in a pizza kit. **o** *Makes enough dough for four 12-inch pizzas or 8 individual-size pizzas*

Packaging: Zip-top sandwich bags, gallon-size zip-top freezer bag

1½ cups water
¼ cup olive oil
2 tablespoons honey or sugar
4½ cups unbleached all-purpose flour (you can substitute up to 1 cup whole-wheat flour
　　for an equivalent amount of all-purpose flour)
1 tablespoon salt
1 tablespoon active dry yeast

If making dough in a bread machine:

1. Combine all of the ingredients in the bread machine pan in the order recommended by the manufacturer. Set the machine to the dough cycle and start it, checking after 10 minutes to make sure all of the ingredients have been incorporated and are not stuck to the side of the pan. Once the mixing cycle is complete, allow the dough to rise for 30 minutes.

If making dough in a stand mixer:

1. Combine the water, oil, honey, 2 cups of the flour, the salt, and yeast in the bowl of a stand mixer fitted with a paddle attachment and beat on low speed. Once the dough starts to come together, 1 to 2 minutes, exchange the paddle for a dough hook. Knead the dough, gradually adding more flour until a dough ball forms. Knead the dough 2 minutes more. Transfer the dough to a greased bowl and turn it to coat it with oil. Allow the dough to rise for 30 minutes.

If making dough by hand:

1. In a large bowl, combine the water, oil, honey, and yeast, and allow to proof for 5 minutes. Add the flour and salt, stirring with a wooden spoon until a stiff dough forms. Turn the dough out onto a lightly floured surface and knead for 5 minutes, or until the dough has a smooth, elastic feel. Add more flour if necessary. Transfer the dough to a greased bowl and turn it to coat it with oil. Allow the dough to rise for 30 minutes.

To finish the dough:

2. When the dough is ready, use greased hands to divide it into 4 or 8 portions, as desired. Shape each portion into a ball. Place each dough ball into a sandwich bag and freeze immediately. The dough will continue to rise and you want to arrest that process, so the sooner it is frozen, the better.

Freezing instructions:

Package the dough balls with other pizza ingredients to make kits or in one large zip-top freezer bag.

To thaw and serve:

Remove the frozen dough from the freezer. Remove the dough from the bag and place in a greased bowl; if thawing more than one dough ball, place on a greased baking pan. Allow the dough to rise for 6 to 8 hours in the refrigerator or for 3 hours at room temperature. If the dough has risen in the refrigerator, let it sit at room temperature for 30 minutes before forming, topping, and baking.

I almost always have several pints or quarts of Easy Slow Cooker Red Sauce (page 205) in the freezer. It's a multipurpose sauce that works well for pizza, lasagna, and pasta.

But when I want to make things a little extra-special, I mix up a bulk batch of this pizza sauce. You can portion it into ½-cup containers—just the right amount for a 12-inch pizza—and store them in the freezer. It's also good on pasta.

Tomato and Herb Pizza Sauce

This flavorful sauce comes together in minutes. Inspired by the sauce at California Pizza Kitchen, it is a delicious topping for pizzas and dip for Calzones (pages 248 to 250) and French Bread Pizza Dippers (page 246). ❍ *Makes about 4½ cups*

Packaging: Plastic containers with lids

¼ **cup olive oil**

2 **teaspoons minced garlic**

One 28-ounce can petite diced tomatoes with juices

3 **tablespoons chopped fresh basil or 1 tablespoon dried basil**

1 **teaspoon salt**

½ **teaspoon dried oregano**

¼ **teaspoon red pepper flakes**

One 6-ounce can tomato paste

1. In a large saucepan, heat the olive oil over medium heat until shimmering. Stir in the garlic and cook until just barely browned.

2. Add the tomatoes, basil, salt, oregano, and red pepper flakes. Simmer until the juices have started to evaporate slightly, about 10 minutes.

3. Stir in the tomato paste and cook 3 minutes more. This is a chunky sauce. Use it as is or puree it with an immersion blender or in a food processor. Let cool.

Freezing instructions:

Divide the sauce into desired portions in plastic containers. Cool completely. Cover and chill in the refrigerator before freezing.

To thaw and serve:

Thaw the sauce in the refrigerator. Use as a topping or dip.

Easy-Peasy Cheesy Pizza

COULDN'T RESIST NAMING THIS PIZZA in a goofy yet accurate way. This cheese pizza is delicious—and easy. It's utterly simple, but it still packs a punch of flavor. The combination of cheeses makes it especially delicious.

o Makes one 12-inch pizza

Packaging: Quart- or pint-size bag, snack-size bag, plastic container with lid or additional snack-size bag, gallon-size zip-top freezer bag

¾ cup shredded mozzarella cheese
¾ cup shredded Monterey Jack cheese
¼ cup Parmesan Herb Blend (page 240)
½ cup Tomato and Herb Pizza Sauce (page 236)
¼ batch frozen, bagged Basic Pizza Dough (page 234)

1. Place the mozzarella and Jack cheeses in the quart- or pint-size bag. Place the Parmesan Herb Blend in the snack-size bag. Place the pizza sauce in a plastic container or a snack-size bag.

2. Place the two bags of cheese and the container of sauce, along with the frozen pizza dough, in the gallon-size zip-top freezer bag. Store in the freezer.

To thaw and serve:

Remove the pizza kit from the freezer. Grease a medium bowl. Unwrap the pizza dough and place it in the greased bowl. Thaw it in the refrigerator for 6 to 8 hours, covered. Thaw the other items in the kit in the refrigerator. Preheat the oven to 475°F. Allow the dough to sit at room temperature for about 30 minutes. Stretch the dough to fit a 12-inch pizza pan. Spread the sauce over the prepared dough. Sprinkle the mozzarella mixture over the sauce. Sprinkle the Parmesan Herb Blend over the top. Bake the pizza for 10 to 12 minutes, or until the crust is crisp and the cheese is melted and starting to brown. Cool slightly before slicing and serving.

Pizza Night Is a Highlight of Our Week— with Pizza Kits on Hand

For many folks, a pizza is a great way to kick off the weekend, celebrate a team's victory, or otherwise enjoy a casual meal with friends and family. And many of us rely on the pizza parlor or the frozen-food section of the grocery store to provide this culinary delight.

But homemade pizza can be as good as or better than commercial versions. And if you've got a few pizza kits in your freezer, you'll be set for a delicious dinner with a minimal amount of work.

I often spend Friday afternoons assembling the makings of homemade pizza, which I bake in the oven or cook on the grill. We enjoy it with vegetable dippers and homemade ranch dressing or a mixed salad. Then after kitchen cleanup (or not), we watch a movie and officially enter the weekend.

Most members of my younger crew prefer simple cheese or pepperoni pizzas, while the more mature ones in our family opt for the Jalapeño Burn Pizza (page 241), Burrito Pizza (page 239), or Pesto Pizza with Shrimp, Feta, and Tomatoes (page 243).

The trick to making these pizza nights relaxing is to have pizza kits at the ready. Homemade sauce, pizza dough, shredded cheese, and other toppings can be prepared ahead and stored in the freezer, ready to grab and thaw in the refrigerator.

All kinds of frozen meal components can come together in a beautiful way for pizza night. A barbecue sauce pairs with shredded chicken on one pizza, while a homemade sauce and shredded cheese come together on another. It's easy to make several kinds of pizza on one night if you have the fixings portioned and ready to go.

Creating pizza kits also helps you make good use of your bulk shopping items, like those large bags of cheese you might buy at a warehouse club. Don't fear the 5-pound bag of cheese. That's the most economical way to buy shredded mozzarella. Simply divide the cheese into quart-size freezer bags when you bring it home. Put ½ pound (about 2 cups) of cheese in each bag, enough for one or two pizzas, depending on how cheesy you like it. Stash the bags in the freezer or, for even greater efficiency, combine them with other components in a pizza kit.

The easiest way to put together pizza kits is to bundle all the components together in a gallon-size zip-top freezer bag. Label the bag (be sure to note what kind of pizza fixings it contains), and include a bag of pizza dough, a bag of cheese, a container of sauce, and any other freezable toppings you would like.

Burrito Pizza

MY RESIDENT CARNIVORE, my 14-year-old son, prefers this pizza to all others, including those with meat. For this simple and delicious pizza, black beans are layered on the crust and topped with cheese and vegetables. Serve it with shredded lettuce, sour cream, salsa, and guacamole.

o Makes one 12-inch pizza, serves 4

Packaging: Quart- or pint-size bag, two snack-size bags, gallon-size zip-top freezer bag

1 cup shredded mozzarella cheese
½ cup shredded cheddar cheese
½ cup chopped onion
1 jalapeño pepper, thinly sliced
¼ batch frozen, bagged Basic Pizza Dough (page 234)

When ready to serve, you will need:

One 15-ounce can black beans, rinsed and drained
½ cup diced tomato
¼ cup sliced black olives
Shredded lettuce
Easy Homemade Salsa (page 71)
Super-Simple Guacamole (page 71)
Sour cream

1. Place the mozzarella and cheddar cheeses in the quart- or pint-size bag. Place the chopped onion in a snack-size bag and seal. Place the sliced jalapeño in another snack-size bag and seal.

2. Place the bagged cheese, jalapeño, and onion, along with the bag of frozen pizza dough, in the gallon-size zip-top freezer bag. Store in the freezer.

To thaw and serve:

Remove the pizza kit from the freezer. Grease a medium bowl. Unwrap the pizza dough and place it in the greased bowl. Thaw it in the refrigerator for 6 to 8 hours, covered. Thaw the other items in the kit in the refrigerator. Preheat the oven to 475°F. Allow the dough to sit at room temperature for about 30 minutes. Stretch the dough to fit a 12-inch pizza pan. Spread the black beans over the prepared dough. Sprinkle with 1 cup of the mozzarella mixture. Layer the tomato, onion, jalapeño, and black olives over the cheese. Sprinkle the remaining ½ cup cheese over the top. Bake for 10 to 12 minutes, or until the crust is crisp and the cheese is melted and golden in spots. Cool slightly before slicing. Serve with the shredded lettuce, salsa, guacamole, and sour cream.

Parmesan Herb Blend

Cheese and herbs make beautiful music together, adding flavor and texture. This mixture of grated Parmesan cheese and herbs is delicious stirred into sauces, sprinkled on salads or steamed vegetables, or used to season herb butters. Toss hot cooked pasta with olive oil and a few tablespoons of this mixture for an easy side dish. Mix up a batch at the beginning of a freezer cooking session and use it to add instant flavor to a number of dishes, including Easy-Peasy Cheesy Pizza (page 237). ○ *Makes about 1 cup*

Packaging: Pint-size zip-top freezer bag or plastic container with lid

1 cup freshly grated Parmesan cheese
1 tablespoon chopped fresh parsley or 1 teaspoon dried parsley flakes
1 teaspoon garlic powder
¾ teaspoon chopped fresh basil or ¼ teaspoon dried basil
¼ teaspoon dried oregano
¼ teaspoon dried thyme
⅛ teaspoon freshly ground black pepper

In a small bowl, gently mix all of the ingredients.

Freezing instructions:

Freeze the cheese blend in a freezer bag or airtight container.

Jalapeño Burn Pizza

THOSE WHO LOVE SPICY FOOD will get a real kick out of this pizza. Red pepper flakes and sliced jalapeños offer heat, while the tomatoes refresh your palate and the cheese helps cool the burn.

○ Makes one 12-inch pizza, serves 4

Packaging: Quart- or pint-size bag, two snack-size bags, sandwich bag, gallon-size zip-top freezer bag

1 cup shredded mozzarella cheese
½ cup shredded cheddar cheese
½ cup chopped onion
2 jalapeño peppers, thinly sliced
1 cup chopped cooked chicken
¼ batch frozen, bagged Basic Pizza Dough (page 234)

When ready to serve, you will need:

1 tablespoon olive oil
Red pepper flakes
1 medium tomato, diced
¼ cup sliced black olives

1. Place the mozzarella and cheddar cheeses in the quart- or pint-size bag. Place the chopped onion in a snack-size bag. Place the sliced jalapeño in another snack-size bag. Place the chopped chicken in the sandwich bag and seal.

2. Place the bagged cheese, onion, jalapeno, and chicken, along with the bag of frozen pizza dough, in the gallon-size zip-top freezer bag. Store in the freezer.

To thaw and serve:

Remove the pizza kit from the freezer. Grease a medium bowl. Unwrap the pizza dough and place it in the greased bowl. Thaw it in the refrigerator for 6 to 8 hours, covered. Thaw the other items in the kit in the refrigerator. Preheat the oven to 475°F. Allow the dough to sit at room temperature for about 30 minutes. Stretch the dough to fit a 12-inch pizza pan. Spread the oil over the prepared pizza dough. Sprinkle with red pepper flakes to taste and 1 cup of the mozzarella mixture.

Layer the chicken, tomato, onion, jalapeños, and black olives over the cheese. Sprinkle the remaining ½ cup cheese over the top. Bake for 10 to 12 minutes, or until the crust is crisp and the cheese is melted and golden in spots. Cool slightly before slicing and serving.

Chicken and Sun-Dried Tomato Pizza with Goat Cheese

LOVE BAKED GOAT CHEESE; something about it just makes the food taste special. This upscale pizza combines rich sun-dried tomato pesto and chicken with goat cheese. ○ *Makes one 12-inch pizza, serves 4*

Packaging: Two sandwich-size bags, plastic container with lid or snack-size bag, quart- or pint-size bag, gallon-size zip-top freezer bag

1 cup chopped cooked chicken
½ cup crumbled goat cheese
½ cup Sun-Dried Tomato Pesto (page 206)
¼ batch frozen, bagged Basic Pizza Dough (page 234)

1. Place the cooked chicken in a sandwich-size bag. Place the goat cheese crumbles in another sandwich-size bag. Place the pesto in a plastic container or snack-size bag.

2. Place the bags of chicken and cheese and the container of pesto, along with the bag of frozen pizza dough, in the gallon-size zip-top freezer bag. Store in the freezer.

To thaw and serve:

Remove the pizza kit from the freezer. Grease a medium bowl. Unwrap the pizza dough and place it in the greased bowl. Thaw it in the refrigerator for 6 to 8 hours, covered. Thaw the other items in the kit in the refrigerator. Preheat the oven to 475°F. Allow the dough to sit at room temperature for about 30 minutes. Stretch the dough to fit a 12-inch pizza pan. Spread the pesto over the prepared dough. Sprinkle the chicken over the sauce. Sprinkle the goat cheese crumbles over the chicken.

Bake the pizza for 10 to 12 minutes, or until the crust is crisp and the cheese is slightly melted and starting to brown. Cool slightly before slicing and serving.

Pesto Pizza with Shrimp, Feta, and Tomatoes

ARESTAURANT I ONCE WORKED IN served a pasta dish with pesto, shrimp, and some salty garnishes. I've re-created it on a pizza, adding feta for tang and tomatoes for sweetness and juicy texture.

o *Makes one 12-inch pizza, serves 4*

Packaging: Quart-size zip-top freezer bag, sandwich-size bag, plastic container with lid or additional sandwich-size bag, gallon-size zip-top freezer bag

16 medium shrimp, peeled and deveined
½ cup crumbled feta cheese
½ cup pesto
¼ batch frozen, bagged Basic Pizza Dough (page 234)

When ready to serve, you will need:

1 cup chopped tomatoes

1. Place the shrimp in the quart-size zip-top freezer bag. Place the feta cheese crumbles in the sandwich-size bag. Place the pesto in a plastic container or snack-size bag.

2. Place the bags of shrimp and cheese and the container of pesto, along with the bag of frozen pizza dough, in the gallon-size zip-top freezer bag. Store in the freezer.

To thaw and serve:

Remove the pizza kit from the freezer. Grease a medium bowl. Unwrap the pizza dough and place it in the greased bowl. Thaw it in the refrigerator for 6 to 8 hours, covered. Thaw the other items in the kit in the refrigerator. Preheat the oven to 475°F. Allow the dough to sit at room temperature for about 30 minutes. Stretch the dough to fit a 12-inch pizza pan. Spread the pesto over the prepared dough. Scatter the shrimp over the sauce. Sprinkle the feta cheese over the shrimp. Sprinkle the tomatoes over the top of the pizza. Bake the pizza for 10 minutes, or until the crust is crisp, the shrimp are pink, and the cheese is slightly melted and starting to brown. Cool slightly before slicing and serving.

Barbecue Cheeseburger Pizza

T'S AMAZING WHAT FLAVORS you can put on a pizza! You really can re-create some of your favorite meals on a flatbread. Fresh toppings make it extra-special. This pizza tastes like a barbecue cheeseburger, complete with a smoky sauce, seasoned ground beef, cheddar cheese, and a topping of red onion, tomatoes, and shredded lettuce. ○ *Makes one 12-inch pizza, serves 4*

Packaging: Quart-size zip-top freezer bag, quart- or pint-size bag, plastic container with lid or snack-size bag, gallon-size zip-top freezer bag

1 cup seasoned taco meat (page 89)
1 cup shredded mozzarella cheese
½ cup shredded cheddar cheese
½ cup Barbecue Sauce for Meatballs (page 98)
¼ batch frozen, bagged Basic Pizza Dough (page 234)

When ready to serve, you will need:

1 cup chopped tomato
1 cup shredded lettuce
¼ cup chopped red onion

1. Place the taco meat in the quart-size zip-top freezer bag. Place the mozzarella and cheddar cheese in the quart- or pint-size bag. Place the barbecue sauce in a plastic container or snack-size bag.

Pizza Baking and Grilling Tips

Make sure the oven is hot! Preheat the oven for at least 30 minutes to ensure a great pizza crust.

You can use a pizza stone if you like, but it isn't necessary. I don't use a special stone, and I've been able to cook beautiful pizzas on regular baking sheets, greased and sometimes sprinkled with cornmeal. I also have a couple of perforated round pizza pans, which I love.

Consider cooking pizza on the grill. If you have the dough and sauce prepared in advance, grilled pizzas come together in a very short time. This method works best for individual pizzas. Brush the grill grate with oil to prevent sticking. Heat the grill. Place the formed pizza dough on the hot grill and close the lid. Cook until the bottom of the dough appears cooked, 5 to 10 minutes, depending on how hot your grill is. Flip the crust and then arrange your sauce and toppings on the cooked side. Continue to cook until the crust is crisp and browned and the toppings are hot, another 5 to 15 minutes, depending on the heat inside your grill.

2. Place the bags of meat and cheese and the container of sauce, along with the bag of frozen pizza dough, in the gallon-size zip-top freezer bag. Store in the freezer.

To thaw and serve:

Remove the pizza kit from the freezer. Grease a medium bowl. Unwrap the pizza dough and place it in the greased bowl. Thaw it in the refrigerator for 6 to 8 hours, covered. Thaw the other items in the kit in the refrigerator. Preheat the oven to 475°F. Allow the dough to sit at room temperature for about 30 minutes. Stretch the dough to fit a 12-inch pizza pan. Spread the barbecue sauce over the prepared dough. Sprinkle the taco meat over the sauce. Sprinkle the mozzarella mixture over the meat. Bake the pizza for 10 minutes, or until the crust is crisp and the cheese is slightly melted and starting to brown. Cool slightly before slicing. Serve topped with the tomato, lettuce, and red onion.

French Bread Pizza Dippers

LOVE TO EXPERIMENT WITH PIZZA, and one way to do that is with different pizza bases. Large flour tortillas work in a pinch for quick lunchtime thin-crust pizzas. And bagel and English muffin pizzas have long been a kids' standby. When I set out to find a way to make French bread pizza work for freezer meals, the answer was a baguette pizza "dipper." Similar in spirit to the baguette spread with butter and jam that I dipped into my breakfast coffee when I lived in France, this is a pizza baguette spread with garlic butter and mozzarella cheese that's dipped in a homemade pizza sauce. The result is a deliciously crisp, cheesy pizza bread that waits happily in the freezer until a pizza craving hits. ○ *Serves 2 generously*

Packaging: Gallon-size zip-top freezer bag

¼ cup (½ stick) salted butter, softened
1 teaspoon chopped garlic
1 traditional French baguette, about 24 inches long, cut into thirds and split horizontally
8 ounces sliced mozzarella cheese

When ready to serve, you will need:

1 cup Tomato and Herb Pizza Sauce (page 236) or other favorite red sauce, warmed

1. In a small mixing bowl, combine the butter and garlic. Spread the garlic butter on each of the six baguette pieces.

2. Layer the mozzarella cheese over the garlic butter.

Freezing instructions:

Place the cheese-topped bread pieces in the freezer bag. Remove as much air as possible and seal. Freeze.

To thaw and serve:

Thaw the bread in the refrigerator. Preheat the oven to 475°F. Place the bread on a baking sheet. Bake for 5 to 10 minutes, until the cheese is melted and starting to brown slightly and the crust is crisp. Serve with the warmed sauce on the side for dipping.

Deep-Dish Focaccia Pizza Your Way

FOCACCIA makes a wonderful base for pizza that's reminiscent of pizza parlor deep-dish pizza. Customize it with whatever toppings you like.

o *Makes three 8-inch deep-dish-style pizzas*

Packaging: Plastic wrap, plastic container with lid, quart- or pint-size zip-top freezer bag, 2-gallon-size zip-top freezer bag

1 recipe Garlic Focaccia (page 318)
¾ cup Tomato and Herb Pizza Sauce (page 236)
1½ cups shredded mozzarella cheese

When ready to serve, you will need:

Your favorite toppings, such as sliced pepperoni, sliced mushrooms, sliced tomatoes, chopped onions, chopped tomatoes—you name it

1. Wrap the baked and cooled focaccia rounds in plastic wrap. Place the sauce in a small plastic container with a lid. Place the cheese in a quart- or pint-size zip-top freezer bag.

2. Place the focaccia, the container of sauce, and the bag of cheese in the 2-gallon bag. Freeze.

To thaw and serve:

Thaw the pizza kit in the refrigerator. Preheat the oven to 475°F. Place the focaccia rounds on baking sheets. Spread the sauce over the bread. Sprinkle the cheese over the sauce. Add any other toppings you desire. Bake the pizza for 5 to 10 minutes, or until the crust is crisp and the cheese is slightly melted and starting to brown. Cool slightly before slicing and serving.

Pepperoni Calzones

ACALZONE IS SIMPLY a pizza folded in half. You can make them with any number of fillings, provided that the fillings do not have a lot of water in them, which would make the crust soggy. Children will go crazy over these "pizza pockets." They're so much better than what you find in the freezer section at the supermarket and such fun to dip into a tasty sauce. Since these are baked prior to freezing, they make great snacks or lunches: Simply reheat them in a toaster oven or microwave. ○ *Serves 8*

Packaging: Plastic wrap, two gallon-size zip-top freezer bags

1 batch Basic Pizza Dough (page 234), prepared through step 1
Cornmeal for sprinkling
4 cups shredded mozzarella cheese
Two 6-ounce packages sliced pepperoni (about 64 slices)

When ready to serve, you will need:

Easy Slow Cooker Red Sauce (page 205) or other favorite red sauce, warmed

1. Once the pizza dough is mixed, allow it to rise for 1 hour or until doubled in bulk.

2. Preheat the oven to 475°F. Grease 2 or 3 baking sheets and sprinkle them with cornmeal.

3. Transfer the dough to a lightly floured surface and divide it into 8 equal portions. Form each portion into a tight ball. Once all the portions are formed, flatten each one into a 6- to 8-inch round.

4. Sprinkle ½ cup mozzarella cheese over half of each dough round, leaving a ½-inch border around the edge. Arrange 8 slices of pepperoni over the cheese.

5. Fold the other half of the dough over the pepperoni and press to seal the edges. You should have a half-moon shape. Gently turn the bottom crust over the top in sections to further seal the rounded edge. As you work your way around the edge of the dough, each turned-up section should build on the previous one, creating a type of braided effect.

6. Place all the formed calzones on the prepared baking sheets. Cut 2 or 3 slits in the top of each one. Bake for 10 to 12 minutes or until crisp. Remove from the baking sheets and cool on a rack.

Freezing instructions:

Wrap each cooled calzone in plastic wrap. Package 4 calzones in each freezer bag and store in the freezer.

To thaw and serve:

Thaw calzones in the refrigerator overnight. Preheat the oven to 350°F. Unwrap the calzones and reheat for 5 to 10 minutes, or until heated through. Serve with the warmed sauce for dipping.

Spinach and Cheese Calzones

SPINACH AND RICOTTA ARE NATURAL PARTNERS and combine into a delicious filling in these calzones, which make an elegant appetizer or light main course. Pair them with Tomato Sauce with Oregano and Kalamata Olives (page 201) for a fresh twist. These are great to pack in lunches and reheat at work or school. ◦ *Serves 8*

Packaging: Plastic wrap, two gallon-size zip-top freezer bags

1 batch Basic Pizza Dough (page 234), prepared through step 1
Cornmeal for sprinkling
2 cups ricotta cheese
One 16-ounce package frozen chopped spinach, thawed and squeezed dry
1 tablespoon Jamie's Spice Mix (page 90)

When ready to serve, you will need:

Tomato Sauce with Oregano and Kalamata Olives (page 201) or
    other favorite tomato sauce, warmed

1. Once the pizza dough is mixed, allow it to rise for 1 hour or until doubled in bulk.

2. Preheat the oven to 475°F. Grease 2 or 3 baking sheets and sprinkle them with cornmeal.

3. Transfer the dough to a lightly floured surface and divide it into 8 equal portions. Form each portion into a tight ball. Once all the portions are formed, flatten each one into a 6- to 8-inch round.

4. In a large bowl, combine the ricotta cheese, spinach, and spice mix. Divide the cheese mixture among the 8 dough rounds, spreading it over half of each dough round and leaving a ½-inch border around the edge.

5. Fold the other half of dough over the cheese filling and press to seal the edges. You should have a half-moon shape. Gently turn the bottom crust over the top in portions to further seal the rounded edge. As you work your way around the edge of the dough, each turned-up section should build on the previous one, creating a type of braided effect.

6. Place all the formed calzones on the prepared baking sheets. Cut 2 or 3 slits in the top of each one. Bake for 10 to 12 minutes or until crisp. Remove from the baking sheets and cool on a rack.

Freezing instructions:

Wrap each calzone in plastic wrap. Package 4 calzones in each freezer bag and store in the freezer.

To thaw and serve:

Thaw calzones in the refrigerator overnight. Preheat the oven to 350°F. Unwrap the calzones and reheat for 5 to 10 minutes, or until heated through. Serve with the warmed sauce for dipping.

Breakfasts for Champions

Quick Tips for Bulk Cooking

"Messy stations slow things down, food doesn't go, orders pile up, disaster! I will make this easier to remember: Keep your station clean—or I will kill you!"

—Colette, Pixar's *Ratatouille*

- Start with a clean kitchen and a stack of clean kitchen towels and sponges.

- Buy in bulk and large containers whenever possible. This saves money because the unit price is usually lower for bulk goods. You will save time because you can open one gigantic can instead of four or five smaller ones. And you send less waste to the landfill.

- Call the butcher in advance and ask if he will cube or preslice any meats that you might be buying in bulk. This also helps ensure they have the quantities you want when you arrive.

- Wear an apron to protect your clothes; you can also dry your hands on it.

- Gather all your containers and wrappings ahead of time.

- If space allows, assemble all your nonperishable ingredients on the counters.

- Prep all the ingredients before assembling your meals (chop onions, shred cheese, and so on).

- Remember that the assembly line is your friend. Use it whenever you can. Don't repeat actions unnecessarily.

- Clean as you go, or at least load the dishwasher or drop dirty dishes into a sink of soapy water.

- Play music to keep you inspired.

Milk and Honey Granola

GRANOLA CAN BE A PRETTY PRICEY grocery store item. However, it is very easy to make this breakfast cereal yourself at home. If you can buy the ingredients in bulk and/or on sale, you will enjoy further savings. An added benefit is that you can add whatever nuts and seeds you like. This basic recipe is flavored with honey and cooks slowly in the oven. Enjoy it as a breakfast cereal, in parfaits layered with yogurt and fruit, or just for snacking. ○ *Serves 6 to 8*

Packaging: Plastic containers with lids or gallon-size zip-top freezer bag

5 cups old-fashioned rolled oats (do not use quick-cooking oats)
1 cup wheat germ
½ cup wheat bran
½ cup sesame seeds
½ teaspoon salt
1 cup honey
½ cup vegetable oil
½ cup powdered nonfat milk
2 teaspoons lemon zest

1. Preheat the oven to 300°F. Grease a large, rimmed baking sheet or line it with parchment paper.

2. In a very large bowl, combine the oats, wheat bran, wheat germ, sesame seeds, and salt. In a separate bowl, combine the honey, oil, powdered milk, and lemon zest. Pour the wet mixture over the dry and toss to coat evenly.

3. Spread the mixture on the prepared baking sheet. Bake for 40 to 45 minutes, stirring every 15 minutes. Do not let the mixture brown too much.

4. Remove the pan from the oven and allow the granola to cool completely.

Freezing instructions:

Store in a plastic container or freezer bag in the freezer.

To thaw and serve:

Thaw the granola in its container on the counter.

Maple Granola with Oats, Nuts, and Seeds

LOVE GRANOLA. And I love it even more with yogurt and fresh fruit. Yum! Almost like dessert—and a great way to get lots of whole grains. If I have a stash of granola, breakfast—or dessert—comes together in a matter of seconds. This granola, inspired by a recipe from cookbook author Ellie Krieger, is the simplest one I've ever made. Just toss oats, nuts, and seeds with a little salt and maple syrup. Bake until crisp. Delicious! o *Serves 6 to 8*

Packaging: Plastic containers with lids or gallon-size zip-top freezer bag

4 cups old-fashioned rolled oats (do not use quick-cooking oats)
½ cup pecans
½ cup walnuts
½ cup whole raw almonds
½ cup raw sunflower seeds
½ cup raw pumpkin seeds
⅜ teaspoon salt
1 cup maple syrup

1. Preheat the oven to 300°F. Grease a large rimmed baking sheet or line it with parchment paper.

2. Combine all of the ingredients in a large bowl, tossing to coat everything with the maple syrup.

3. Spread the mixture on the prepared baking sheet. Bake for 30 to 45 minutes, stirring often, until toasted and crisp. Cool completely.

Freezing instructions:

Store in a plastic container or freezer bag in the freezer.

To thaw and serve:

Thaw the granola in its container on the counter.

Cranberry-Orange Granola

THIS GRANOLA MAKES A BEAUTIFUL GIFT at the holidays, as well as a fantastic breakfast any time of year. Store the cranberries separately from the granola until you're ready to serve it, so they retain their tenderness and moisture. ○ *Serves 6 to 8*

Packaging: Plastic containers with lids or gallon-size zip-top freezer bag

5 cups old-fashioned rolled oats (do not use quick-cooking oats)
1 cup chopped nuts, such as walnuts or pecans
1 cup light brown sugar
½ cup vegetable oil
½ cup powdered nonfat milk, optional
¼ cup water
1 tablespoon ground cinnamon
Grated zest of 1 orange
1 teaspoon vanilla extract
½ teaspoon salt

When ready to serve, you will need:

1 cup dried cranberries

1. Preheat the oven to 300°F. Grease a large rimmed baking sheet or line it with parchment paper.

2. In a large bowl, combine the oats and nuts.

3. In a medium saucepan over low heat, combine the brown sugar, oil, powdered milk (if using), water, cinnamon, orange zest, vanilla, and salt. Heat, stirring, until just simmering. Pour this mixture over the oats and nuts, stirring to combine.

4. Spread the mixture on the prepared baking sheet. Bake for 40 to 45 minutes, stirring every 10 to 15 minutes. Cool completely.

Freezing instructions:

Store in a plastic container or freezer bag in the freezer.

Breakfast of Champions

Breakfast can be a tough meal. You know it's beneficial for you and your family to eat a good breakfast each morning, but getting it together can be a difficult job to tackle. Freezer cooking comes to the rescue! You'll be pleasantly surprised to see what great breakfasts you can pull off if you do some advance prep work.

Here are a few ways you can make breakfast ahead of time:

Prepare Your Own Breakfast Cereals

My kids love this, especially the younger ones. I make a million little packets of homemade instant oatmeal, and breakfast for the early birds is ready before my coffee is brewed. Homemade granola is another easy cereal solution.

Assemble Breakfast Sandwiches

Make a detour from the fast-food lane in the morning by assembling your own English muffin or biscuit sandwiches. Wrap them in foil and freeze them to reheat on a busy morning.

Enjoy Homemade Baked Goods

Homemade cinnamon rolls are a staple at our house since my friend Amy McGuire (who blogs at AmysFinerThings.com) taught me the best way to freeze them. Simply freeze individual unbaked rolls on a tray and store them in a bag in the freezer. The night before you want fresh-baked rolls, thaw the rolls overnight in a pan, and bake them in the morning. Brilliant! I keep a bag of cinnamon rolls in the freezer at all times (see page 311 for my whole-grain recipe). And I use this same freezing method for a multitude of scone recipes as well.

Freeze Egg Dishes to Bake Later

Easy-to-prepare recipes like quiche and egg casseroles also go from freezer to oven in a flash, making brunch or a hearty breakfast simple to pull off.

Make a Mix

Waffle, pancake, and muffin mixes can be made quickly and efficiently via the assembly-line method. Keep a stash of homemade baking mixes on hand for fast and healthy breakfasts any day.

To thaw and serve:

Thaw the granola in its container on the counter. Add the cranberries right before serving.

Better Instant Oatmeal Packets

LOVE BREAKFAST IN A BOX! It makes our mornings go so much more smoothly when I serve food that is easy to prepare and clean up. Even the little kids can do it all by themselves! Cold cereal and instant oatmeal are favorites, but since my children can eat through one box of instant oatmeal packets in a single morning, I've learned to make my own, inspired by a recipe on the blog The Simple Dollar. It takes just minutes to assemble a few dozen packets. I store the packets in a bin the pantry, but you can freeze them for longer storage. To reduce waste, save the empty snack-size bags to refill next month or next week. ○ *Serves 1*

Packaging: Snack-size zip-top bag

¼ cup quick-cooking rolled oats
1½ teaspoons brown sugar
1 tablespoon raisins, dried cranberries, or dried blueberries (optional)
1 teaspoon powdered nonfat milk (optional)
⅛ teaspoon salt

Place the oats, brown sugar, fruit (if using), milk (if using), and salt in the bag. Shake gently to combine. Repeat to make as many additional servings as desired.

Freezing instructions:

Store the bags in the freezer.

To serve:

Empty the contents of one bag into a heatproof bowl. Add ¼ to ½ cup boiling water. If you omitted the milk powder, you can use hot milk instead of boiling water. Let sit for 1 to 2 minutes, then stir before serving.

Bulk-Batch Pancakes

ONE THING I LOVE ABOUT PANCAKES is that I can vary the batter recipe as well as the toppings to suit my mood or whatever's in the pantry. I've even been known to prepare them for a quick dinner when my other plans don't pan out.

You can combine the dry ingredients in this bulk pancake recipe ahead of time, for a mix that can be stored in the pantry or freezer. Or cook and cool the pancakes, wrap them in stacks of three, and store them in the freezer. Simply reheat cooked pancakes in the microwave or oven before serving.

If you decide to package the recipe as a mix, be sure to mark the bag with a list of the wet ingredients to add right before cooking, as well as the cooking instructions.

o *Serves 4 to 6*

Packaging: Quart-size zip-top freezer bag *or* plastic wrap and gallon-size zip-top freezer bags

Dry ingredients:

1½ cups unbleached all-purpose flour
1½ cups whole-wheat pastry flour
¼ cup sugar
1 tablespoon baking powder
1 teaspoon baking soda
1 teaspoon salt

Wet ingredients:

3½ cups buttermilk
2 large eggs
⅓ cup unsalted butter, melted

Melted butter, for the griddle

To package as a mix:

Place all of the dry ingredients in the quart-size freezer bag. Seal the bag and shake it gently to combine. Store in the freezer.

Cooking instructions:

1. In a large bowl, combine the buttermilk, eggs, and melted butter, blending well. Stir in the dry ingredients. There may be a few small lumps, but that's fine. Add some more buttermilk if the batter is too thick.

2. Heat a large skillet or griddle over medium heat until a few droplets of water sizzle when sprinkled onto the cooking surface. Brush the griddle with melted butter. Pour the batter onto the griddle in ¼-cup portions.

3. Cook the pancakes until bubbles form in the batter and start to pop. Flip the pancakes with a pancake turner. Brush the cooked tops of the cakes with more melted butter. Cook a minute or two more. Stack on a plate and continue until all are cooked.

Freezing instructions:

Cool completely. Wrap pancakes in plastic wrap in stacks of three and place in the large freezer bag. Freeze.

To thaw and serve:

Thaw the pancakes in the refrigerator or on the counter. Reheat in the microwave or oven until hot.

Oatmeal–Chocolate Chip Pancakes

THESE DELICIOUS, WHOLE-GRAIN PANCAKES are reminiscent of oatmeal–chocolate chip cookies, with a tad less guilt. You can combine the dry ingredients ahead of time, for a mix that can be stored in the pantry or freezer. Or cook and cool the pancakes, wrap them in stacks of three, and store them in the freezer. Simply reheat cooked pancakes in the microwave or oven before serving. If you decide to package the recipe as a mix, be sure to mark the bag with a list of the wet ingredients to add right before cooking, as well as the cooking instructions.

o Serves 4 to 6

Packaging: Quart-size zip-top freezer bag *or* plastic wrap and
gallon-size zip-top freezer bags

Dry ingredients:

1 cup unbleached all-purpose flour
1 cup whole-wheat pastry flour
1 cup oat flour
½ cup quick-cooking oats
¼ cup brown sugar
1 tablespoon baking powder
1 teaspoon baking soda
1 teaspoon salt
½ cup mini chocolate chips

Wet ingredients:

3½ cups buttermilk
2 large eggs
⅓ cup vegetable oil
1 teaspoon vanilla extract
1 teaspoon grated orange zest

Butter, for the griddle

To package as a mix:

Place all of the dry ingredients in the quart-size freezer bag. Seal the bag and shake it gently to combine the ingredients. Store in the freezer.

Cooking instructions:

1. In a large bowl, combine the buttermilk, eggs, oil, vanilla, and orange zest, blending well. Add the dry ingredients, whisking until smooth. There may be a few lumps, but that's fine. Add some more buttermilk if the batter is too thick or a tablespoon or two of flour if it is too thin.

2. Heat a large skillet or griddle over medium heat until a few droplets of water sizzle when sprinkled onto the cooking surface. Brush the griddle with melted butter. Pour the batter onto the griddle in ¼-cup portions.

3. Cook the pancakes until bubbles form in the batter and start to pop. Flip the pancakes with a pancake turner. Brush the cooked tops of the cakes with more melted butter. Cook a minute or two more. Stack on a plate and continue until all are cooked.

Freezing instructions:

Cool completely. Wrap pancakes in plastic wrap in stacks of three and place in the large freezer bag. Freeze.

To thaw and serve:

Thaw the pancakes in the refrigerator or on the counter. Reheat in the microwave or oven until hot.

Maple-Oat Waffles

THESE TASTY WAFFLES get even better under cold storage. The tang of the buttermilk mellows and the maple flavor shines through. Full of whole grains, they are a hearty way to start your morning. Serve them with butter and a little more maple syrup to make the day sing. Prepare the dry ingredients as a mix, or cook and freeze the waffles to reheat later for breakfasts on the go. If you decide to package the recipe as a mix, be sure to mark the bag with a list of the wet ingredients to add right before cooking, as well as the cooking instructions.

o *Serves 4 to 6*

Packaging: Gallon-size zip-top freezer bag

Dry ingredients:

2½ cups unbleached all-purpose flour
2 cups whole-wheat pastry flour
1 cup oat flour
½ cup quick-cooking oats
¼ cup baking powder
1½ teaspoons salt

Wet ingredients:

5 cups buttermilk
1 cup (2 sticks) unsalted butter, melted
¼ cup maple syrup
4 large eggs

To package as a mix:

Place all of the dry ingredients in the freezer bag. Seal the bag and shake it gently to combine the ingredients. Store in the freezer.

Cooking instructions:

In a large bowl, combine the dry ingredients with the wet ingredients. Allow the batter to rest for 5 minutes before cooking in your waffle iron according to the manufacturer's instructions. Cool the cooked waffles on a rack.

Freezing instructions:

Place the cooked waffles in the labeled freezer bag and store in the freezer.

To serve:

Reheat frozen waffles (no need to thaw) in the toaster or toaster oven.

Spiced Whole-Grain Waffles

WAFFLES ARE A WONDERFUL MAKE-AHEAD MEAL. You can prepare this recipe as a mix or cook all the waffles at one time, cool, and freeze. Either way, you've cut out a significant amount of prep time. These spiced waffles are packed with whole grains and have so much flavor that you can eat them out of hand, without any toppings. My mother, however, says they beg for a scoop of vanilla ice cream. (Obviously, not all your mother's ideas need be discarded.) If you decide to package the recipe as a mix, be sure to mark the bag with a list of the wet ingredients to add right before cooking, as well as the cooking instructions. ○ *Serves 4 to 6*

Packaging: Gallon-size zip-top freezer bag

Dry ingredients:

3½ cups unbleached all-purpose flour
2 cups whole-wheat pastry flour
¼ cup quick-cooking oats
¼ cup cornmeal
¼ cup dark brown sugar
¼ cup baking powder
1½ teaspoons salt
1½ teaspoons ground cinnamon
1 teaspoon ground nutmeg
1 teaspoon grated orange zest
1 teaspoon ground ginger

Wet ingredients:

4 cups milk
1 cup (2 sticks) unsalted butter, melted
4 large eggs
1 teaspoon vanilla extract

To package as a mix:

Place all of the dry ingredients in the freezer bag. Seal the bag and shake it gently to combine the ingredients. Store in the freezer.

Cooking instructions:

In a large bowl, combine the milk, melted butter, eggs, and vanilla until well blended. Stir in the dry ingredients. Allow the batter to rest for 5 minutes before cooking in your waffle iron according to the manufacturer's instructions. Cool the cooked waffles on a rack.

Freezing instructions:

Place the cooked waffles in the freezer bag and store in the freezer.

To serve:

Reheat frozen waffles (no need to thaw) in the toaster or toaster oven.

Lemon-and-Honey Flax Waffles

TALK ABOUT YOUR DAY-BRIGHTENERS! These waffles positively buzz with honey and lemon zest. The touch of flax brings fiber, antioxidants, and omega-3s to the table. These waffles are out of this world when served with berries and freshly whipped cream. Prepare the dry ingredients as a mix, or cook and freeze the waffles to reheat later for breakfasts on the go. If you decide to package the recipe as a mix, be sure to mark the bag with a list of the wet ingredients to add right before cooking, as well as the cooking instructions. ● *Serves 4 to 6*

Packaging: Gallon-size zip-top freezer bag

Dry ingredients:

3 cups whole-wheat pastry flour
3 cups unbleached all-purpose flour
¼ cup baking powder
½ tablespoon salt

Wet ingredients:

3½ cups milk
1 cup olive oil
3 large eggs
¼ cup honey
1 tablespoon ground flax seed meal, combined with 3 tablespoons water
Grated zest of 1 lemon

To package as a mix:

Place all of the dry ingredients in the freezer bag. Seal the bag and shake it gently to combine the ingredients. Store in the freezer.

Cooking instructions:

In a large bowl, combine the dry ingredients with the wet ingredients. Allow the batter to rest for 5 minutes before cooking in your waffle iron according to the manufacturer's instructions. Cool the cooked waffles on a rack.

Freezing instructions:

Place the cooked waffles in the freezer bag and store in the freezer.

To serve:

Reheat frozen waffles (no need to thaw) in the toaster or toaster oven.

Cinnamon French Toast Dippers

FRENCH TOAST IS A TASTY WAY to make use of day-old bread. With this recipe you can prepare a large batch of this crispy, crunchy, battered bread at one time, making it a perfect recipe for a crowd. I've updated a vintage recipe by stirring in some spices and using large French rolls sliced on the diagonal, which creates ideal "dippers." ○ *Serves 6 to 8*

Packaging: Gallon-size zip-top freezer bag

5 large eggs
1 cup milk
1½ tablespoons brown sugar
½ teaspoon salt
1 teaspoon vanilla extract
¼ teaspoon grated orange zest
½ teaspoon ground cinnamon
Three 8-inch French or sub rolls, sliced on the diagonal into 8 slices each

1. Preheat the oven to 500°F. Line 2 to 3 baking sheets with parchment paper or silicone baking mats.

2. In a wide, shallow dish, mix the eggs, milk, brown sugar, salt, vanilla, orange zest, and cinnamon until well blended.

3. Dip both sides of the bread pieces into the egg mixture and arrange them on the prepared baking sheets.

4. Bake the bread slices until the undersides are golden, about 5 minutes. Turn the slices over. Bake until the bread is golden brown, 2 to 5 minutes more. Watch carefully to prevent burning.

Freezing instructions:

Cool the French toast dippers completely on a wire rack. Place the dippers in the zip-top freezer bag and freeze.

To serve:

Preheat the oven to 375°F. Place the frozen dippers (no need to thaw) on an ungreased baking sheet. Bake until heated through, 8 to 10 minutes. You can warm smaller quantities in the toaster or toaster oven.

Buttered French Toast Casserole with Almonds and Ginger

A BREAKFAST CASSEROLE is one of the easiest ways to start the morning. This elegant dish is bursting with color and sweetness from the cranberries and raisins, crunch from the almonds, and a little kick from the ginger. Leftovers are delicious served cold. For a crisper texture, omit the dried fruit and leave the dish uncovered for the entire baking time. Use a softer, Italian-style bread rather than a crusty French loaf for this dish, and serve with maple syrup, if you like. o *Serves 4 to 6*

Packaging: 9 × 13-inch baking dish with lid

1 loaf Italian or brioche bread, 14 to 16 inches long, sliced into 1½-inch slices
¼ cup (½ stick) unsalted butter, softened
¼ cup golden raisins or dark raisins, or a combination
2 tablespoons dried cranberries
2 tablespoons sliced almonds

2 tablespoons chopped crystallized ginger

3 large eggs, beaten

1 cup half-and-half

¼ cup sugar

2 tablespoons unbleached all-purpose flour

1. Spray the baking dish with nonstick cooking spray.

2. Butter the bread slices on one side and fit the slices, buttered side up, in the bottom of the prepared baking dish.

3. Sprinkle the raisins, cranberries, almonds, and ginger over the top of the bread.

4. In a bowl, combine the eggs, half-and-half, sugar, and flour, whisking well to combine. Pour the egg mixture over the bread slices.

Freezing instructions:

Cover and freeze.

To thaw and serve:

Thaw the casserole in the refrigerator. Preheat the oven to 350°F. Bake, covered, for 25 minutes, then remove the cover and bake 20 minutes more.

Breakfast Cookies

M Y HUSBAND LEAVES FOR WORK before most of the household is awake. He often grabs a cup of coffee and a protein bar, then hits the road. I am always on the hunt for a more economical yet still nourishing option. I took one of my favorite cookie recipes and tweaked it by substituting healthier ingredients like honey, whole-wheat flour, and lots of nuts and grains. The result is a hearty, portable breakfast cookie. Whole-wheat pastry flour can usually be found in the bulk section of your health food store and in larger supermarkets. If you can't find it, you can substitute regular whole-wheat flour, though the cookie will be denser. If you don't have coconut oil, use butter or your preferred vegetable oil instead. ○ *Makes 3 dozen cookies*

Packaging: Gallon-size zip-top freezer bag

½ cup honey
¾ cup light or dark brown sugar
¾ cup coconut oil
2 large eggs
2 teaspoons vanilla extract
½ cup ground flax seed meal
1½ cups whole-wheat pastry flour
1 teaspoon salt
1 teaspoon baking soda
2 cups quick-cooking oats
¼ cup dried cranberries
¼ cup semisweet chocolate chips
¼ cup raw pumpkin seeds
¼ cup sesame seeds
¼ cup chopped nuts of your choice

1. Preheat the oven to 350°F. Line 2 or 3 baking sheets with silicone baking mats or parchment paper.

2. In a large bowl, combine the honey, brown sugar, and coconut oil. Blend well. Beat in the eggs and vanilla. Stir in all of the remaining ingredients.

3. Drop the batter by tablespoonfuls onto the prepared baking sheets. Bake for 10 to 15 minutes or until the tops are set and golden. Cool on racks.

Freezing instructions:

Place the cooled cookies into the freezer bag. Store in the freezer. Cookies can also be packed into sandwich-size bags and then placed in a larger freezer bag, to make them that much easier to grab and go.

To thaw and serve:

The cookies thaw in a few minutes at room temperature.

Breakfast Smoothies

WHILE BLENDING A SMOOTHIE doesn't take that long, it's nice to be able to grab a quick, cold snack or breakfast. Freezer smoothies are just the ticket! Dishwasher- and microwave-safe 8-ounce plastic freezer jars with screw-on lids are perfect for storing freezer smoothies.

Making smoothies can be really simple. Just blend different combinations of fruits, juices, and ice. To make dairy-based smoothies, add yogurt and/or milk. Or use soy milk or almond milk, for creaminess without dairy. I even use homemade fruit jam to flavor milk-based smoothies. Test out some of your favorite fruits and see what combinations you like best. And then keep your freezer stocked for all sorts of cool snacking.

A smoothie is great to pack in the lunch box or to grab and go. Thaw in the refrigerator for 4 hours before serving or on the counter for about an hour, or microwave it for 20 seconds on 50 percent power for a perfect slushy consistency.

The Red Banana

There's a smoothie bar in Santa Barbara that serves up some of the best smoothies on the planet, including the Red Banana, a milk-based smoothie with strawberries and bananas. It is delicious simplicity. ○ *Serves 6*

Packaging: Six plastic freezer jars with lids

2½ cups nonfat milk
1 cup sliced strawberries
2 bananas, broken into pieces

Mix the milk, strawberries, and bananas in the blender until smooth. Pour the mixture into the freezer jars, leaving ½ inch headspace.

Freezing instructions:

Cover the jars and freeze.

To thaw and serve:

Thaw smoothies in the refrigerator for 4 hours or on the counter for about an hour, or microwave them for 20 seconds on 50 percent power. Serve immediately.

The Red Orange

This nondairy fruit-based smoothie is a great way to get one of your five daily servings of produce. The riper the strawberries, the sweeter the treat. Add a teaspoon or two of honey to adjust the sweetness, if desired. ○ *Serves 6*

Packaging: Six plastic freezer jars with lids

2 cups orange juice
2 cups sliced strawberries
½ cup raspberry-grape juice blend
1 to 2 teaspoons honey (optional)

Mix the orange juice, strawberries, and raspberry-grape juice in the blender until smooth. Taste and adjust the sweetness if necessary by adding honey. Pour the mixture into the freezer jars, leaving ½ inch headspace.

Freezing instructions:

Cover the jars and freeze.

To thaw and serve:

Thaw smoothies in the refrigerator for 4 hours or on the counter for about an hour, or microwave them for 20 seconds on 50 percent power. Serve immediately.

The Blue Maple

This milky treat features blueberries and gets a little zip from the maple syrup.
○ *Serves 6*

Packaging: Six plastic freezer jars with lids

2 cups milk
1½ cups blueberries
¾ cup plain yogurt
2 tablespoons maple syrup

Mix the milk, blueberries, yogurt, and maple syrup in the blender until smooth. Pour the mixture into the freezer jars, leaving ½ inch headspace.

Freezing instructions:

Cover the jars and freeze.

To thaw and serve:

Thaw smoothies in the refrigerator for 4 hours or on the counter for about and hour, or microwave them for 20 seconds on 50 percent power. Serve immediately.

The Blue Pineapple

Canned pineapple and fresh blueberries blend beautifully with plain yogurt for a nutritious smoothie. ◉ *Serves 6*

Packaging: Six plastic freezer jars with lids

One 20-ounce can sliced or chunk pineapple in juice
1 cup blueberries
8 ounces plain yogurt

Mix the pineapple, blueberries, and yogurt in the blender until smooth. Pour the mixture into the freezer jars, leaving ½ inch headspace.

Freezing instructions:

Cover the jars and freeze.

To thaw and serve:

Thaw smoothies in the refrigerator for 4 hours or on the counter for about an hour, or microwave them for 20 seconds on 50 percent power. Serve immediately.

Cooking with Friends

Cooking is a very relaxing pursuit for me. If I have a nice drink and a snack, soft music and someone to talk with while I work, I am happy as can be. And while filling my freezer for a week or a month might be considered "work," the load is lightened when I have a cooking partner.

Years ago, my friend Jessika and I cooked together, split the costs, and shared the benefits. Since our husbands had similar tastes in food, we were able to make quite a few dishes to please everyone. We enjoyed talking girl talk while we chopped and mixed and cooked—and when we were done, we had a month's worth of dinners at our fingertips. We've both since moved to different cities, but we still get together a couple times a year to eat and talk.

I introduced my friend Tami to this method of batch cooking at about the same time Jessika and I started. Tami found a cooking buddy, too, and they've been dishing together for almost 13 years! They've perfected their routine after all this time. Four times a year, the husbands watch the kids while the ladies cook enough meals to last for three months. They only make about 25 meals at each session, but they stretch those meals with leftovers, take-out, and dinners with friends mixed in. They are a great example of tweaking bulk cooking to fit individual lifestyles.

Cooking with friends can be a great habit. Not only do you experience the companionship and camaraderie of spending time with a friend, you also have someone to share the workload and another kitchen full of equipment to draw upon. I've heard from some people, though, whose experiences haven't been so positive or long-lasting. So consider the following tips to make your cooking partnership a success:

1. Discuss recipes carefully. Spend a fair amount of time talking about the foods that your respective households prefer. Flip through this book, making lists of the recipes you want to make. Choose the recipes that you both want to try.

2. Keep a careful record of receipts. When you are buying so much food in bulk, it can be easy to lose track of purchases, but it's important to make sure no one feels "stiffed." Collect the receipts after shopping, or better yet, set a budget before you go shopping, so that you can each pay your fair share.

3. Split the meals evenly. As you assemble the meals, use the same packaging for both families whenever possible. Even though you may have different needs or appetites, you are sharing the workload and costs equally, so it's important to remember to split the benefits evenly. Sour grapes don't make for tasty dinners.

4. Prepare adequately for transporting the food. You probably aren't going to cook at both homes, so there will be some transportation of utensils, ingredients, and prepared meals involved. Plan for this. Large coolers are ideal for carrying home chilled food. Laundry baskets or plastic totes are good for carrying spices, utensils, and other shared items.

5. Plan to eat out or get takeout afterward. Depending on how long your cooking session lasts, you may be too tired to do anything but eat food someone else has prepared. Celebrate your accomplishment by ordering a couple of pizzas and putting your feet up.

6. Be flexible about the cooking relationship. Bulk cooking doesn't work for everybody all the time. Seasons change, and so do the needs, food tastes, and preferences of every family. It's okay if this doesn't become a shared activity that stretches over decades. But be sure to enjoy it if it does.

Bacon-Cheddar Egg Bake

T HE EGG BAKE IS A FANTASTIC make-ahead breakfast dish. It's basically bread, cheese, and cooked meat and/or vegetables soaked in a custard mixture, refrigerated overnight, and then baked in the morning. An egg bake is ideal to serve for brunch or, paired with a salad, as an elegant lunch. Egg dishes also freeze well, further freeing up your time.

Usually egg bakes are prepared in 9 × 13-inch baking dishes. However, I enjoy making them in individual servings as well. Following are instructions for both a single serving and a bigger batch. You can customize the individual egg bakes by adding different cheeses, meats, or precooked vegetables and prepare as many as you would like. Just lay out several small baking dishes and assemble a variety of egg bakes at one time.

Individual Bacon-Cheddar Egg Bake o *Serves 1*

Packaging: 2-cup baking dish with lid

1 cup soft bread cubes
⅓ cup shredded cheddar cheese
2 slices bacon, cooked and chopped
2 large eggs, beaten
½ cup milk
Pinch of freshly ground black pepper

1. Grease the baking dish. Spread the bread cubes across the bottom of the dish. Sprinkle the cheese and bacon over the bread cubes.

2. In a small bowl, combine the eggs, milk, and black pepper. Pour the egg mixture over the bread and cheese.

Freezing instructions:

Cover and freeze.

To thaw and serve:

Thaw the egg bake in the refrigerator. Preheat the oven to 350°F. Bake for 25 minutes, or until the top is puffy and a tester inserted in the center comes out clean.

Bacon-Cheddar Egg Bake for a Crowd o *Serves 6 to 8*

Packaging: 9 × 13-inch baking dish with lid

6 cups soft bread cubes
1⅓ cups shredded cheddar cheese
4 slices bacon, cooked and chopped
9 large eggs, beaten
2 cups milk
¼ teaspoon freshly ground black pepper

1. Grease the baking dish. Spread the bread cubes across the bottom of the dish. Sprinkle the cheese and bacon over the bread cubes.

2. In a large bowl, combine the eggs, milk, and black pepper. Pour the egg mixture over the bread and cheese.

Freezing instructions:

Cover and freeze.

To thaw and serve:

Thaw the casserole in the refrigerator. Preheat the oven to 350°F. Bake for 45 minutes to 1 hour, or until the top is puffy and a tester inserted in the center comes out clean.

Eggs Florentine Casserole

BREAKFAST HAS ALWAYS BEEN an enjoyable meal for our family. One of my favorite morning meals is this easy make-ahead casserole. It was served to my husband and me at the little bed and breakfast where we stayed on our honeymoon. It's a delicious way to get your children to eat spinach. Thanks to hearty portions of rich cheeses, it is both filling and flavorful. ○ *Serves 6 to 10*

Packaging: 9 × 13-inch baking dish with lid or two 8-inch round baking dishes with lids

9 large eggs
16 ounces cottage cheese
2 cups shredded Swiss cheese
2 cups crumbled feta cheese
One 10-ounce package frozen chopped spinach, thawed and squeezed dry

1. Spray the baking dish(es) with nonstick cooking spray.

2. In a large bowl, beat the eggs. Add the cheeses and stir to combine well. Stir in the spinach. Pour the mixture into the prepared dish(es).

Freezing instructions:

Cover and freeze.

To thaw and serve:

Thaw the casserole in the refrigerator. Preheat the oven to 350°F. Bake the casserole for 45 minutes to 1 hour, or until the eggs are cooked through. Cool slightly before cutting into squares. Serve hot or warm.

Bacon and Spinach Quiche

QUICHE, A FRENCH CLASSIC, is a basic custard pie that can be varied in any number of ways. It's also unbelievably easy to make ahead and freeze. Just make sure you can store the unbaked pie level in your freezer until it freezes solid. Then wrap it tightly in foil and slip the frozen quiche into a freezer bag before returning it to the freezer. To make it even easier, feel free to use a frozen pie shell—but it won't be as good as my Buttery Pie Crust. An 8-inch pie pan works best for this recipe. ○ *Serves 4 to 6*

Packaging: 9-inch pie plate, heavy-duty aluminum foil

1 cup shredded Swiss cheese mixed with 2 tablespoons unbleached all-purpose flour
½ cup frozen chopped spinach, thawed and squeezed dry
2 tablespoons crumbled cooked bacon
1 recipe Versatile Buttery Pie Crust (page 356) or other favorite pie crust, pressed into an
    8-inch pie plate
3 large eggs
1½ cups cream or half-and-half
⅛ teaspoon freshly ground black pepper

1. Sprinkle the cheese, spinach, and bacon over the bottom of the unbaked pie shell.

2. In a bowl, beat the eggs with the cream and pepper. Pour the egg mixture into the pie shell.

Freezing instructions:

Place the pie plate flat in the freezer. Freeze until firm. Cover the frozen quiche with foil. Return to the freezer.

Preheat the oven to 400°F. Unwrap the frozen quiche and bake it (no need to thaw) for 30 to 45 minutes, or until a knife inserted in the center comes out clean.

Savory Ham and Swiss Clafouti

A CLAFOUTI IS TRADITIONALLY a fruit-and-custard dessert. However, savory clafouti has recently arrived on the scene. Similar to a crustless quiche, this rich ham-and-cheese custard makes an elegant breakfast or brunch entrée. ○ *Serves 4 to 6*

Packaging: 9-inch baking dish with lid, heavy-duty aluminum foil

3 large eggs
1½ cups cream or half-and-half
1 teaspoon Dijon mustard
1 tablespoon chopped fresh parsley or 1 teaspoon dried parsley flakes
⅛ teaspoon freshly ground black pepper
1 cup shredded Swiss cheese mixed with 2 tablespoons unbleached all-purpose flour
1¾ cups diced ham (about 8 ounces)

1. Grease the baking dish.

2. In a large bowl, beat the eggs. Stir in the cream, Dijon mustard, parsley, and pepper. Stir in the shredded cheese and diced ham. Pour the egg mixture into the prepared baking dish.

Freezing instructions:

Place the baking dish flat in the freezer. Freeze until firm. Cover the frozen clafouti or wrap well with foil. Return to the freezer.

To thaw and serve:

Thaw the clafouti in the refrigerator. Preheat the oven to 350°F. Bake the thawed clafouti, uncovered, for 30 to 45 minutes. Alternatively, bake the frozen clafouti for 45 minutes to 1 hour, or until a knife inserted in the center comes out clean.

Chile and Sausage Oven Frittata

THIS OVEN-BAKED EGG DISH is full of flavor from the sausage and green chiles. It is also a breeze to prepare. Mix up and freeze several at a time, and enjoy this easy, protein-packed main dish later. The frittata also makes a delicious and simple lunch or dinner when served with a side salad or a bowl of soup. ○ *Serves 4 to 6*

Packaging: 9-inch deep-dish pie plate, heavy-duty aluminum foil

4 ounces sweet Italian sausage, casings removed
¾ cup shredded Monterey Jack cheese mixed with
    1 tablespoon unbleached all-purpose flour
One 4-ounce can diced green chiles
6 large eggs, beaten
½ teaspoon ground cumin
⅛ teaspoon freshly ground black pepper
1 tablespoon chopped fresh cilantro

1. In a large skillet over medium-high heat, cook the sausage until no longer pink, breaking up the chunks with the back of a spoon. Drain the sausage and let cool.

2. Grease the deep-dish pie plate. Sprinkle the sausage, cheese, and chiles over the bottom of the pie plate.

3. In a large bowl, beat the eggs. Stir in the cumin and pepper. Pour the egg mixture into the pie plate. Sprinkle the cilantro over the top.

Freezing instructions:

Place the pie plate flat in the freezer. Freeze until firm. Cover the frozen frittata with foil. Return to the freezer.

To thaw and serve:

Thaw frittata in the refrigerator. Preheat the oven to 400°F. Remove the foil from the frittata and bake it for 20 to 30 minutes, or until the eggs are set.

Slow Cooker Applesauce

WHEN APPLES ARE IN SEASON, stock up. Make several batches of this easier-than-pie applesauce and stash them in 2-cup portions in the freezer. You can eat the applesauce straight up or use it in recipes; try it in Applesauce-Walnut Bread (page 283).

If you don't have a slow cooker, you can make this on the stovetop. Cook it over low heat in a heavy saucepan for about an hour, checking often to make sure the water doesn't completely evaporate. ○ *Serves 12*

Packaging: Plastic containers with lids

16 large apples, such as Granny Smith, Gravenstein, or
    Braeburn, peeled, cored, and cut into quarters
¼ cup water
¼ cup brown sugar (optional)

1. Place the apples and water in a 5-quart slow cooker. Cook on HIGH for about 4 hours or until the apples have softened.

2. Mash the apples with a potato masher to achieve a chunky consistency. Use an immersion blender if you prefer a smooth texture. Stir in the brown sugar, if desired.

Freezing instructions:

Divide the applesauce into 2-cup portions in plastic containers. Cool completely before covering and freezing.

To thaw and serve:

Thaw the applesauce in the refrigerator. Serve warm, at room temperature, or chilled.

Breakfast Sliders

BREAKFAST SANDWICHES are a favorite with everyone. However, a quick morning trip to the drive-through can leave your wallet empty and your blood pressure elevated. Instead, prepare and freeze your own breakfast sandwiches to reheat while you get ready for the day. These sandwiches contain homemade pork sausage, but feel free to use commercially made sausage or substitute a different breakfast meat, such as bacon or Canadian bacon. ○ *Serves 6*

Packaging: Plastic wrap or heavy-duty aluminum foil,
gallon-size zip-top freezer bag

6 Herbed Pork Sausage Patties (page 173), cooked and cooled
6 slices cheddar cheese
6 English muffins, split

Assemble the breakfast sandwiches by placing one sausage patty and one slice of cheese between two English muffin halves.

Freezing instructions:

Wrap each sandwich individually, using plastic wrap if you plan to reheat in the microwave or foil if you plan to reheat in the oven. Place all the sandwiches in the freezer bag, squeezing out as much air as possible from the bag, and freeze.

To thaw and serve:

Sandwiches can be reheated thawed or frozen. For microwave heating, heat thawed plastic-wrapped sandwiches for 1 to 2 minutes or until heated through. Increase cooking time by 30 seconds to 1 minute for frozen sandwiches. For oven heating, preheat the oven to 375°F. Reheat thawed foil-wrapped sandwiches for 15 minutes or until heated through. Increase cooking time by 10 minutes for frozen sandwiches.

Breads, Muffins, Scones, Rolls, and Then Some

Buttermilk Cornbread

THIS BUTTERMILK-AND-BROWN-SUGAR cornbread is a favorite with friends and family. I serve it as a side dish with dinner, but we also love it for breakfast with a little honey butter. Since this recipe mixes and bakes so quickly, it's most efficient to package several batches of the "dry team" and store them in the freezer for later use, rather than freezing a finished bread. The honey butter can be prepared ahead of time and stored in the refrigerator.

o *Makes one 8-inch square pan*

Packaging: Quart-size freezer bag

Dry ingredients:

¾ cup whole-wheat pastry flour
¾ cup unbleached all-purpose flour
½ cup cornmeal
½ cup dark brown sugar
1 tablespoon baking powder
½ teaspoon salt

Wet ingredients:

½ cup vegetable oil or melted unsalted butter
2 large eggs
1¼ cups buttermilk

Honey Butter (recipe follows)

To package as a mix:

Place all of the dry ingredients in the freezer bag. Seal the bag and shake it gently to combine the ingredients. Store it in the pantry or freezer.

Baking instructions:

Preheat the oven to 350°F. Grease an 8-inch square baking pan. In a large bowl, combine the oil, eggs, and buttermilk. Whisk to blend. Add the bag of cornbread mix. Mix well. Pour the batter into the prepared pan and bake for about 30 minutes, or until the cornbread is golden and a tester inserted in the center comes out with only a few crumbs attached. Serve with the honey butter.

Honey Butter

½ cup (1 stick) salted butter, softened
2 tablespoons honey

In a small bowl, blend the butter and honey. Spoon the butter into a small plastic container with a lid. Store in the refrigerator.

Applesauce-Walnut Bread

QUICK BREADS ARE WONDERFUL to keep on hand in the freezer. They make delicious breakfasts, snacks, and hostess gifts. This bread is a comfort, full of applesauce, spices, and crunchy nuts. It's delicious with or without the icing. To be really fancy, use homemade Slow Cooker Applesauce (page 279). Oh my! Yummy and good for you. ○ *Makes two 4½ × 8½ loaves*

Packaging: Plastic wrap, two gallon-size zip-top freezer bags

¾ cup vegetable oil
1 cup dark brown sugar
2 large eggs
2 cups Slow Cooker Applesauce (page 279; don't include the optional brown sugar) or other
    favorite unsweetened applesauce
1 teaspoon vanilla extract
1 cup whole-wheat pastry flour
2 cups unbleached all-purpose flour
2 teaspoons ground cinnamon
2 teaspoons baking soda
1 cup chopped walnuts

When ready to serve, you will need:

1 cup confectioners' sugar
½ teaspoon ground cinnamon
3 tablespoons freshly squeezed orange juice

1. Preheat the oven to 325°F. Spray two 4½ × 8½ loaf pans with nonstick cooking spray.

2. In a large bowl, combine the oil and brown sugar. Add the eggs and beat until combined. Stir in the applesauce and vanilla extract.

3. In another large bowl, whisk together the flours, cinnamon, and baking soda. Add this dry mixture to the wet mixture. Before stirring, sprinkle the walnuts over the dry ingredients. Gently fold everything together until well combined.

4. Pour the batter into the prepared pans. Bake for 60 to 65 minutes, or until a tester inserted in the center comes out with only a few crumbs attached. Transfer the pans to a rack and let cool for 10 minutes, then remove the loaves from the pans and place on a rack to cool completely.

Freezing instructions:

Wrap the cooled loaves in plastic wrap and place them in the zip-top freezer bags. Store in the freezer.

To thaw and serve:

Thaw the breads, wrapped, at room temperature for about 1 hour. Unwrap and place on a rack. In a small bowl, stir together the confectioners' sugar, cinnamon, and orange juice, and drizzle this icing over the tops of the breads. Once the icing is set, transfer the loaves to a serving tray. Slice and serve.

Chocolate Chip Banana Bread with Oats

N COLLEGE there was always a mad dash at the cafeteria when this bread was on the menu. At the time, I had never heard of such a thing. Now it's an item regularly stashed in our freezer. Banana bread is wonderfully adaptable for bulk baking and freezing. ○ *Makes one 9 × 5-inch loaf*

Packaging: Plastic wrap, gallon-size zip-top freezer bag

1 cup sugar
⅔ cup vegetable oil
2 large eggs
¼ cup buttermilk
1 teaspoon baking soda
1 cup mashed banana
⅔ cup unbleached all-purpose flour
⅔ cup whole-wheat flour
⅓ cup quick-cooking rolled oats
1 teaspoon vanilla extract
½ cup chocolate chips

1. Preheat the oven to 350°F. Spray a 9 × 5-inch loaf pan with nonstick cooking spray.

2. In a large bowl, combine all of the ingredients until well blended.

3. Pour the batter into the prepared pan. Bake for about 1 hour, or until a tester inserted in the center comes out clean.

4. Transfer to a rack and let cool for 10 minutes, then remove from the pan and place on a rack to cool completely.

Freezing instructions:

Wrap the cooled loaf in plastic wrap and place it in the zip-top freezer bag. Store in the freezer.

To thaw and serve:

Thaw the loaf, wrapped, at room temperature for about 1 hour. Slice and serve.

NOTE: To make a big batch (four loaves) of this banana bread, simply multiply all the ingredients by four. The cooking method remains the same. You should be able to fit two wrapped loaves into a gallon-size freezer bag.

Should You Buy a Deep Freezer?

Not all refrigerators are created equal. In fact, some are equipped with freezer compartments that won't even hold a 9 × 13-inch pan. If this describes your situation, you have to get creative if you want to cook in bulk. But never fear! There are a number of ways to make bulk cooking work with a small freezer.

1. Do shorter, more frequent cooking sessions. Chances are you can fit 10 meals into your freezer, even if it is a smaller model. Two or three times a month, you can spend an hour or two prepping those 10 meals, then stash them away to use over the coming weeks. When your supply dwindles, hold another mini cooking session.

2. Use zip-top freezer bags as your main form of packaging, as these are the most compact option. Seal the bag carefully and freeze the food flat. Once the package is frozen, you can flip the bags on their sides and line them up like books on a shelf.

If you'd like to expand your frozen storage resources, having a dedicated freezer might be the best route. Owning a deep freezer can be very useful, especially if you want to cook a month's worth of meals, are feeding large numbers of people, or would like to invest in significant bulk purchases, such as a side of beef.

There are two basic styles of deep freezer to choose from: the chest freezer and the upright. There are pros and cons to both.

We have owned a chest freezer for more than 10 years. It has served us well through everyday life with a large family, two cross-country moves, one power failure, and a few sides of beef. We bought our freezer used from a friend, so there wasn't a ton of research involved in our purchase. I had investigated upright freezers, but this was simply too good of a deal to pass up.

A chest freezer has a number of potential drawbacks:

1. It can be a safety hazard if small children try to remove items unsupervised. Yes, there have been cases of children falling in and becoming trapped. Our freezer can be locked, which is an excellent safety feature.

2. It can accumulate ice crystals on the walls. I defrost it once or twice a year.

3. Things can get "lost," since you have to pile the frozen entrees on top of one another and can't see beneath them.

In its defense, however, a chest freezer can't be left open accidentally, causing the contents to thaw.

A reader of my blog, LifeasMOM.com, wrote asking what kind of freezer to buy. I shared my experience and then opened it up to the blog readership to get their feedback. Here's a summary of what they had to say, which may help you decide:

Chest freezers

Pros

- Energy Star chest freezers are more efficient in energy usage than uprights.
- They are less expensive than uprights.

Cons

- They are too deep for short people to reach the bottom.
- They are difficult to organize efficiently.
- They need to be defrosted regularly.

Upright freezers

Pros

- All the contents are visible.
- They are easy to organize.
- They are more flexible for storage.
- They have a smaller footprint than a chest freezer.

Cons

- Upright freezers can be left ajar accidentally.
- They are less energy efficient because ambient air pours in when the door is opened.

Spiced Pumpkin Flax Bread

THIS RECIPE IS AN EGG-FREE, nut-free spiced pumpkin bread that is not overly sweet. (And if you use vegetable oil, it's also vegan.) It mixes up quickly, fills your home with a tantalizing aroma, and freezes beautifully. Flax seed meal is a great source of omega-3 fatty acids. If you prefer to use eggs, just substitute 3 beaten eggs for the flax seed meal and water.

○ *Makes two 9 × 5-inch loaves*

Packaging: Plastic wrap, gallon-size zip-top freezer bag

3 tablespoons flax seed meal
½ cup plus 1 tablespoon water
2 cups sugar
¾ cup (1½ sticks) plus 2 tablespoons melted unsalted butter or vegetable oil
2 cups pumpkin puree or solid-pack pumpkin (one 15-ounce can is fine)
3 cups unbleached all-purpose flour
½ teaspoon ground ginger
½ teaspoon ground cinnamon
½ teaspoon ground nutmeg
1 teaspoon baking soda
½ teaspoon salt
½ teaspoon baking powder

1. Preheat the oven to 350°F. Grease two 9 × 5-inch loaf pans.

2. In a small bowl, combine the flax seed meal and the water. Let it rest for 2 minutes.

3. In a large bowl, beat together the sugar and the butter. Mix in the flax seed mixture and the pumpkin.

4. In another large bowl, sift together the flour, ginger, cinnamon, nutmeg, baking soda, salt, and baking powder. Stir the flour mixture into the pumpkin mixture in two additions.

5. Pour the batter into the prepared pans. Bake for 50 minutes to 1 hour, or until a tester inserted in the center comes out clean.

6. Transfer to racks and let cool for 10 minutes. Loosen the loaves from the edges of the pans. Remove from the pans and place on racks to cool completely.

Freezing instructions:

Wrap the cooled loaves in plastic wrap. Place both loaves in the freezer bag and freeze.

Serving instructions:

Thaw the bread, wrapped, at room temperature for about 1 hour. Slice and serve.

Nutty Zucchini Bread

AH, ZUCCHINI. The vegetable you love to hate, or hate to love. They are such prolific little buggers. I know—my dad grows them every summer. Correction: My dad grows "too many of them" every summer. Thankfully, my mom picks them while they are smallish, instead of the gargantuan things Dad likes to drop on my doorstep. When I have a wealth of zucchini from his garden, I bake up a big batch of this bread. A food processor is very handy for this sort of thing, making quick work of grating zucchini. Feel free to stir in chopped nuts or chocolate chips, or both. Still got extra zucchini? Be sure to make the Chocolate-Zucchini Cake (page 340). ○ *Makes four 9 × 5-inch loaves*

Packaging: Plastic wrap, 2 gallon-size zip-top freezer bags

3 cups vegetable oil
9 large eggs, beaten
5 cups sugar
2 tablespoons vanilla extract
9 cups unbleached all-purpose flour
6 cups shredded zucchini
1 tablespoon baking soda
¾ teaspoon baking powder
1 tablespoon salt
1 tablespoon ground cinnamon
1½ cups chopped nuts of your choice, chocolate chips, or a combination

1. Preheat the oven to 325°F. Spray four 9 × 5-inch loaf pans with nonstick cooking spray.

2. In a very large bowl, combine the oil, eggs, sugar, and vanilla. Mix well.

3. Stir in the flour, shredded zucchini, baking soda, baking powder, salt, cinnamon, and nuts. Stir until just mixed.

4. Pour the batter into the prepared pans and bake for 1 hour or until a tester inserted in the center comes out clean. Transfer to a rack and let cool for 10 minutes, then remove from the pan and place on a rack to cool completely.

Freezing instructions:

Wrap the cooled loaves in plastic wrap. Place two wrapped loaves in each freezer bag and freeze.

To thaw and serve:

Thaw the bread, wrapped, at room temperature for about 1 hour. Slice and serve.

Cinnamon Banana Bread

LOVE BAKING BANANA BREAD in big batches. When you're rich in golden loaves fragrant with cinnamon and banana, it's easy to share—and to stash a few away for a rainy day. Baking in muffin tins can save you time and provide you with individual breads, ready to pack for work, school, or play.

o Makes four 9 × 5-inch loaves or 36 to 40 mini breads

Packaging: Plastic wrap, gallon-size zip-top freezer bags

6 bananas, mashed
1½ cups half-and-half
3 large eggs
¾ cup vegetable oil or melted unsalted butter
2 cups light or dark brown sugar
3 cups unbleached all-purpose flour

3 cups whole-wheat pastry flour
1 tablespoon baking powder
1½ teaspoons baking soda
1½ teaspoons salt
1½ teaspoons ground cinnamon

1. Preheat the oven to 350°F. Spray four loaf pans with nonstick cooking spray or line muffin tins with paper liners. You can bake some of both sizes, if you prefer.

2. In a very large bowl, blend the bananas, half-and-half, eggs, and oil until smooth. Add the brown sugar and stir, smoothing out any lumps.

3. Add the flours, baking powder, baking soda, salt, and cinnamon. Fold the wet and dry ingredients together just until mixed.

4. Pour the batter into the prepared pans. Bake the loaves for about 1 hour, or until a tester inserted in the center comes out clean. Bake the mini breads for 20 to 22 minutes, or until a tester inserted in the center comes out clean.

5. Transfer the pans to a rack and let cool for 10 minutes, then remove the breads from the pans and place on a rack to cool completely.

Freezing instructions:

Wrap each cooled loaf in plastic wrap. Place two wrapped loaves in each freezer bag and freeze. Mini breads can be placed in freezer bags; remove as much air as possible before sealing the bags.

To thaw and serve:

Thaw banana bread, wrapped, at room temperature for about 1 hour.

Vanilla Cranberry Bread

THIS CRANBERRY BREAD is delightful at tea or breakfast, and makes a perfect addition to a holiday breadbasket. The sweet bread, tangy cranberries, and warm vanilla blend together harmoniously. Keep several loaves stashed in the freezer for a tasty snack anytime. ○ *Makes three 9 × 5-inch loaves*

Make Your Own Mixes

I love to bake, and I know that baking from scratch is usually the most frugal option. But I confess, I'm often lazy and just don't want to haul out the flour and leavening and measuring cups. A boxed mix could come to my rescue, but there is a better, healthier, less expensive way: homemade baking mixes. Any of the recipes in this chapter can be prepared as mixes, except for the yeast breads.

About once a month, I spend an hour or so making and packaging my own mixes. In assembly-line fashion, I measure out the dry ingredients for some of my favorite recipes. I make two to four batches of each, storing them in quart- or gallon-size freezer bags. I mark the bags clearly, noting which wet ingredients and mix-ins to add later, as well as the baking instructions; I don't want to have to hunt down a recipe at baking time. I often store my mixes in the freezer since many of them contain whole-wheat flour, which doesn't have as long a shelf life as all-purpose white flour. Then, when Coconut-Lime Muffins with Chocolate Chips (page 295) sound good one morning, or the family is begging for Buttermilk Cornbread (page 282) with dinner, I just mix up the wet ingredients, dump in a bag of mix, and we're good to go. You can even take some baking mixes camping with you!

Homemade mixes also play a major role in my gift giving. When I need a hostess gift or a quick thank-you, I can grab a mix from the freezer, pair it with a jar of jam or a bag of coffee, tie it all with a ribbon, and have a gift ready in just minutes. Instant friendship in a gift bag!

Great Recipes for Mix-Making:

- Bulk-Batch Pancakes, page 258
- Oatmeal–Chocolate Chip Pancakes, page 259
- Spiced Whole-Grain Waffles, page 262
- Maple-Oat Waffles, page 261
- Lemon-and-Honey Flax Waffles, page 264
- Buttermilk Cornbread, page 282
- Mix-and-Match Muffins, page 294
- Coconut-Lime Muffins with Chocolate Chips, page 295
- Crumb-Topped Zucchini Muffins, page 297
- Raspberry Jam Cream Scones, page 299
- Lemon-Blueberry Scones, page 300
- Ginger-Coconut Scones, page 302
- Lime Chocolate Chip Scones, page 303
- Make-Ahead Drop Biscuits, page 306
- Garlic-Parmesan Swirl Biscuits, page 308
- Cocoa Brownies, page 333

Packaging: Plastic wrap, gallon-size zip-top freezer bags

1 cup (2 sticks) unsalted butter, softened
2¼ cups sugar
6 large eggs
1 cup plain yogurt
1 cup milk
1 tablespoon vanilla extract
4 cups unbleached all-purpose flour
2 cups whole-wheat pastry flour
1½ teaspoons salt
1½ teaspoons baking soda
1½ teaspoons baking powder
3 cups fresh cranberries

1. Preheat the oven to 350°F. Spray three loaf pans with nonstick cooking spray.

2. In a very large bowl, cream the butter and sugar until smooth. Add the eggs and beat until well incorporated. Stir in the yogurt, milk, and vanilla.

3. Add the flours, salt, baking soda, and baking powder. Fold the wet and dry ingredients together just until mixed. Fold in the cranberries.

4. Spoon the batter into the prepared pans. Bake the breads for 50 minutes to 1 hour, or until a tester inserted in the center comes out clean.

5. Transfer the pans to a rack and let cool for 10 minutes, then remove the loaves from the pans and place on a rack to cool completely.

Freezing instructions:

Wrap each cooled loaf in plastic wrap and store them in freezer bags. Freeze.

To thaw and serve:

Thaw the bread, wrapped, at room temperature for about 1 hour. Slice and serve.

Mix-and-Match Muffins

HOME-BAKED MUFFINS are hard to beat—unless you add more sugar and call them cupcakes. This recipe, inspired by one from bakery owner and cookbook author Joanne Chang, has endless possibilities. I've adapted it by adding plain yogurt and a little whole-wheat flour. Prepare the baking mix ahead of time for fresh muffins in a matter of minutes on busy mornings. If you decide to package the recipe as a mix, be sure to mark the bag with a list of the wet ingredients to add right before baking, as well as the baking instructions. ○ *Makes 24 muffins*

Packaging: Zip-top freezer bags (gallon size for baked muffins, quart size for mix)

Dry ingredients:

3 cups unbleached all-purpose flour
½ cup whole-wheat flour
4 teaspoons baking powder
½ teaspoon baking soda
½ teaspoon salt
1 cup granulated or light brown sugar

Wet ingredients:

½ cup vegetable oil
1 cup milk
½ cup plain yogurt
2 large eggs

MIX-INS: Your choice of 1 teaspoon extract (such as vanilla, almond, butterscotch, or coconut), 1½ cups any combination of fruit (such as mashed bananas, finely chopped apples, blueberries, raspberries, or fresh or dried cranberries), chopped nuts, and/or chocolate chips

To package as a mix:

Place all of the dry ingredients in the quart-size freezer bag. Seal the bag and shake it gently to combine the ingredients. Store in the freezer.

Baking instructions:

1. Preheat the oven to 350°F. Line two muffin tins with paper liners or spray them with nonstick cooking spray.

2. In a large bowl, combine the oil, milk, yogurt, and eggs. Whisk to blend. Add the dry ingredients to the wet ingredients and fold gently with a rubber spatula just until combined. Fold in the desired mix-ins.

3. Scoop the batter into the prepared muffin tins. Bake for 25 to 30 minutes, until the muffins are golden brown and a tester comes out clean. Cool the muffins on a rack.

Freezing instructions:

Place the cooled muffins in the gallon-size freezer bags, removing as much air as possible before sealing the bag. Freeze.

To thaw and serve:

Thaw the muffins in bags at room temperature.

Coconut-Lime Muffins with Chocolate Chips

WHEN WE WERE NEWLYWEDS, my husband and I enjoyed a local restaurant that served flourless chocolate cake with a lime sauce. It was heavenly. While we can't have chocolate cake for breakfast, I can recreate some of those flavors in these delectable muffins bursting with tart lime, buttery coconut, and sweet chocolate. Use the dry ingredients from Mix-and-Match Muffins (page 294), then add the wet ingredients and mix-ins right before baking. Alternatively, bake up these muffins and stash them in the freezer for on-the-go snacking. Just before serving, you can drizzle the icing over the tops, though the muffins are delicious without it as well. o *Makes 24 muffins*

Packaging: 2 gallon-size zip-top freezer bags

½ cup vegetable oil
1 cup coconut milk
½ cup plain yogurt
2 large eggs
1 tablespoon freshly squeezed lime juice
Grated zest of 1 lime
1 batch Mix-and-Match Muffins, dry ingredients only (page 294)
1 cup chocolate chips

When ready to serve, you will need:

1 cup confectioners' sugar
Juice of 1 lime
Grated zest of 1 lime

1. Preheat the oven to 350°F. Line two muffin tins with paper liners or spray them with nonstick cooking spray.

2. In a large bowl, combine the oil, coconut milk, yogurt, eggs, the 1 tablespoon lime juice, and zest of 1 lime. Whisk to blend.

3. Add the dry ingredients. Fold gently until mostly moistened but still lumpy. Fold in the chocolate chips.

4. Scoop the batter into the prepared muffin tins. Bake for 25 to 30 minutes, until the muffins are golden brown and a tester comes out clean. Cool the muffins on a rack.

Freezing instructions:

Place the cooled muffins in the freezer bags, removing as much air as possible before sealing the bags. Freeze.

To thaw and serve:

Thaw the muffins in bags at room temperature. Stir together the confectioners' sugar, remaining lime juice, and remaining lime zest. Drizzle this icing over the muffins.

Crumb-Topped Zucchini Muffins

LOVE THE VERSATILITY of baking mixes because I can stir in all kinds of goodies, like zucchini. Your kids might not think of zucchini as a "goodie," but when it's baked into these muffins they will! Summertime tip: If you don't feel like baking up your whole zucchini harvest at once, simply freeze the shredded vegetable in quart-size zip-top freezer bags. Thaw and drain the zucchini before adding it to recipes. ○ *Makes 24 muffins*

Packaging: 2 gallon-size zip-top freezer bags

½ cup vegetable oil
1 cup milk
½ cup plain yogurt
2 large eggs
1 teaspoon vanilla extract
½ teaspoon ground nutmeg
1 batch Mix-and-Match Muffins, dry ingredients only (page 294)
1½ cups shredded zucchini

Streusel topping:

½ cup unbleached all-purpose flour
2 tablespoons unsalted butter, cubed
¼ cup brown sugar
½ cup chopped walnuts, pecans, or almonds
1 teaspoon ground cinnamon
½ teaspoon almond extract

1. Preheat the oven to 350°F. Line two muffin tins with paper liners or spray them with nonstick cooking spray.

2. In a large bowl, combine the oil, milk, yogurt, eggs, vanilla, and nutmeg. Whisk to blend.

3. Add the bag dry ingredients. Fold gently until mostly moistened but still lumpy. Fold in the zucchini.

4. To prepare the streusel topping, place all the topping ingredients in the bowl of a food processor. Pulse until coarse crumbs are formed. Alternatively, combine the flour and butter in a small bowl. Cut the butter into the flour with a pastry blender or two knives. Stir in the sugar, nuts, cinnamon, and almond extract.

5. Scoop the batter into the prepared muffin tins. Sprinkle the streusel topping over the batter. Bake for 25 to 30 minutes, until the muffins are golden brown and a tester comes out clean. Cool the muffins on a rack.

Freezing instructions:

Place the cooled muffins in the freezer bags, removing as much air as possible before sealing the bag. Freeze.

To thaw and serve:

Thaw the muffins in bags at room temperature.

Scones and Biscuits

Scones and biscuits are easy shortbreads to pull together. But making them still involves mess and time. I've found three successful methods for preparing scones and biscuits ahead of time. Each allows me flexibility in baking—and makes good use of my freezer.

Make a Mix

Combine the dry ingredients in a quart-size freezer bag. Label it with a list of the wet ingredients to be added later and the baking instructions. Half the work is already done next time you want a fresh scone or biscuit.

Quick Freeze

This method involves mixing and forming the dough and then freezing it. Frozen unbaked scones can be pulled from the freezer and slid into the oven. They are hot on the table within 20 minutes.

Bake and Freeze

For this method, completely prepare the scone or biscuit recipe. Once the baked goods have cooled, wrap them well and freeze. This method allows for quick breakfasts, lunches, and snacks on the go.

Raspberry Jam Cream Scones

MY HUSBAND LOVES the raspberry scones at a certain coffee shop. I found a way to make them at home, and now I can freeze them and pop them in the oven at any time. Feel free to make scone "bites" by cutting the dough into smaller squares. ○ *Makes 12 scones*

Packaging: Zip-top freezer bags (gallon size for pre-formed or baked scones, quart size for mix)

Dry ingredients:

2 cups whole-wheat pastry flour
3 cups unbleached all-purpose flour
1 cup sugar
1 tablespoon baking powder
1 teaspoon baking soda
½ teaspoon salt

Wet ingredients:

1 teaspoon grated orange zest
¾ cup (1½ sticks) unsalted butter, cut into cubes
1¾ cups cream
⅓ cup seedless raspberry jam

To package as a mix:

Place all of the dry ingredients in the quart-size freezer bag. Seal the bag and shake it gently to combine the ingredients. Store in the pantry or freezer.

To prepare scones:

1. Line baking sheets with parchment paper.

2. In a large bowl, combine dry ingredients and orange zest. Cut in the butter with a pastry blender or two knives until coarse crumbs form. (To speed up the process, do this in batches in a food processor, then transfer to a large bowl.)

3. Add the cream. Fold gently until combined. The dough will be sticky.

4. Turn the dough out onto a floured surface and fold 2 or 3 turns, or until the dough comes together.

5. Pat or roll the dough into a 1-inch-thick rectangle. Spread the jam over one half of the dough. Fold the side without jam over the jam side and press to flatten again to a 1-inch thickness. The jam and dough should swirl together a bit. Cut the dough into 12 rectangles. Scones can be baked at this point.

Freezing instructions:

Place the scones on parchment-lined baking sheets and freeze until firm. Once the scones are firm, transfer them to the gallon-size freezer bags, removing as much air as possible. Freeze.

To serve:

Preheat the oven to 375°F. Bake scones for 20 minutes, or 25 minutes for frozen scones (no need to thaw). Cool and serve. Baked scones can also be frozen in an airtight container or freezer bag.

Lemon-Blueberry Scones

LEMONS AND BLUEBERRIES are a classic flavor combination, and for good reason. They just burst with sunshiny flavor. What better way to start a morning than with fresh-baked lemony scones, popping with blueberries? Mix up a batch to freeze. On a busy morning, you can pull them from the freezer and pop them in the oven. They'll be ready in no time. ○ *Makes 12 scones*

Packaging: Zip-top freezer bags (gallon size for pre-formed or baked scones, quart size for mix)

Dry ingredients:

3 cups whole-wheat pastry flour
2 cups unbleached all-purpose flour
1 cup sugar

1 tablespoon baking powder
1 teaspoon baking soda
½ teaspoon salt

Wet ingredients:

Grated zest of 1 lemon
1 cup (2 sticks) unsalted butter, cut into cubes
2 cups buttermilk
1½ cups frozen blueberries (no need to thaw)

To package as a mix:

Place all of the dry ingredients in the quart-size freezer bag. Seal the bag and shake it gently to combine the ingredients. Store in the pantry or freezer.

To prepare scones:

1. Line baking sheets with parchment paper.

2. In a large bowl, combine the dry ingredients and lemon zest. Cut in the butter with a pastry blender or two knives until coarse crumbs form. (To speed up the process, you can do this in batches in a food processor, then remove the mixture to a large bowl.)

3. Add the buttermilk and blueberries. Fold gently until combined. The dough will be sticky.

4. Turn the dough out onto a floured surface and fold 2 or 3 turns, or until the dough comes together.

5. Gently pat or roll the dough into a 1-inch-thick rectangle, taking care not to squash the berries. Cut the dough into 12 rectangles. Scones can be baked at this point.

Freezing instructions:

Place the scones on parchment-lined baking sheets and freeze until firm. Once the scones are firm, transfer them to the gallon-size freezer bags, removing as much air as possible. Freeze.

To serve:

Preheat the oven to 375°F. Bake scones for 20 minutes, or 25 minutes for frozen scones (no need to thaw). Cool and serve. Baked scones can also be frozen in an airtight container or freezer bag.

Ginger-Coconut Scones

LOVE THE WAY GINGER and coconut work together. There's a warm, buttery zip to these scones, making them perfect with a cup of tea. Feel free to cut them into smaller squares for snack-size scones. ○ *Makes 12 large or 24 small scones*

Packaging: Zip-top freezer bags (gallon size for pre-formed or baked scones, quart size for mix)

Dry ingredients:

2 cups whole-wheat pastry flour
3 cups unbleached all-purpose flour
1 cup sugar
1 tablespoon baking powder
½ teaspoon ground ginger
½ teaspoon salt

Wet ingredients:

1 cup (2 sticks) unsalted butter, cut into cubes
1½ cups light coconut milk
½ cup unsweetened shredded coconut
¼ cup chopped crystallized ginger

To package as a mix:

Place all of the dry ingredients in the quart-size freezer bag. Seal the bag and shake it gently to combine the ingredients. Store in the pantry or freezer.

To prepare scones:

1. Line baking sheets with parchment paper.

2. Place the dry ingredients in a large bowl. Cut in the butter with a pastry blender or two knives until coarse crumbs form. (To speed up the process, you can do this in batches in a food processor, then remove the mixture to a large bowl.)

3. Add the coconut milk, shredded coconut, and crystallized ginger. Fold gently until combined. The dough will be sticky.

4. Turn the dough out onto a floured surface and fold 2 or 3 turns, or until the dough comes together.

5. Pat or roll the dough into a 1-inch-thick rectangle. Cut into 12 or 24 squares. Scones can be baked at this point.

Freezing instructions:

Place the scones on parchment-lined baking sheets and freeze until firm. Once the scones are firm, transfer them to the gallon-size freezer bags, removing as much air as possible. Freeze.

To serve:

Preheat the oven to 375°F. Bake scones for 20 minutes, or 25 minutes for frozen scones (no need to thaw). Cool and serve. Baked scones can also be frozen in an airtight container or freezer bag.

Lime Chocolate Chip Scones

N**O SCONE REPERTOIRE** is complete without a chocolate recipe. These make use of the ease of self-rising flour and combine lime zest and chocolate, two friends that go very well together. If you make the smaller scones, consider using mini chocolate chips. ○ *Makes 12 large or 24 small scones*

Packaging: Zip-top freezer bags (gallon size for pre-formed or baked scones, quart size for mix)

Dry ingredients:

4 cups self-rising flour
½ cup granulated sugar or light brown sugar

Wet ingredients:

½ cup (1 stick) unsalted butter, cubed

½ cup milk

¼ cup cream

2 large eggs

Zest of 2 limes

1 cup chocolate chips

To package as a mix:

Place all of the dry ingredients in the quart-size freezer bag. Seal the bag ʼand shake it gently to combine the ingredients. Store in the pantry or freezer.

To prepare scones:

1. Line baking sheets with parchment paper.

2. Place the dry ingredients in a large bowl. Cut in the butter with a pastry blender or two knives until coarse crumbs form. (To speed up the process, you can do this in batches in a food processor, then remove the mixture to a large bowl.)

3. In another mixing bowl, combine the milk, cream, eggs, and lime zest. Add this to the dry mixture. Sprinkle the chocolate chips over the dough and fold gently until combined. The dough will be sticky.

4. Turn the dough out onto a floured surface and fold 2 or 3 turns, or until the dough comes together.

5. Pat or roll the dough into a 1-inch-thick rectangle. Cut into 12 or 24 rectangles. Scones can be baked at this point.

Freezing instructions:

Place the scones on parchment-lined baking sheets and freeze until firm. Once the scones are firm, transfer them to the gallon-size freezer bags, removing as much air as possible. Freeze.

To serve:

Preheat the oven to 375°F. Bake scones for 20 minutes, or 25 minutes for frozen scones (no need to thaw). Cool and serve. Baked scones can also be frozen in an airtight container or freezer bag.

Forming a Bulk Cooking Co-Op

> "If more of us valued food and cheer and song above
> hoarded gold, it would be a merrier world."
> — **J.R.R. Tolkien**

Food is a great equalizer. We all need it. We all love it. And we know it's fun to share it. A bulk cooking co-op can be a great way to do just that.

A co-op can take different forms, but the general idea is that each person in the group makes one or two recipes in quantities large enough to share with everyone in the group. Like a traditional Christmas cookie exchange, the group members gather with their pre-made, pre-frozen meals and then swap, so that everyone goes home with one container of each meal. This method of bulk cooking allows you to capitalize on the assembly-line method of cooking and bulk buying while adding more variety to your freezer choices.

Certainly you can make your co-op as big and complicated, or as small and simple, as you like. The point is to help one another serve great food at home and create a little community spirit at the same time.

Here are some basic tips to help you start a bulk freezer cooking cooperative:

1. Decide on the size of the group. Four to six people is probably ideal. You'll need to make that number of batches of one recipe at a time, and you don't want the adventure to become too unwieldy by including too many people.

2. Choose the recipes. Coordinating the tastes and food preferences of several households is a little more complicated than cooking on your own or with just one friend. Be diplomatic, as well as respectful of food allergies and aversions. You aren't doing your partners any favors if you make food their families can't or won't eat.

3. Assign the recipes. This is a great way to build on one another's strengths. Does someone in the group just rock the tamale making? Assign that dish to her. Is someone else a whiz with pastry? Let him make the Best-Ever Chicken Pot Pie (page 121). Arrange who will cook what, and then choose a day to convene to swap meals. At the same time, find out what kind of freezer storage each person has at home. Some freezers can't hold larger pans easily, so make sure that the other group members will be able to stash your meals.

4. Cook up a storm on your own. Remember to label carefully and make each share more or less the same size, even if you need to use smaller pans to accommodate smaller freezers. Two 8-inch square pans are about equal to one 9 × 13-inch baking dish.

(continued)

5. Get together to swap. Bring coolers full of frozen meals to one location; go home with those coolers full of different frozen meals.

6. Compare notes. As you prepare for the next round of cooking, discuss what meals worked—or didn't—in the previous go-round. Try to have a thick skin about this. Different folks like different flavors. If you thoroughly discussed the recipes at the outset, this shouldn't be a big problem. But things will invariably come up ("Oh, I forgot that Joe doesn't like olives"). Go with it.

Make-Ahead Drop Biscuits

M Y KIDS LOVE BISCUITS. One night they ate a full dozen before I could get dinner on the table. Homemade biscuits are so much tastier and healthier than the kind you buy in a can. Although it's nice to make the fluffy cutout variety, drop biscuits are much easier and more forgiving.

o *Makes 12 biscuits*

Packaging: Quart-size zip-top freezer bag, gallon-size zip-top freezer bag

Dry ingredients:

1 cup unbleached all-purpose flour
1 cup whole-wheat pastry flour
1 tablespoon baking powder
½ teaspoon salt

Wet ingredients:

3 tablespoons olive oil
1 large egg
¾ cup milk

To package as a mix:

Place all of the dry ingredients in the quart-size freezer bag. Seal the bag and shake it gently to combine the ingredients. Store in the pantry or freezer.

To prepare the biscuits:

1. Preheat the oven to 450°F and line a baking sheet with parchment paper or a silicone baking mat.

2. Place the dry ingredients in a large bowl. In another bowl, combine the oil, egg, and milk.

3. Fold the wet mixture into the dry gently until combined.

4. Drop the batter by scant ¼ cupfuls onto the prepared baking sheet. See directions below for freezing unbaked biscuits.

5. Bake for 10 to 15 minutes, or until golden brown. Cool the biscuits completely on a rack.

Freezing instructions:

Place the cooled biscuits in the gallon-size freezer bag, removing as much air as possible. Freeze.

To thaw and serve:

Thaw the biscuits at room temperature and warm in a low oven until heated through.

To freeze unbaked biscuits:

Place the unbaked biscuits on baking sheets or trays in the freezer. Once they are firm, transfer them to the gallon-size freezer bag, removing as much air as possible. Freeze.

To serve:

Preheat the oven to 450°F. Bake frozen biscuits (no need to thaw) on a baking sheet lined with parchment paper or a silicone baking mat for 15 to 20 minutes.

Herb Biscuits

Stir the following into the dry ingredients:

¼ teaspoon garlic powder
¼ teaspoon dried basil
⅛ teaspoon dried oregano
⅛ teaspoon dried thyme

Proceed as directed.

Garlic-Parmesan Swirl Biscuits

THESE BISCUITS take a little extra work, but they look elegant and really dress up the plate. I have found that preparing and freezing them in advance of baking is the best approach. ○ *Makes 12 biscuits*

Packaging: Gallon-size zip-top freezer bag

Garlic butter:

¼ cup (½ stick) unsalted butter, softened
3 cloves garlic, crushed
2 tablespoons freshly grated Parmesan cheese
¼ teaspoon dried parsley flakes

Biscuit dough:

2 cups unbleached all-purpose flour
1 teaspoon salt
1 tablespoon baking powder
⅓ cup unsalted butter
¾ cup milk

1. Grease a 12-cup muffin tin.

2. In a small bowl, combine the garlic butter ingredients. Set aside.

3. In a large bowl, combine the flour, salt, and baking powder. Cut in the ⅓ cup butter with a pastry blender or two knives until coarse crumbs are formed. Stir in the milk until combined.

4. Turn the dough out onto a floured surface. Knead the dough a few times and flatten into a 9 × 12-inch rectangle.

5. Spread the garlic butter over the surface of the dough. Roll the dough up from the long side and pinch the edges to seal.

6. Cut the rolled dough into twelve 1-inch-wide pieces. Place each spiral in a prepared muffin cup.

Freezing instructions:

Place the muffin pan in the freezer. Freeze until the biscuits are firm to the touch. Pop the biscuits out of the pan and store them in the freezer bag in the freezer.

To thaw and serve:

Preheat the oven to 425°F. Place the desired number of frozen biscuits (no need to thaw) on a baking sheet and bake for 15 minutes, or until golden brown. Serve warm.

Cheddar Coins

MOST OF US CAN GO THROUGH a box of snack crackers in one sitting. To combat the expense and the number of ingredients whose names I can't pronounce in store-bought snack crackers, I experimented with making a healthier cheese cracker. This is adapted from a version I found in *Fine Cooking* magazine; I make it with whole-wheat flour and simplify the process. The end result was a crisp, salty, cheddary cracker that smacks of the "I-could-eat-the-whole-box" packaged cheese crackers. ○ *Makes about 4 dozen crackers*

Packaging: Quart-size zip-top freezer bag

1 cup unbleached all-purpose flour
⅓ cup whole-wheat flour
1⅓ cups finely shredded sharp cheddar cheese
1 teaspoon salt
½ teaspoon garlic powder
½ cup (1 stick) unsalted butter, cubed
1 large egg

1. In the bowl of a food processor, combine the flours, cheese, salt, and garlic powder. Add the butter cubes and pulse until crumbs are formed. Blend in the egg until the dough comes together around the blade.

2. Turn the dough out onto a sheet of plastic wrap. Form the dough into a 1-inch-diameter log. Wrap tightly in plastic wrap and chill in the refrigerator for at least 2 hours.

3. Preheat the oven to 375°F. Line baking sheets with parchment paper or silicone baking mats.

4. Slice the log into thin coins, rolling the log on the cutting board so as to maintain its rounded shape.

5. Place the coins on the prepared baking sheets and bake for 15 minutes. Cool on a rack.

Freezing instructions:

Store the cooled crackers in the freezer bag, removing as much air as possible from the bag. Freeze.

To thaw and serve:

These crackers thaw quickly. They will be ready to devour after just a few minutes on the counter.

Whole-Grain Cinnamon Rolls

USED TO MIX UP cinnamon rolls every Saturday night so we could enjoy them on Sunday mornings. While we loved the morning ritual, I wasn't crazy about the messy Saturday night kitchen. My friend Amy McGuire, from AmysFinerThings.com, taught me how to adapt my cinnamon rolls for the freezer. Now we can enjoy cinnamon rolls any day of the week—without the huge mess! I use a bread machine to make the process even easier. ○ *Makes 18 rolls*

Packaging: Gallon-size zip-top freezer bags

Dough:

2 cups milk
4½ tablespoons unsalted butter
1½ teaspoons vanilla extract
¼ cup granulated sugar
3¾ teaspoons active dry yeast
½ cup quick-cooking rolled oats
1 cup whole-wheat flour
3 to 3½ cups unbleached all-purpose flour
1¾ teaspoons salt

Filling:

3½ tablespoons unsalted butter, softened
¾ cup light or dark brown sugar
1 tablespoon ground cinnamon

When ready to serve, you will need:

¾ cup confectioners' sugar
1 to 2 tablespoons milk
½ teaspoon vanilla extract

1. Line baking sheets with parchment paper.

2. If making the dough in the bread machine, combine the dough ingredients in the bread machine according to the manufacturer's instructions. Program the machine for the dough setting and start it.

If making the dough by hand, place the milk and butter in a medium saucepan and warm slightly. Transfer the mixture to a large bowl and add the vanilla, sugar, and yeast. Stir and allow the yeast to proof for 5 minutes. Add the oats, whole-wheat flour, 3 cups of the all-purpose flour, and the salt. Stir to combine well. Turn the mixture onto a lightly floured surface and knead. Continue kneading for 5 minutes to create a smooth, elastic dough, adding more of the all-purpose flour as necessary. Transfer to a greased bowl and turn the dough ball to coat. Let rise until doubled in bulk, about 1 hour.

3. When the dough is ready, roll it out on a lightly floured surface to form a 12 × 15-inch rectangle.

4. Spread the softened butter over the surface.

5. In a small bowl, combine the brown sugar and cinnamon. Sprinkle this mixture over the butter.

6. Roll up the dough, jelly-roll fashion, starting from a long edge and pinching the seam to seal.

7. Cut the rolled dough into 18 slices, each about ⅔ inch wide, and arrange them on the prepared baking sheets 1 to 2 inches apart.

Freezing instructions:

Place the trays in the freezer and freeze the rolls until they are firm. Remove the trays from the freezer and place the rolls on their sides in the freezer bags, in stacks of six. Place the bags in the freezer immediately.

To thaw and serve:

The night before baking, remove as many rolls as desired from the freezer and place them in a greased 9 × 13-inch baking dish. You may need two pans if you bake all 18 rolls at once. Cover the dish with plastic wrap and refrigerate overnight. The rolls will thaw and rise in the refrigerator. In the morning, remove the dish from the refrigerator and let the rolls rest for 20 minutes at room temperature. Preheat the oven to 350°F. Bake the rolls until browned, 20 to 30 minutes. Remove the pans from the oven and cool on a wire rack. To make the icing, stir together the confectioners' sugar, milk, and vanilla until smooth. Glaze with the icing before serving.

Crystal's Butterhorn Rolls

MY FRIEND CRYSTAL PAINE, from the blog Money Saving Mom, shared her butterhorn recipe years ago. These rolls freeze, thaw, rise, and bake beautifully; they can be frozen baked or unbaked. Our family enjoys them immensely. I adapted her recipe to work in my bread machine, thereby enabling me to multitask a little bit better in the kitchen. The bread machine can do most of the work while I do something else. ○ *Makes 32 rolls*

Packaging: Gallon-size zip-top freezer bags

1 cup milk
½ cup (1 stick) unsalted butter, cubed
2 large eggs
½ cup sugar
4 to 4½ cups unbleached all-purpose flour
1 teaspoon salt
1 heaping tablespoon active dry yeast
Melted butter for brushing

1. Grease baking sheets or line them with parchment paper or silicone baking mats.

2. Combine the milk, cubed butter, eggs, sugar, 4 cups of the flour, the salt, and yeast in your bread machine, according to the manufacturer's instructions. Program the machine for the dough setting and start it. If the dough is very sticky during the mixing phase, add up to ½ cup additional flour, until a soft dough is formed.

3. When the dough cycle is complete, remove the dough from the pan and place it on a lightly floured surface. Divide it into four equal parts.

4. Roll each piece of dough into a 12-inch circle and cut each circle into 8 wedges. Brush the melted butter over the surface of each wedge. Roll each wedge like a crescent roll, starting with the wide bottom of the triangular wedge and ending with the point.

5. Place the rolls, point down, on the prepared baking sheets, about 2 inches apart.

Freezing instructions:

To bake and freeze: Allow the rolls to rise for 30 minutes. Preheat the oven to 375°F. Bake for 12 to 15 minutes, or until lightly browned. Let cool, then place in freezer bags and seal, removing as much air as possible. Freeze.

To freeze unbaked rolls: Place the rolls on their sheets or trays in the freezer and freeze until firm. Place the frozen rolls in freezer bags and store in the freezer.

To thaw and serve:

To serve baked rolls: Thaw the rolls at room temperature in their bags before warming in a low oven.

To serve unbaked rolls: Grease baking sheets or line them with parchment paper or silicone baking mats. Place the frozen rolls on the prepared sheets. Let thaw and rise, covered, in the refrigerator for at least 5 hours or as long as overnight, until doubled in size. Preheat the oven to 375°F and bake the rolls for 12 to 15 minutes, or until lightly browned. Cool on wire racks.

Cinnamon Twist Loaves

OUR FAMILY LOVES Crystal's Butterhorn Rolls (page 313) so much that I experimented with the dough and came up with several variations. This one is a delicious braided cinnamon loaf. For variety in your freezer stash, prepare one batch of dough and make Crystal's Butterhorn Rolls, Chocolate Butterhorns (page 316), and these loaves. ○ *Makes 4 large braids*

Packaging: Gallon-size zip-top freezer bags

1 cup milk
½ cup (1 stick) unsalted butter, cubed
2 large eggs
½ cup sugar
4 to 4½ cups unbleached all-purpose flour
1 teaspoon salt
1 heaping tablespoon active dry yeast
½ cup sugar mixed with 2 tablespoons ground cinnamon

1. Line 2 baking sheets with parchment paper.

2. Combine the milk, cubed butter, eggs, sugar, 4 cups of the flour, the salt, and yeast in your bread machine, according to the manufacturer's instructions. Program the machine for the dough setting and start it. If the dough is very sticky during the mixing phase, add up to ½ cup additional flour, until a soft dough is formed.

3. When the dough cycle is complete, remove the dough from the pan and place it on a lightly floured surface. Divide it into four equal parts.

4. Roll each piece of dough into a 12-inch-long oval and sprinkle 2 tablespoons cinnamon sugar over the surface of each oval.

5. Slice each oval into three strips, leaving them attached at the top edge. Braid the dough, press the ends to seal, and tuck under slightly.

Freezing instructions:

Place the braided loaves on prepared baking sheets and freeze. Once the braids are frozen, place them in freezer bags and store in the freezer until needed.

To thaw and serve:

Grease a baking sheet or line it with parchment paper or a silicone baking mat. Place 1 or 2 cinnamon braids on the prepared sheet, leaving several inches of space between the loaves on the pan. Let thaw and rise for at least 5 hours and as long as overnight in the refrigerator, until doubled in size. Preheat the oven to 375°F and bake the braid(s) for 12 to 15 minutes, or until lightly browned. Cool on wire racks.

You can also freeze the baked braids. Simply place cooled, baked bread braids in gallon-size zip-top freezer bags and seal, removing as much air as possible before closing the bag. Thaw in bags at room temperature.

Chocolate Butterhorn Rolls

SINCE I HAVE A LITTLE BIT of a sweet tooth, I played around with that butterhorn dough a little more, adding chocolate to the finished product. Oh, my word! In my initial recipe testing, the first batch of 32 small rolls never even made it to the freezer. Easy, make-ahead, and delicious—what more could you ask for in a recipe? Reminiscent of chocolate croissants, these rolls will make you a star at your next brunch get-together. ● *Makes 32 rolls*

Packaging: Gallon-size zip-top freezer bags

1 cup milk
½ cup (1 stick) unsalted butter, cubed
2 large eggs
½ cup sugar
4 to 4½ cups unbleached all-purpose flour
1 teaspoon salt
1 heaping tablespoon active dry yeast
1 to 2 cups chocolate chips, depending on how chocolaty you want the rolls

1. Grease baking sheets or line them with parchment paper or silicone baking mats.

2. Combine the milk, cubed butter, eggs, sugar, 4 cups of the flour, the salt, and yeast in your bread machine, according to the manufacturer's instructions. Program the machine for the dough setting and start it. If the dough is very sticky during the mixing phase, add up to ½ cup additional flour until a soft dough is formed.

3. When the dough cycle is complete, remove the dough from the pan and place it on a lightly floured surface. Divide it into four equal parts.

4. Roll each piece of dough into a 12-inch circle and cut each circle into 8 wedges. Sprinkle chocolate chips over the surface of each wedge. Roll each wedge like a crescent roll, starting with the wide bottom of the triangular wedge and ending with the point.

5. If baking before freezing, place the rolls, point down, on the prepared baking sheets, about 2 inches apart. If freezing unbaked rolls, place the rolls on trays or baking sheets (no need to line with parchment paper or use a mat).

Freezing instructions:

To bake and freeze: Allow the rolls to rise for 30 minutes. Preheat the oven to 375°F. Bake for 12 to 15 minutes, or until lightly browned. Let cool, then place in freezer bags and seal, removing as much air as possible. Freeze.

To freeze unbaked rolls: Place the rolls on their sheets or trays in the freezer and freeze until firm. Place the frozen rolls in freezer bags and store in the freezer.

To thaw and serve:

To serve baked rolls: Thaw the rolls at room temperature in their bags before warming in a low oven.

To serve unbaked rolls: Grease baking sheets or line them with parchment paper or silicone baking mats. Place the frozen rolls on the prepared sheets. Let thaw and rise, covered, in the refrigerator for at least 5 hours or as long as overnight, until doubled in size. Preheat the oven to 375°F and bake the rolls for 12 to 15 minutes, or until lightly browned. Cool on wire racks.

Honey Multi-Grain Rolls

THESE ROLLS don't taste overly "healthy," but they are packed with whole-grain goodness. Oat flour, whole-wheat flour, and ground corn combine in a hearty roll that is perfect alongside a bowl of soup on a rainy day.

o *Makes 8 large rolls*

Packaging: Gallon-size zip-top freezer bag

1 cup milk
2½ tablespoons unsalted butter, cut into cubes
2 tablespoons honey
1¼ cups whole-wheat flour
1 cup unbleached all-purpose flour
½ cup oat flour
¼ cup cornmeal
2¼ teaspoons active dry yeast
1 teaspoon salt

1. Combine all of the ingredients in your bread machine according to the manufacturer's instructions. Program the machine for the dough setting and start it.

2. Grease a baking sheet or line it with parchment paper or a silicone baking mat. When the cycle is complete, remove the dough from the pan and divide it into eight equal parts. Form each piece of dough into a tight round and place on the prepared baking sheet to rise until doubled in bulk, about 1 hour.

3. Preheat the oven to 350°F.

4. Bake the rolls for 20 minutes, or until golden brown. Cool completely.

Freezing instructions:

Place the cooled rolls into the freezer bag and seal, removing as much air as possible. Freeze.

To thaw and serve:

Thaw the rolls in their bag at room temperature before reheating in a low oven for about 5 minutes.

Garlic Focaccia

FRESHLY BAKED BREAD IS A JOY. But sometimes, even with handy gadgets and small kitchen appliances, there just aren't enough hours in the day to pull together a fresh loaf. That's when homemade breads prepared in advance and stashed in the freezer can save the day—or the dinner. Inspired by a recipe from cookbook author Beth Hensperger, this recipe is a family favorite. Bake it in 8-inch round cake pans for easy wrapping and freezing. I use a bread machine to speed things up. These rounds make delicious bases for Deep-Dish Focaccia Pizza Your Way (page 247). ○ *Makes 3 focaccia rounds*

Packaging: Plastic wrap, 3 gallon-size zip-top freezer bags

1¼ cups water

¼ cup plus 2 tablespoons olive oil

2¼ cups unbleached all-purpose flour

1 cup whole-wheat flour

1½ teaspoons salt

1 teaspoon garlic powder

¼ teaspoon dried oregano

2½ teaspoons active dry yeast

Coarse salt

1. Combine the water, the 2 tablespoons olive oil, the flours, the 1½ teaspoons salt, garlic powder, oregano, and yeast in your bread machine according to the manufacturer's instructions. Program the machine for the dough setting and start it.

2. Meanwhile, generously grease three 8-inch round cake pans with some of the remaining olive oil.

3. When the dough cycle is complete, remove the dough to a lightly greased surface and divide it into three portions. Press each portion into a prepared cake pan.

4. Flip each dough round over so that both sides are oiled. Spread the dough to the edges of the pans.

5. Cover the pans with plastic wrap and let the dough rise for at least 30 minutes, or longer if possible, until about doubled in bulk.

6. About 30 minutes before baking, preheat the oven to 450°F. Remove the plastic wrap and drizzle the remaining olive oil over the bread rounds. Sprinkle the tops with coarse salt and bake the rounds for 15 minutes, or until golden brown.

Freezing instructions:

Cool the rounds completely on a wire rack. Remove from the pans, wrap securely in plastic wrap, and place each in a freezer bag. Freeze.

To thaw and serve:

Thaw the breads in their wrappings at room temperature. It thaws very quickly. Preheat the oven to 350°F. Unwrap and warm the bread in the oven for about 5 minutes before serving.

How Day-Old Bread and Your Freezer Can Work Together

I often buy marked-down artisan bread a day or two before the sell-by date. The grocery store or bakery wants to move it before the loaves are no longer saleable, so the price is marked down, sometimes to as little as 25 percent of the original price. Day-old bread becomes frozen bread cubes, to use later for egg dishes or homemade croutons. I cube all the bread and put the cubes back into the bread bags to freeze for a day when I want to make croutons or homemade bread crumbs or something like the Bacon-Cheddar Egg Bake (page 273).

Homemade Croutons

My toddler once ate an entire box of packaged croutons in one sitting. Not the most nutritious of snacks—packaged croutons are often full of additives. And don't ask me how he got hold of the box! Nowadays, I make croutons in minutes. Whether I've got a marked-down artisan bread or a loaf of home-baked bread that didn't turn out as light and fluffy as I'd hoped, homemade croutons make the most of bread that might otherwise go to waste.

◉ Makes 5 cups

5 cups cubed bread
2 tablespoons olive oil

1. Preheat the oven to 375°F.

2. In a large bowl, combine the bread cubes with the olive oil. Toss well to coat.

3. Pour the bread cubes onto a large rimmed baking sheet. Bake in the oven for 10 to 15 minutes, stirring every 5 minutes to prevent burning.

4. Cool completely before storing in an airtight container or zip-top bags.

Variation: Add ½ teaspoon garlic powder to the bread when you add the oil.

Bread Crumbs

Bread crumbs are an essential ingredient in meatloaves, meatballs, breaded chicken, and lots of other great dishes. Packaged bread crumbs are quite costly and often contain unwanted ingredients. Many people don't realize that bread crumbs are actually quite inexpensive and easy to make yourself. After all, they're just dried bread! Tear dry bread into chunks and place in the bowl of a food processor or blender. Pulse until you have the consistency you'd like. Store the bread crumbs in the freezer in an airtight container or zip-top freezer bag. Three regular slices of sandwich bread should make about 1 cup of fresh bread crumbs.

Wholesome Energy Bars

YEARS AGO, I worked in a Santa Barbara bakery and restaurant that sold delicious nut-and-fruit bars. They were extremely popular with the customers. Here, I've created my own version, full of flavor; they're delicious toasted for breakfast or a quick snack. They are a lot healthier than most of the so-called energy bars you can buy. ○ *Makes 12 bars*

Packaging: Gallon-size zip-top freezer bag

1 cup milk
3 tablespoons olive oil
3 tablespoons honey
1 teaspoon vanilla extract
1 cup whole-wheat flour
2 cups unbleached all-purpose flour
½ cup oat flour
¼ cup cornmeal
Grated zest of 1 orange
1 teaspoon ground cinnamon
2¼ teaspoons active dry yeast
1 teaspoon salt
¼ cup dried cranberries
¼ cup golden raisins
¼ cup dark raisins
¼ cup raw sunflower seeds

1. Combine all of the ingredients in your bread machine according to the manufacturer's instructions. Program the machine for the dough setting and start it.

2. Grease a baking sheet. When the cycle is complete, turn the dough out onto a lightly floured surface.

3. Press the dough into a 1-inch-thick rectangle. Cut into 12 rectangles and place them on the prepared baking sheet.

4. Preheat the oven to 350°F. Allow the bars to rise for about 20 minutes.

5. Bake the bars for 20 minutes, or until golden brown. Cool the bars on a rack.

Freezing instructions:

Place the cooled bars in the freezer bag and seal, removing as much air as possible. Freeze.

To thaw and serve:

Thaw the desired number of bars at room temperature. Serve at room temperature, or cut the bars in half horizontally, toast, and serve with butter.

Easy Make-Ahead Garlic Bread

WHILE PREPARING homemade garlic bread is inarguably easy, it does take a few minutes. Get that time back on a busy weeknight by keeping a few loaves stashed in the freezer, ready to throw on the grill or toss in the oven alongside the rest of the dinner. For a crispier top, unwrap the foil at the end of the baking time and broil the bread briefly. ○ *Makes 1 large loaf*

Packaging: Heavy-duty aluminum foil

½ cup (1 stick) unsalted butter, softened
2 cloves garlic, minced
1 tablespoon chopped fresh basil or oregano or 1 teaspoon dried basil or oregano (optional)
1½ teaspoons chopped fresh parsley or ½ teaspoon dried parsley flakes
1 large loaf French or Italian bread, halved lengthwise

1. In a small bowl, combine the butter, garlic, basil (if using), and parsley.

2. Spread the butter in a thick layer over the surface of each bread half.

Freezing instructions:

Put the two bread halves back together and wrap with foil. Freeze.

To thaw and serve:

Thaw the bread in the refrigerator. Bake, still wrapped in foil, at 375°F for 25 minutes. Or bake the frozen bread for 35 to 40 minutes.

Desserts When You Crave Them

Cranberry-Oatmeal Cookies

O ATMEAL-RAISIN is a traditional cookie favorite. I've updated a vintage, egg-free recipe with dried cranberries for a tart and chewy sweet treat. Bake up several batches to keep in the freezer for spur-of-the-moment snacks, or freeze the dough balls to bake later. o *Makes about 2 dozen cookies*

Packaging: Plastic containers with lids, waxed paper

1½ cups packed light or dark brown sugar
1 cup (2 sticks) unsalted butter, softened
½ cup buttermilk
1 teaspoon vanilla extract
3½ cups quick-cooking rolled oats
½ cup old-fashioned rolled oats
1¾ cups unbleached all-purpose flour
Grated zest of 1 lemon
1 teaspoon baking soda
1 teaspoon cinnamon
¾ teaspoon salt
2 cups dried cranberries

1. Preheat the oven to 375°F. Line baking sheets with parchment paper or silicone baking mats.

2. In a large bowl, cream together the sugar and butter. Add the buttermilk and vanilla. Blend well. Stir in both kinds of oats, the flour, lemon zest, baking soda, cinnamon, salt, and dried cranberries.

3. Drop the batter by rounded tablespoonfuls about 3 inches apart on the prepared baking sheets. Flatten each cookie with the bottom of a glass dipped in water.

4. Bake until set and lightly browned, about 10 minutes. Remove to racks to cool.

Freezing instructions:

Layer the cookies in a plastic container between sheets of waxed paper. Cover and freeze.

To thaw and serve:

Remove as many cookies as desired from the freezer and thaw them at room temperature. They should thaw within 30 minutes.

White Chocolate–Walnut Jumbles

M Y GRANDMOTHER WAS FAMOUS for her baking, winning blue ribbons at the county fair every year. Family lore has it that when the time came for her to share her recipe on the radio, she would change some of the ingredients so that no one could duplicate her prize-winning baking. Even her daughters-in-law always wondered if they had "the real recipe." These white chocolate jumbles are based on Grandma's blue ribbon chocolate chip cookies. I've updated the recipe with whole-wheat flour, white chocolate chips, and Sucanat (a whole cane sugar), but it's still just as tasty. o *Makes about 3 dozen cookies*

Packaging: Plastic containers with lids, waxed paper

1 cup Sucanat or light or dark brown sugar
1 cup (2 sticks) unsalted butter, softened
2 large eggs
2 teaspoons vanilla extract
2 cups unbleached all-purpose flour
2 cups whole-wheat pastry flour
2 teaspoons baking soda
1 teaspoon salt
One 12-ounce bag white chocolate chips
1 cup chopped walnuts

1. Preheat the oven to 350°F. Line baking sheets with parchment paper or silicone baking mats.

2. In a large bowl, cream together the sugar and butter. Add the eggs and vanilla, mixing thoroughly.

3. Blend in the flours, baking soda, and salt until well combined. Stir in the white chocolate chips and walnuts.

4. Drop the batter onto the baking sheets by rounded tablespoonfuls. Bake for 8 to 10 minutes, or until set. Remove to racks to cool.

Freezing instructions:

Layer the cookies in plastic containers between sheets of waxed paper. Cover and freeze.

To thaw and serve:

Remove as many cookies as desired from the freezer and thaw them at room temperature. They should thaw within 30 minutes.

Cookies and Bulk Cooking

I love the idea of serving a wide variety of Christmas cookies at one time. My goal is to bake a dozen kinds during the holiday season, but this can be a tricky feat. Who wants to spend three days baking? And who has the willpower to resist eating that "wide variety of Christmas cookies" before the holiday arrives?

This is where your freezer can make things a little easier for you at the holidays! There are several techniques that can help you during this hectic month. You *can* have 12 kinds of cookies and not go insane.

Use a food processor or stand mixer

With a food processor or stand mixer, you can quickly prepare many batches of dough in quick succession. In fact, start with the plainest cookie dough and work your way up to the chocolate and the peppermint. Since these cookies most likely all start with butter, sugar, and flour, you don't need to wash the bowl between each batch.

Of course, if you'd rather wash the bowl in between batches, feel free to do so. You'll still save time by using a machine and by preparing many batches of dough in quick succession.

As each batch of dough is prepared, wrap it in plastic wrap or place it in an airtight container and stash it in the refrigerator. By performing all your like tasks together—mixing, forming, and baking—you'll save time and energy.

Make and freeze bulk cookie dough

Once you have your dough prepared, you can freeze the different varieties "as is" until you want freshly baked cookies. Wrap the dough well in plastic wrap and slip it into a zip-top freezer bag before storing it in the freezer. Thaw the dough overnight in the refrigerator, and it should be ready to roll and bake the next day. If you freeze the dough in logs, you don't even need the overnight thaw; the frozen dough will be ready to slice and bake in about an hour.

Make and freeze individual cookie dough balls

Another option is to freeze the dough in ready-to-bake dough balls. Simply form your cookies and place them on baking sheets. Place the sheets in the freezer. Once the cookies are firm, transfer them to a zip-top freezer bag or plastic containers with lids and return them to the freezer for longer storage.

Bake and freeze the cookies

This is probably the easiest—and my favorite—way to get a jump on holiday baking. I prepare the different dough varieties and then roll and bake several kinds of cookies in quick succession. I do three or four kinds at a time. Once the cookies are cooled, I layer them between sheets of waxed paper in airtight containers. Baked cookies should keep well in the freezer for at least a month if wrapped properly. When I want to assemble cookie trays, I pull my containers out of the freezer and place a few of each kind of cookie on each tray. The cookies thaw in a matter of minutes, and I have a great gift or dessert without a lot of last-minute prep work. This gives me a breather during the busy holiday season. I can also spend this "extra" time making my cookie presentation a little prettier.

Tackle your baking in stages

Unless you want to bake all day, consider scheduling three or four baking sessions. One year, I just made a batch of cookies every day for a couple weeks. It didn't take more than an hour each day, and since I was stashing it all in the freezer right away, I built a sweet little stockpile very quickly.

Include the family

It goes without saying that kids love to help bake cookies. I quiz my kids as the holidays approach to hear their cookie choices. They have so much fun helping me bake. While there's invariably a mess in the kitchen—and we have had some hilarious flops—it is always a great time. And our freezer holds enough cookies to last us at least a month.

Lemon Whole-Wheat Spritz Cookies

SPRITZ COOKIES ARE WHIMSICAL and fun. The cookie press makes quick work of preparing these elegant cookies to complement tea or coffee. Whole-wheat pastry flour gives them more substance and a nutty texture.

o *Makes 5 to 6 dozen cookies*

Packaging: Plastic containers with lids, waxed paper

1½ cups (3 sticks) unsalted butter, softened
1 cup granulated sugar
1 teaspoon baking powder
1 large egg
1 teaspoon vanilla extract
Grated zest of 1 lemon
¼ teaspoon lemon extract
3½ cups whole-wheat pastry flour
Turbinado sugar or candy sprinkles

1. Preheat the oven to 375°F. Line baking sheets with parchment paper or silicone baking mats.

2. In a large bowl, beat the butter until light and fluffy. Add the granulated sugar and baking powder and blend until smooth.

3. Beat in the egg, vanilla, lemon zest, and lemon extract. Beat in the flour until smooth.

4. Put the dough into a cookie press fitted with a template and press cookies onto the prepared baking sheets, leaving about 2 inches of space between cookies. Sprinkle the tops of the cookies with turbinado sugar or candy sprinkles.

5. Bake the cookies for 8 minutes. Remove to racks to cool.

Freezing instructions:

Layer the cookies in plastic containers between sheets of waxed paper. Cover and freeze.

To thaw and serve:

Remove as many cookies as desired from the freezer and thaw them at room temperature. They should thaw within 30 minutes.

Chocolate-Almond Biscotti

THIS IS MY FAMILY'S favorite biscotti recipe, and it fits well into the heart-healthier changes we're trying to make in our diet. Almonds and dark chocolate both are considered helpful in lowering cholesterol and blood pressure. And this relatively low-fat recipe does not call for butter or oil.

○ *Makes 2 dozen biscotti*

Packaging: Plastic containers with lids, waxed paper

3 large eggs
1 teaspoon vanilla extract
½ teaspoon almond extract
1 cup dark brown sugar
1¾ cups unbleached all-purpose flour
⅓ cup unsweetened cocoa powder
½ teaspoon finely ground decaf coffee
1 teaspoon baking soda
¼ teaspoon salt
1 cup whole almonds, toasted
¾ cup mini or regular semisweet chocolate chips

1. Preheat the oven to 300°F. Line a large baking sheet with parchment paper or a silicone baking mat.

2. In a large bowl, beat the eggs and extracts with a hand mixer. Blend in the sugar.

3. In another bowl, sift together the flour, cocoa, coffee, baking soda, and salt.

4. Add the dry ingredients to the wet ingredients, and mix. Stir in the almonds and chocolate chips.

5. Spoon the batter into one log, about 16 × 3 inches, down the center of the parchment. Bake for 50 minutes. The dough will spread during baking.

6. Remove the pan from the oven and let cool for 5 to 10 minutes.

7. Slice the large cookie log crosswise into ½-inch-thick slices. Lay the cookie slices, with a cut side down, on one or two baking sheets, and bake 25 minutes. Turn the cookie slices over and bake 25 minutes more. Remove to racks to cool.

Freezing instructions:

Layer the baked cookies in plastic containers between sheets of waxed paper. Cover and freeze.

To thaw and serve:

Remove as many cookies as desired from the freezer and thaw them at room temperature. They should thaw within 30 minutes.

Chocolate-Toffee Cookies

T HESE COOKIES WILL PLEASE chocolate lovers. Enriched with toffee bits, they are a perfect snack with a glass of milk or a cup of coffee.

○ *Makes 3 dozen cookies*

Packaging: Plastic containers with lids, waxed paper

2 cups unbleached all-purpose flour
1½ teaspoons baking powder
¼ teaspoon salt
6 tablespoons (¾ stick) unsalted butter, softened
1 cup dark brown sugar
1 cup semisweet chocolate chips
2 large eggs

1½ teaspoons vanilla extract

1 cup toffee bits (such as Heath) *or* **½ cup chocolate chips and ½ cup toffee bits**

1. Preheat the oven to 350°F. Line baking sheets with parchment paper or silicone baking mats.

2. In a large bowl, whisk together the flour, baking powder, and salt.

3. In another large bowl, beat the butter until light and fluffy. Add the sugar and continue beating until incorporated. Heat the chocolate chips in a microwave-safe bowl in the microwave for 1 to 2 minutes at 50 percent power. Check after 1 minute. The chips will not lose their shape but will soften enough to stir together easily and smoothly. Beat the eggs, melted chocolate, and vanilla extract into the butter mixture. Beat until well combined.

4. Beat in the dry ingredients just until combined. Stir in the toffee bits.

5. Spoon the dough onto the prepared sheets by rounded tablespoonfuls. Bake for 10 to 12 minutes, or until set. Remove to racks to cool.

Freezing instructions:

Layer the cookies in plastic containers between sheets of waxed paper. Cover and freeze.

To thaw and serve:

Remove as many cookies as desired from the freezer and thaw them at room temperature. They should thaw within 30 minutes.

Chocolate Minty Melts

THESE COOKIES, RICH IN CHOCOLATE and peppermint, are a family favorite come holiday time. I often bake double or triple batches so that there's no shortage of them. They are delicious eaten straight from the freezer!

○ Makes about 42 cookies

Packaging: Plastic containers with lids, waxed paper

1½ cups unbleached all-purpose flour
1½ teaspoons baking powder
¼ teaspoon salt
½ cup unsweetened cocoa powder
½ cup (1 stick) unsalted butter, softened
1 cup granulated sugar
6 tablespoons light brown sugar
2 large eggs
1½ teaspoons vanilla extract
¼ teaspoon peppermint extract
Confectioners' sugar for rolling
About 42 mint-flavored Hershey's Kisses, unwrapped

1. Preheat the oven to 350°F. Line baking sheets with parchment paper or silicone baking mats.

2. In a large bowl, combine the flour, baking powder, salt, and cocoa.

3. In another large bowl, cream the butter and sugars until well combined. Beat in the eggs, vanilla, and peppermint extract. Stir in the flour mixture until just combined.

4. Shape the dough into 1-inch balls and roll the balls in confectioners' sugar. Place the balls about 2 inches apart on the prepared sheets. Press a Hershey's Kiss into the center of each cookie ball.

5. Bake the cookies for 10 to 12 minutes, or until the tops are crackled. The kisses may look a little sunken.

6. Cool the cookies for 2 minutes on the baking sheets. Transfer them to racks. Smooth the tops of the chocolate kisses into flat disks with an offset spatula. Let cool completely.

Freezing instructions:

Layer the cookies in plastic containers between sheets of waxed paper. Cover and freeze.

To thaw and serve:

Remove as many cookies as desired from the freezer and thaw them at room temperature. They should thaw within 30 minutes.

Cocoa Brownies

LOVE BROWNIES. But I consider the price of a box of brownie mix ridiculous. Instead of buying commercial versions, I make my own mixes, preparing several batches at once to stash in the pantry or freezer for later baking. You can customize each batch by adding any of the mix-ins listed below. Of course, you can also bake the brownies and freeze them as you would other cookies. However, if you package the recipe as a mix, be sure to label the bag of dry ingredients with the baking instructions and a list of wet ingredients to add right before baking. Bags of mix and mix-ins make great holiday and hostess gifts. ○ *Makes 16 brownies*

Packaging: Quart-size zip-top freezer bag, plastic container with lid, waxed paper

Dry ingredients:

1 cup sugar
⅔ cup unbleached all-purpose flour
⅔ cup unsweetened cocoa powder
½ teaspoon baking powder
½ teaspoon salt

Wet ingredients:

½ cup vegetable oil
2 large eggs
1 teaspoon vanilla extract

Optional mix-ins (choose one or two):

¼ cup chopped walnuts, chocolate chips, or M&Ms
2 teaspoons instant coffee crystals
¼ teaspoon ground cinnamon
1 teaspoon mint extract

To package as a mix:

Place all of the dry ingredients in the quart-size freezer bag. Seal the bag and shake it gently to combine the ingredients. Store in the pantry or freezer.

Baking instructions:

1. Preheat the oven to 350°F. Grease an 8-inch square pan, or line the pan with aluminum foil or parchment paper, letting the ends hang over the sides for easier removal.

2. In a large bowl, combine the wet ingredients and whisk to blend. Add the dry ingredients to the bowl. Stir gently to combine. Fold in the mix-ins, if using. Spoon the batter into the prepared baking pan. Bake for 20 to 25 minutes, or until a tester comes out with a few crumbs attached. Cool and cut into squares.

Other Ways to Put Your Freezer to Work

"I am not a glutton—I am an explorer of food."
—Erma Bombeck

Lasagna? Check. Taco meat? Check. Pizza dough? Check.

Clearly the freezer can be a wonderful storehouse of meals and meal components. It's been known to hold a few quarts of ice cream and boxes of popsicles, too, and it does a great job with ice and ice packs. But there are even more ways that you can put your freezer to work, and they all make good eats.

Homemade TV dinners

Repackage leftovers from a large holiday meal. Portion out cooled turkey, mashed potatoes, gravy, stuffing, and vegetables into aluminum pie plates. Wrap securely with heavy-duty aluminum foil and stash in the freezer for quick individual meals. Thaw in the refrigerator, and then reheat in the oven.

Roasted garlic, peppers, and chiles

These roasted vegetables add flavor to many dishes. I regularly roast big pans of fresh chiles to peel, seed, and chop. I store them in the freezer and add them as desired to egg scrambles, enchiladas, and other dishes that could benefit from an added punch. Roasted garlic and peppers complement salads, sandwiches, and pastas. Cook up bulk batches and package them in appropriately sized containers for adding to meals. Call on these rich flavors at any time for great taste without the wait.

Summer fruits and vegetables

Make use of your freezer to preserve fresh fruits and vegetables, so you can enjoy them throughout the year. Each type of produce has a different recommended method of freezing;

Freezing instructions:

Layer the brownies in a plastic container between sheets of waxed paper. Cover and freeze.

To thaw and serve:

Remove as many brownies as desired from the freezer and thaw them at room temperature. They should thaw within 30 minutes.

some items need to be blanched first, whereas others should be treated with sugar and citric acid. Find a good book on food preservation to get the lowdown.

Many items, like bananas, berries, peppers, onions, and fresh herbs, can be frozen without blanching or pretreating. Chop or slice these items and freeze them on open trays in the freezer. Once the food is firm, place the items in a labeled freezer bag. This method of freezing allows you to uses small quantities at a time without having to thaw the entire bag. Zucchini can be shredded and stored in pint-size freezer bags. Be sure to thaw and drain the zucchini thoroughly before adding it to recipes. Citrus juices can be frozen in small plastic containers or in ice cube trays.

Bulk purchases

Make the most of your warehouse club purchases. Bulk packages of chicken or 5-pound bags of shredded cheese can be broken down into smaller packages and frozen. Even milk and buttermilk can go in the freezer. Just pour out a bit or transfer to other containers, if needed, before you freeze, to allow for expansion.

Good stuff that doesn't come in small packages

There are some pantry ingredients, like tomato paste and chipotle peppers in adobo sauce, that are usually used only in small quantities. When you don't use the whole package, divide the leftovers into small portions wrapped in squares of plastic wrap and freeze the lot in bags to pull out as needed.

Seasonal sales

Certain foods go on sale at certain seasons: hot dogs and sausages in the summer; butter, flour, and cranberries in the winter. Stock up and freeze them to enjoy all year long.

Kahlúa Brownies

THESE BROWNIES WERE ALWAYS A BIG HIT with my mom and her friends when I was growing up. Could it have been the Kahlúa? Though the alcohol had obviously cooked out, Mom and the girls still perked up whenever these brownies were served. I've updated Mom's recipe with homemade brownie mix, dark chocolate chips, and unsweetened coconut. The result is a pan of chewy, chocolaty brownies that are rich without being overly sweet. ○ *Makes 16 brownies*

Packaging: Plastic container with lid, waxed paper

2 large eggs
¼ cup vegetable oil
¼ cup Kahlúa
1 batch Cocoa Brownies, dry ingredients only (page 333)
½ cup chopped pecans
½ cup unsweetened shredded coconut
½ cup dark chocolate chips

1. Preheat the oven to 350°F. Line an 8-inch square pan with parchment paper or aluminum foil, letting the ends hang over the sides for easier removal.

2. In a large bowl, combine the eggs, oil, and Kahlúa. Blend in the dry brownie ingredients just until combined. Stir in the pecans, coconut, and chocolate chips.

3. Spoon the batter into the prepared pan and bake for 25 to 30 minutes, or until a tester comes out with a few crumbs attached. Cool completely on a wire rack.

4. Remove the brownies from the pan by lifting the edges of the parchment. Place on a flat surface and cut into squares.

Freezing instructions:

Layer the brownies in a plastic container between sheets of waxed paper. Cover and freeze.

To thaw and serve:

Remove as many brownies as desired from the freezer and thaw them at room temperature. They should thaw within 30 minutes.

Double Chocolate Magic Bars

MAGIC BARS ARE AN ADDICTIVE, gooey, crunchy sweet treat. I've updated them by using Oreo cookie crumbs instead of graham crackers and unsweetened coconut instead of sweetened. The result is a rich and chocolaty dessert bar. They taste fantastic served cold from the freezer.

o *Makes about 18 bars*

Packaging: Plastic container with lid

1½ cups Oreo cookie crumbs
½ cup (1 stick) unsalted butter, melted
1 cup semisweet chocolate chips
1 cup unsweetened flaked coconut
One 14-ounce can sweetened condensed milk (the fat-free variety is fine)

1. Preheat the oven to 350°F.

2. In a 9 × 13-inch baking dish, combine the cookie crumbs and the melted butter. Press the mixture lightly into the dish to form a crust.

3. Sprinkle the crumb layer with the chocolate chips, then the coconut.

4. Drizzle the sweetened condensed milk over all. Bake for 25 minutes, or until golden brown. Cool, then cut into bars.

Freezing instructions:

Layer the bars in a plastic container between sheets of waxed paper. Cover and freeze.

To thaw and serve:

Remove as many bars as desired from the freezer and thaw them at room temperature. They should thaw within 30 minutes.

Caramel-Lime Bars

REMINISCENT OF KEY LIME PIE, these sweet, tart bars are a refreshing dessert with a hint of caramel in the topping. Serve with a dollop of freshly whipped cream for an elegant presentation. ○ *Makes about 18 bars*

Packaging: 9 × 13-inch baking dish with lid

2 cups graham cracker crumbs
½ cup (1 stick) unsalted butter, melted
4 egg yolks
One 14-ounce can sweetened condensed milk
⅔ cup freshly squeezed lime juice
2 teaspoons grated lime zest
1 cup sour cream
¼ cup dark brown sugar
½ teaspoon vanilla extract

1. Preheat the oven to 350°F.

2. In the baking dish, combine the graham cracker crumbs and the melted butter, pressing the mixture lightly into the dish to form a crust. Bake the crust for 8 minutes.

3. Meanwhile, in a large bowl, combine the egg yolks, sweetened condensed milk, lime juice, and lime zest. Blend well. Pour the filling over the crust and spread to cover. Bake for 8 minutes.

4. In another bowl, combine the sour cream, brown sugar, and vanilla. Spread this over the lime layer and bake for 5 minutes.

5. Cool the pan on a wire rack.

Freezing instructions:

Cover the cooled pan and freeze.

To thaw and serve:

Thaw at room temperature for 10 minutes, or until bars can be cut easily. Cut and serve semi-frozen.

Chocolate-Banana Marble Cake

CHOCOLATE AND BANANAS are a natural pairing; the flavors complement one another so well. And snack cakes are perfect for freezing. You can wrap the whole cake in plastic wrap or package individual slices to freeze, making for quick brown-bag desserts. If you can't find whole-wheat pastry flour, simply use unbleached all-purpose flour. o *Serves 12 to 16*

Packaging: Plastic wrap, gallon-size zip-top freezer bag

1 cup whole-wheat pastry flour
1 cup unbleached all-purpose flour
2 teaspoons baking powder
¼ teaspoon baking soda
¼ teaspoon salt
¾ cup vegetable oil
1¼ cups dark brown sugar
3 ripe bananas, mashed
2 teaspoons vanilla extract
3 large eggs
⅓ cup plain nonfat yogurt
½ cup unsweetened cocoa powder

When ready to serve, you will need:

Confectioners' sugar for dusting

1. Preheat the oven to 350°F. Spray a bundt pan with nonstick cooking spray.

2. In a large bowl, whisk together the flours, baking powder, baking soda, and salt.

3. In another bowl, combine the oil, sugar, and bananas. Beat until smooth. Mix in the vanilla, eggs, and yogurt. Blend until smooth.

4. Add the wet ingredients to the dry ingredients, stirring just until blended.

5. Spoon half the batter into the prepared bundt pan.

6. Add the cocoa to the remaining batter in the bowl and stir until just combined. Spoon the chocolate batter on top of the white batter in sections, leaving some non-chocolate spaces in between chocolate sections.

7. Use a knife to swirl the two batters together, taking care not to mix them too much.

8. Bake the cake for 35 to 40 minutes, or until a tester comes out with just a few crumbs attached.

9. Cool the cake in the pan on a wire rack for 15 minutes. Carefully run a rubber spatula around the edges of the pan to loosen the cake. Invert the cake onto a cooling rack and remove the pan. Cool the cake completely.

Freezing instructions:

Once the cake has cooled, wrap it securely in plastic wrap and place it in the freezer bag. Remove as much air from the bag as possible and freeze. Alternatively, you can wrap individual slices in plastic wrap and place them in the freezer bag. Remove as much air from the bag as possible and freeze.

To thaw and serve:

Thaw the cake, wrapped, at room temperature. Unwrap the thawed cake and place it on a serving platter. Sift the confectioners' sugar over the top of the cake before serving.

Chocolate-Zucchini Cake

THE TOO-PROLIFIC SQUASH that all your neighbors are apt to ditch on your front doorstep becomes something new and delicious when baked into this cake. It is moist and flavorful, best served simply with a dusting of confectioners' sugar and a glass of cold milk. I often freeze slices wrapped in pairs, making them easy to slip into lunches or grab for a snack on the go. If you can't find whole-wheat pastry flour, just substitute additional all-purpose flour.

o *Serves 12 to 16*

Packaging: Plastic wrap, gallon-size zip-top freezer bag

1 cup unbleached all-purpose flour
1½ cups whole-wheat pastry flour

½ cup unsweetened cocoa powder

2½ teaspoons baking powder

1½ teaspoons baking soda

1 teaspoon salt

1 tablespoon ground cinnamon

¾ cup olive oil

1 cup granulated sugar

1 cup light or dark brown sugar

3 large eggs

2 teaspoons vanilla extract

2 cups shredded zucchini

½ cup buttermilk

1 cup chopped pecans or chocolate chips (optional)

When ready to serve, you will need:

Confectioners' sugar for dusting

1. Preheat the oven to 350°F. Spray a bundt pan with nonstick cooking spray.

2. In a large bowl, combine the flours, cocoa, baking powder, baking soda, salt, and cinnamon.

3. In a second bowl, beat together the oil and sugars until smooth. Add the eggs, one at a time. Beat well. Stir in the vanilla and zucchini.

4. Alternately stir the dry ingredients and buttermilk into the wet ingredients. Fold in the nuts or chocolate chips, if using.

5. Pour the batter into the prepared pan. Bake for 1 hour, or until a tester comes out with just a few crumbs attached.

6. Cool the cake in the pan on a wire rack for 15 minutes. Carefully run a rubber spatula around the edges of the pan to loosen the cake. Invert the cake onto a cooling rack and remove the pan. Cool the cake completely.

Freezing instructions:

Once the cake has cooled, wrap it securely in plastic wrap and place it in the freezer bag. Remove as much air from the bag as possible and freeze. Alternatively, you can wrap individual slices in plastic wrap and place them in the freezer bag. Remove as much air from the bag as possible and freeze.

To thaw and serve:

Thaw the cake, wrapped, at room temperature. Unwrap the thawed cake and place it on a serving platter. Sift the confectioners' sugar over the top of the cake before serving.

Pretzel Berry Cheesecake

A **FAMILY FAVORITE** for our holiday get-togethers is a gelatin dessert featuring berries and cream cheese layered atop a pretzel crust. I've re-created that dessert in cheesecake form. It's a delicious, contemporary version of a vintage favorite. Serve it topped with fresh berries. ○ *Serves 8 to 12*

Packaging: Plastic wrap, gallon-size zip-top freezer bag

2 cups pretzel crumbs
¾ cup plus 2 tablespoons sugar
¾ cup (1½ sticks) unsalted butter, melted
Two 8-ounce packages cream cheese, softened
3 large eggs
¾ cup whipping cream
1 teaspoon vanilla extract
½ cup raspberry or other berry jam, warmed to liquid consistency

When ready to serve, you will need:

Fresh raspberries

1. Preheat the oven to 400°F.

2. In a large bowl, combine the pretzel crumbs, 2 tablespoons sugar, and the melted butter. Stir well to combine.

3. Press the crumb mixture into the bottom and up the sides of a 9-inch springform pan.

4. Bake the crust for 8 minutes. Remove the pan from the oven and set on a rack. Reduce the oven temperature to 325°F.

5. In a large bowl, beat the cream cheese and remaining ¾ cup sugar until smooth. Beat in the eggs, one at a time, scraping the sides of the bowl as needed. Beat in the whipping cream and vanilla.

6. Remove and reserve ½ cup of the batter. Pour the rest of the batter into the prepared crust.

7. Stir the jam and the reserved ½ cup of batter together. Drizzle this mixture gently over the top of the cheesecake. Swirl by running a knife in figure eights across the top of the cake.

8. Place a pan of water on the lower shelf of the oven. Place the cheesecake on the rack above it. Bake the cheesecake for 50 to 60 minutes, or until set in the center.

9. Cool the cheesecake for 15 minutes on a rack. Carefully run a knife around the edge of the cake. Remove the sides of the pan and allow the cake to cool to room temperature on the rack. Chill the cake for several hours in the refrigerator.

Freezing instructions:

Carefully remove the bottom of the springform pan, wrap the chilled cake in plastic wrap, and place it in the freezer bag. Remove as much air from the bag as possible and freeze.

To thaw and serve:

Thaw the cake, wrapped, in the refrigerator. Once thawed, unwrap the cake and place it on a serving platter. Cut into slices and serve with fresh raspberries.

Mocha Hot Fudge Cake

WHEN I WAS A kid, the local diner served a hot fudge cake to rave reviews. This one is reminiscent of that childhood cake but made a bit more sophisticated with coffee in both the cake and the ice cream.

○ *Serves 16*

Packaging: Plastic wrap

2 cups sugar
2 cups unbleached all-purpose flour
½ cup unsweetened cocoa powder
1 teaspoon baking powder
1 teaspoon salt
1 cup vegetable oil
4 large eggs
1 teaspoon vanilla extract
1 teaspoon instant coffee crystals
1 pint mocha ice cream

When ready to serve, you will need:

Hot fudge sauce
Whipped cream
Fresh or maraschino cherries (optional)

1. Preheat the oven to 350°F. Line a 9 × 13-inch baking dish with parchment paper, letting the ends of the paper hang over the sides of the pan for easier removal.

2. In a large bowl, whisk together the sugar, flour, cocoa, baking powder, and salt. Add the oil, eggs, vanilla, and instant coffee crystals. Stir gently just until combined.

3. Spread the batter in the prepared baking dish and bake for 25 to 30 minutes, or until a tester comes out with just a few crumbs attached. Cool the cake in its pan on a rack.

4. Remove the ice cream from the freezer to soften slightly at room temperature.

5. Lift the cooled cake out of the pan by grasping each side of the parchment. Invert the cake on a flat surface and carefully loosen the parchment from the cake. Cut the cake in half horizontally.

6. Lay out a large length of plastic wrap on a flat surface. Place one half of the cake in the middle of the plastic wrap. Spread the softened ice cream evenly over the surface of the cake, working quickly.

7. Place the second half of the cake atop the ice cream layer. Wrap the ice cream cake securely with the plastic wrap and freeze immediately.

To serve:

Allow the cake to soften for 5 minutes on the counter. Cut the cake into rectangular slices and place each piece on a serving plate, turning the slices on their sides. Top each portion with hot fudge sauce, whipped cream, and a cherry, if desired.

Spiced Pumpkin Custards

THIS RECIPE IS SO EASY—open a few cans, crack an egg, add some spices, and whisk away. It comes together in minutes. Served in individual ramekins with dollops of freshly whipped cream, it makes for an easy and elegant presentation. ○ *Serves 6*

Packaging: Six 5-ounce ramekins, plastic wrap

One 15-ounce can solid-pack pumpkin
One 14-ounce can sweetened condensed milk
1 large egg
1 teaspoon ground cinnamon
½ teaspoon ground ginger
½ teaspoon salt

When ready to serve, you will need:

1 cup heavy whipping cream
1 tablespoon sugar

1. Preheat the oven to 350°F. Grease six 5-ounce ramekins.

2. In a large bowl, whisk together the pumpkin, sweetened condensed milk, egg, cinnamon, ginger, and salt.

3. Pour the mixture into the ramekins.

4. Place the ramekins in a 9 × 13-inch baking pan. Place the pan in the oven and fill it with hot water to a depth of about 1 inch. Bake the custards for 20 to 30 minutes, or until set.

5. Remove the custards from the oven and cool on a rack.

Freezing instructions:

Cover each cooled ramekin with plastic wrap. Chill the custards in the refrigerator before freezing.

To thaw and serve:

Thaw the custards in the refrigerator. In a large bowl, combine the whipping cream and sugar. Beat with an electric mixer until soft peaks form. Serve each custard with a dollop of whipped cream.

Not Your Ice Cream Truck's Ice Cream Sandwiches

WHEN YOU WERE A KID, you probably enjoyed those cheap ice cream sandwiches from the corner store or the ice cream truck. Two soggy chocolate cookies with ice cream sandwiched in the middle? The taste can take us back to third grade in an instant. These chewy, fudgy ice cream sandwiches update that frozen treat for today's palates. You're going to want to make several batches so as to keep your freezer well stocked.

o *Makes 8 ice cream sandwiches*

Packaging: Plastic wrap, gallon-size zip-top freezer bag

6 tablespoons (¾ stick) unsalted butter, melted
1 cup sugar
¾ cup unsweetened cocoa powder

3 large eggs
½ cup unbleached all-purpose flour
1 teaspoon vanilla extract
½ teaspoon baking powder
½ to 1 quart ice cream of your choice

1. Preheat the oven to 350°F. Line baking sheets with parchment paper.

2. In a large bowl, combine the butter, sugar, cocoa, eggs, flour, vanilla, and baking powder. Stir until well blended.

3. Drop rounded tablespoonfuls of the batter onto the prepared sheets, leaving at least 2 inches between them. You should have 16 cookies.

4. Bake for 8 to 10 minutes, or until set. Remove to racks to cool.

5. Remove the ice cream from the freezer to soften slightly at room temperature.

6. Place one cookie, flat side up, on a small sheet of plastic wrap. Place a scoop of ice cream on the cookie. Place a second cookie, flat side down, on top of the ice cream. Press the cookies together until the ice cream flattens and spreads to the edges of the cookies. Wrap the sandwich tightly in plastic wrap and place immediately in the freezer. Continue assembling the sandwiches and placing them in the freezer. When all the sandwiches are have been assembled and wrapped, place them all in the freezer bag and store in the freezer.

To serve:

Serve frozen.

Easy Chocolate Fudge Sundae Cups

SUNDAE CUPS ready and waiting in the freezer are a treat for all ages. These sundaes feature a simple yet rich homemade fudge sauce that comes together quickly. The sauce can also be customized with a variety of flavorings.

o *Serves 16*

Packaging: Sixteen 8-ounce plastic containers with lids

⅓ cup evaporated milk, plus more for thinning if needed
2 cups semisweet chocolate chips
Optional flavorings: ½ teaspoon ground cinnamon, 1 teaspoon mint extract, 1 teaspoon vanilla
  extract, ½ teaspoon almond extract, or ¼ cup Kahlúa
1 gallon ice cream of your choice

When ready to serve, you will need:

Whipped cream
Chopped nuts
Maraschino cherries (optional)

1. In a small saucepan, combine the evaporated milk and chocolate chips. Heat over low heat, stirring, until the chocolate is melted and the mixture is smooth. Thin with additional evaporated milk, if desired.

2. Add one of the optional flavorings, if desired. Remove the pan from the heat and let cool to room temperature.

3. Remove the ice cream from the freezer to soften slightly at room temperature.

4. Scoop enough ice cream into the plastic containers to fill them about halfway. Spoon some fudge sauce over the ice cream. Scoop more ice cream, filling the containers to within 1 inch of the top. Spoon more fudge sauce on top, leaving ½ inch headspace. Cover and freeze the sundaes immediately.

To serve:

Let the sundaes soften briefly at room temperature. Top with whipped cream, chopped nuts, and a cherry, if desired, prior to serving.

Mint Chocolate Fudge Ice Cream Pie

CE CREAM PIES ARE AN ELEGANT WAY to dress up plain old ice cream. This version combines fudge and mint, a classic favorite. The whipped cream that tops the pie is unsweetened, helping to balance the sweetness of the pie. But if you prefer a sweeter topping, simply add 1 tablespoon of sugar to the cream before you whip it. ○ *Serves 8*

Packaging: 8-inch pie pan, heavy-duty aluminum foil, gallon-size zip-top freezer bag

1½ cups chocolate cookie crumbs
⅓ cup unsalted butter, melted
One 5-ounce can evaporated milk
2 cups semisweet chocolate chips
1 teaspoon peppermint extract
1 pint chocolate ice cream

When ready to serve, you will need:

1 cup heavy whipping cream

1. Preheat the oven to 350°F.

2. In a medium bowl, combine the cookie crumbs and melted butter. Pat this crumb mixture into the bottom and up the sides of the pie pan. Bake for 8 minutes. Let cool on a rack.

3. In a small saucepan, combine the evaporated milk and chocolate chips. Heat over low heat, stirring, until the chocolate is melted and the mixture is smooth. Stir in the peppermint extract. Remove the pan from the heat and let the sauce cool to room temperature.

4. Pour ½ cup of the sauce into the bottom of the cooled cookie crust, spreading to cover the bottom of the crust. Chill in the freezer for 10 minutes.

5. Remove the ice cream from the freezer to soften slightly at room temperature.

6. Spoon the softened ice cream into the frozen pie shell, spreading to distribute it evenly.

7. Pour 1 cup of the remaining cooled sauce over the ice cream and place the pie in the freezer. Reserve any remaining sauce for another recipe.

Freezing instructions:

Wrap the frozen pie with aluminum foil, slip it into the freezer bag, and store it in the freezer for up to 1 month.

To thaw and serve:

Unwrap the pie. Let stand at room temperature for about 10 minutes. While the pie is softening, whip the cream until soft peaks are formed. Serve the sliced pie with dollops of whipped cream.

Blueberry-Raspberry Croustades

HAVING A STASH OF READY-TO-BAKE homemade pies in the freezer brings me such joy. I don't have to do much prep work, but the rewards are huge: I can serve my family or guests a berry pie à la mode without breaking a sweat. These croustades are quick and simple, since they need no pie pan. Simply form the crust around the frozen berries and wrap carefully for freezing. Bake the frozen croustades for a delicious berry dessert. ○ *Makes 4 croustades*

Packaging: Plastic wrap, gallon-size zip-top freezer bags

2 batches Versatile Buttery Pie Crust (page 356) or other favorite pie crust
2½ cups frozen raspberries
2 cups frozen blueberries
½ cup unbleached all-purpose flour
1 cup sugar
2 tablespoons cold unsalted butter, cut into 8 cubes

1. Divide the pie crust into 4 disks and chill.

2. On a lightly floured surface, roll each disk into a ¼-inch-thick round, 6 to 8 inches in diameter. Place the disks on 1 or 2 parchment paper–lined baking sheets.

3. In a large bowl, combine the frozen berries, flour, and sugar. Spoon a quarter of the berry mixture into the center of each pie crust round, leaving a 1- to 2-inch border around the edges.

4. Fold the edges of the pie crust toward the center, overlapping as necessary and leaving the center uncovered. Place 2 cubes of butter on the filling of each croustade.

Freezing instructions:

Place the trays of croustades in the freezer and freeze until set. Once they are set, wrap each one in plastic wrap and place in a zip-top freezer bag. Store in the freezer.

To serve:

Remove the desired number of croustades from the freezer. Preheat the oven to 425°F. Line a rimmed baking sheet or sheets with parchment paper. Unwrap each croustade and place it on the parchment paper. Bake the frozen croustade(s) for 25 minutes. Reduce the oven temperature to 375°F and bake 25 minutes more, or until crust is brown and the filling bubbles. Remove the croustade(s) to a rack to cool to room temperature before serving.

Coconut Crunch Pie

THIS PIE EVOKES THE TASTE of a coconut cream pie—but you don't have to spend any time slaving over a hot stove to make it. It comes together in minutes and provides cool refreshment on a hot summer evening. ○ *Serves 8*

Packaging: 8-inch pie pan, heavy-duty aluminum foil, gallon-size zip-top freezer bag

½ cup unsweetened shredded coconut
2 cups shortbread cookie crumbs
¼ cup (½ stick) unsalted butter, melted
1½ cups whipping cream
⅓ cup confectioners' sugar
1 cup coarsely crushed shortbread cookies

1. Preheat the oven to 350°F. Spread the shredded coconut on a rimmed baking sheet and toast for 5 to 10 minutes, stirring frequently. Remove from the oven and let cool completely.

2. In a small bowl, combine the cookie crumbs and melted butter. Pat the crumb mixture into the pie plate. Chill in the freezer.

3. In a large bowl, whip the cream and the confectioners' sugar until soft peaks form. Fold in the crushed cookies and coconut.

4. Spoon the whipped cream mixture into the shortbread crust. Freeze until firm.

Freezing instructions:

Wrap the frozen pie with foil and place in the freezer bag. Store in the freezer for up to 1 month.

To serve:

Unwrap the pie. Let it stand at room temperature for about 10 minutes before slicing and serving.

Nanna's Apple Pie

FROZEN FRUIT PIES are ubiquitous in the grocery store, but their flavor is sadly lacking. Prepping several homemade pies and stashing them in the freezer is a wonderful way to have spur-of-the-moment desserts that burst with flavor. Set up an assembly line: Make four pie crusts, fill four pie crusts, top four pies with streusel mixed up in the food processor. Easy-peasy. This apple pie, a family favorite, comes together easily and quickly, and it bakes perfectly straight from the freezer. ○ *Serves 8*

Packaging: 9-inch deep-dish pie pan, heavy-duty aluminum foil

1 batch Versatile Buttery Pie Crust (page 356)
½ cup unbleached all-purpose flour

½ cup chopped walnuts

¼ cup brown sugar

2 tablespoons unsalted butter

1 tablespoon plus 1 teaspoon ground cinnamon

½ teaspoon almond extract

6 tart apples (such Granny Smith, Gravenstein, or Braeburn), peeled, cored, and sliced

½ cup granulated sugar

1 tablespoon freshly squeezed lemon juice

1. Line a 9-inch deep-dish pie pan with the pie crust. Chill the crust in the refrigerator while you make the filling and the topping.

2. In the bowl of a food processor, combine the flour, walnuts, brown sugar, butter, 1 teaspoon cinnamon, and almond extract. Pulse until coarse crumbs are formed. Alternatively, in a large bowl, combine the flour, butter, and brown sugar, cutting the butter into the sugar and flour with a pastry blender or two knives until coarse crumbs are formed. Stir in the walnuts, 1 teaspoon cinnamon, and almond extract.

3. In a large bowl, combine the apples, granulated sugar, the remaining 1 tablespoon cinnamon, and the lemon juice. Pile this filling into the prepared pie shell.

4. Sprinkle the crumb mixture evenly over the apples.

Freezing instructions:

Wrap the pie securely with heavy-duty aluminum foil. Freeze.

To serve:

Preheat the oven to 425°F. Unwrap the pie and place it on a rimmed baking sheet to catch any drips. Bake the frozen pie for 15 minutes. Reduce the oven temperature to 375°F and bake 45 minutes to 1 hour more, or until the crust is browned and the filling bubbles. To prevent excessive browning, cover the pie with a sheet of aluminum foil. Allow the pie to cool before serving. Serve warm or at room temperature.

Slab Apple Pie

ONE DAY, I EXPERIMENTED with my usual apple pie recipe by baking it in a 9 × 13-inch baking dish. What I'd discovered was an even easier and equally delicious way to serve apple pie. This dessert has several things going for it: It's super easy to throw together, since you don't have to worry about fluting edges or getting the topping to form a perfect mound. There's a bigger crust-to-apple ratio. And it freezes just as well as a regular pie but has a shape that's more freezer-friendly. ○ *Serves 8 to 12*

Packaging: 9 × 13-inch baking dish with lid

1 batch Versatile Buttery Pie Crust (page 356)
6 tart apples (such as Granny Smith, Gravenstein, or Braeburn), peeled, cored, and sliced
½ cup granulated sugar
1 tablespoon freshly squeezed lemon juice
1 tablespoon ground cinnamon
1 cup unbleached all-purpose flour
½ cup (1 stick) unsalted butter
½ cup brown sugar
½ cup quick-cooking rolled oats

1. Line the bottom of the baking dish with the crust.

2. In a large bowl, combine the apple slices, granulated sugar, lemon juice, and cinnamon. Spread the apple mixture in an even layer over the crust.

3. In a food processor, combine the flour, butter, and brown sugar, pulsing until coarse crumbs are formed. Alternatively, combine these ingredients in a large bowl, cutting the butter into the sugar and flour with a pastry blender or two knives until coarse crumbs are formed.

4. Stir the oats into the crumb topping. Sprinkle the crumb topping over the apple layer.

Freezing instructions:

Cover the dish and label before freezing.

To serve:

Preheat the oven to 425°F. Uncover the frozen pie and bake it for 15 minutes. Reduce the oven temperature to 375°F and bake 45 minutes to 1 hour more, or until browned and bubbly.

Lemon-Ginger Freezer Pie

CREAMY AND LEMONY, with a little warmth from the ginger, this pie comes together easily and quickly. Stash it in the freezer for a "ready when you are" dessert. ○ *Serves 8*

Packaging: 8-inch pie pan, plastic wrap, gallon-size zip-top freezer bag

1½ cups graham cracker crumbs
2 tablespoons sugar
⅓ cup unsalted butter, melted
½ cup prepared lemon curd
8 ounces cream cheese, softened
One 14-ounce can sweetened condensed milk
½ teaspoon ground ginger
1 cup whipping cream

1. Preheat the oven to 350°F.

2. In a medium bowl, combine the graham cracker crumbs, sugar, and melted butter. Pat this crumb mixture into an 8-inch pie pan. Bake for 8 minutes. Let cool on a rack.

3. In a large bowl, blend the lemon curd and cream cheese until light and fluffy. Blend in the sweetened condensed milk and ginger.

4. In a separate bowl, beat the whipped cream until stiff peaks form. Fold half of the whipped cream into the lemon mixture. Spoon this mixture into the cooled pie crust. Smooth the top.

5. Spread the remaining whipped cream over the top of the pie.

Freezing instructions:

Freeze the pie until firm. Wrap the pie securely with plastic wrap and place in the freezer bag. Store in the freezer for up to 1 month.

To thaw and serve:

Unwrap the pie. Let it stand at room temperature for about 10 minutes, until it can be cut easily. Serve cold.

Versatile Buttery Pie Crust

MAKING THIS PIE CRUST is as easy as, well, pie. Using a food processor makes quick work of it; the dough can be ready in less than five minutes. You can freeze the pie crust, tightly wrapped, in a disk and roll it out later or assemble your pies and freeze them prior to baking. This particular crust also works well as a "pat in the pan" crust. You don't need to roll it out if you don't want to—simply press it gently into the pan and up the sides.

○ *Makes enough for 1 single-crust pie*

Packaging: Plastic wrap, gallon-size zip-top freezer bag

1 cup unbleached all-purpose flour
½ cup (1 stick) unsalted butter, cut into chunks
½ teaspoon salt
1 to 2 tablespoons cold water

1. In the bowl of a food processor, combine the flour, butter, and salt. Run the processor for 15 to 20 seconds, or until coarse crumbs are formed. Alternatively, in a medium bowl, combine the flour, butter, and salt with a pastry blender or two knives. Work these ingredients together until coarse crumbs are formed.

2. Quickly pulse or stir in the cold water and mix until a dough forms. Form into a ball.

Freezing instructions:

If using the dough in a recipe, proceed with the recipe. Otherwise, wrap the dough securely in plastic wrap, slip into a zip-top freezer bag, and store in the freezer.

To thaw and serve:

Thaw the dough in the refrigerator overnight. Let stand at room temperature for a few minutes to soften before rolling it out or patting it into a pie pan, pressing the dough across the bottom of the pie plate and up the sides. Use as is in recipes that call for an unbaked pie shell. For recipes that require a prebaked crust, preheat the oven to 350°F and prebake the crust for 10 to 15 minutes, until light golden brown. Cool completely before filling.

Measurement Equivalents

Please note that all conversions are approximate.

Liquid Conversions

U.S.	Metric	U.S.	Metric
1 tsp	5 ml	1 cup	240 ml
1 tbs	15 ml	1 cup + 2 tbs	275 ml
2 tbs	30 ml	1¼ cups	300 ml
3 tbs	45 ml	1⅓ cups	325 ml
¼ cup	60 ml	1½ cups	350 ml
⅓ cup	75 ml	1⅔ cups	375 ml
⅓ cup + 1 tbs	90 ml	1¾ cups	400 ml
⅓ cup + 2 tbs	100 ml	1¾ cups + 2 tbs	450 ml
½ cup	120 ml	2 cups (1 pint)	475 ml
⅔ cup	150 ml	2½ cups	600 ml
¾ cup	180 ml	3 cups	720 ml
¾ cup + 2 tbs	200 ml	4 cups (1 quart)	945 ml
			(1,000 ml is 1 liter)

Weight Conversions

U.S. / U.K.	Metric	U.S. / U.K.	Metric
½ oz	14 g	7 oz	200 g
1 oz	28 g	8 oz	227 g
1½ oz	43 g	9 oz	255 g
2 oz	57 g	10 oz	284 g
2½ oz	71 g	11 oz	312 g
3 oz	85 g	12 oz	340 g
3½ oz	100 g	13 oz	368 g
4 oz	113 g	14 oz	400 g
5 oz	142 g	15 oz	425 g
6 oz	170 g	1 lb	454 g

Oven Temperature Conversions

°F	Gas Mark	°C
250	½	120
275	1	140
300	2	150
325	3	165
350	4	180
375	5	190
400	6	200
425	7	220
450	8	230
475	9	240
500	10	260
550	Broil	290

Index